Colossians, Philemon, Ephesians

Good News Commentaries

MARK, by Larry W. Hurtado

JOHN, by J. Ramsey Michaels

PHILIPPIANS, by F. F. Bruce

1 AND 2 THESSALONIANS, by Earl F. Palmer

HEBREWS, by Donald A. Hagner

JAMES, by Peter H. Davids

1 AND 2 TIMOTHY AND TITUS, by Gordon D. Fee

COLOSSIANS, PHILEMON, EPHESIANS, by Arthur G. Patzia

Colossians, Philemon, Ephesians

Arthur G. Patzia

A GOOD NEWS COMMENTARY

New Testament Editor

W. Ward Gasque

1817

HARPER & ROW, PUBLISHERS, SAN FRANCISCO

Cambridge, Hagerstown, New York, Philadelphia
London, Mexico City, São Paulo, Singapore, Sydney

Dedicated to my wife
DOROTHY
who is a living expression
of God's love, grace, and forgiveness

COLOSSIANS, PHILEMON, EPHESIANS: *A Good News
Commentary.* Copyright © 1984 by Arthur G. Patzia.
All rights reserved. Printed in the United States of
America. No part of this book may be used or reproduced in any manner whatsoever without written permission except in the case of brief quotations embodied
in critical articles and reviews. For information address Harper & Row, Publishers, Inc., 10 East 53rd
Street, New York, NY 10022. Published simulta-
neously in Canada by Fitzhenry & Whiteside, Limited, Toronto.

FIRST EDITION

Designed by Design Office Bruce Kortebein

Library of Congress Cataloging in Publication
Data
Patzia, Arthur G.
    COLOSSIANS, PHILEMON, EPHESIANS.

    (A Good News Commentary)
    Bibliography: p.
    Includes indexes.
    1. Bible. N.T. Colossians—Commentaries.
2. Bible. N.T. Philemon—Commentaries. 3. Bible.
N.T. Ephesians—Commentaries. I. Bible. N.T.
Epistles of Paul. English. Today's English. Selections.
1984. II. Title. III. Series.
BS2650.3.P37   1984   227   83-48996
ISBN 0-06-066479-7

84 85 86 87 88 10 9 8 7 6 5 4 3 2 1

About the Series

This is the first major series to use the popular Good News Bible, which has sold in the millions. Each volume is informed by solid scholarship and the most up-to-date research, yet each is biblically faithful and readily understandable to the general reader. Features include:

Introductory material highlighting authorship, dating, background information, and thematic emphases—plus a map

Full text of each Good News Bible book, with running commentary

Special end notes giving references for key words and concepts and providing suggestions for further reading

Full indexes for Scripture and Subjects/Persons/Places

Series Editor W. Ward Gasque is Vice-Principal and Professor of New Testament at Regent College in Vancouver. A former editor-at-large for *Christianity Today*, he is the author of numerous articles and books and has edited *In God's Community: Studies in the Church and Its Ministry, Handbook of Biblical Prophecy, Apostolic History and the Gospel,* and *Scripture, Tradition, and Interpretation.* Dr. Gasque's major involvement is in the provision of theological resources and education for the laity.

Contents

Foreword

The Good News Bible Commentary Series

Although it does not appear on the standard best-seller lists, the
Bible continues to outsell all other books. And in spite of growing
secularism in the West, there are no signs that interest in its
message is abating. Quite to the contrary, more and more men and women
are turning to its pages for insight and guidance in the midst of the ever-
increasing complexity of modern life.

This renewed interest in Scripture is found outside of, as well as in,
the church. It is found among people in Asia and Africa as well as in
Europe and North America; indeed, as one moves outside of the tradition-
ally Christian countries, interest in the Bible seems to quicken. Believers
associated with the traditional Catholic and Protestant churches manifest
the same eagerness for the word that is found in the newer evangelical
churches and fellowships.

Millions of individuals read the Bible daily for inspiration. Many of
these lay Bible students join with others in small study groups in homes,
office buildings, factories, and churches to discuss a passage of Scripture
on a weekly basis. This small-group movement is one that seems certain
to grow even more in the future, since leadership of nearly all churches is
encouraging these groups, and they certainly seem to be filling a significant gap in people's lives. In addition, there is renewed concern for biblical preaching throughout the church. Congregations where systematic
Bible teaching ranks high on the agenda seem to have no difficulty filling
their pews, and "secular" men and women who have no particular interest in joining a church are often quite willing to join a nonthreatening,
informal Bible discussion group in their neighborhood or place of work.

We wish to encourage and, indeed, strengthen this worldwide movement of lay Bible study by offering this new commentary series. Although
we hope that pastors and teachers will find these volumes helpful in both
understanding and communicating the Word of God, we do not write
primarily for them. Our aim is, rather, to provide for the benefit of the
ordinary Bible reader reliable guides to the books of the Bible, represent-
ing the best of contemporary scholarship presented in a form that does not
require formal theological education to understand.

The conviction of editors and authors alike is that the Bible belongs to
the people and not merely to the academy. The message of the Bible is too
important to be locked up in erudite and esoteric essays and monographs

written for the eyes of theological specialists. Although exact scholarship has its place in the service of Christ, those who share in the teaching office of the church have a responsibility to make the results of their research accessible to the Christian community at large. Thus, the Bible scholars who join in the presentation of this series write with these broader concerns in view.

A wide range of modern translations is available to the contemporary Bible student. We have chosen to use the Good News Bible (Today's English Version) as the basis of our series for three reasons. First, it has become the most widely used translation, both geographically and ecclesiastically. It is read wherever English is spoken and is immensely popular with people who speak English as a second language and among people who were not brought up in the church. In addition, it is endorsed by nearly every denominational group.

Second, the Good News Bible seeks to do what we are seeking to do in our comments, namely, translate the teaching of the Bible into terms that can be understood by the person who has not had a strong Christian background or formal theological education. Though its idiomatic and sometimes paraphrastic style has occasionally frustrated the scholar who is concerned with a minute examination of the original Greek and Hebrew words, there can be no question but that this translation makes the Scripture more accessible to the ordinary reader than any other English translation currently available.

Third, we wish to encourage group study of the Bible, particularly by people who have not yet become a part of the church but who are interested in investigating for themselves the claims of Christ. We believe that the Good News Bible is by far the best translation for group discussion. It is both accurate and fresh, free from jargon, and, above all, contemporary. No longer does the Bible seem like an ancient book, belonging more to the museum than to the modern metropolis. Rather, it is as comprehensible and up-to-date as the daily newspaper.

We have decided to print the full text of the Good News Bible—and we are grateful for the kind permission of the United Bible Societies to do this—in our commentary series. This takes up valuable space, but we believe that it will prove to be very convenient for those who make use of the commentary, since it will enable them to read it straight through like an ordinary book as well as use it for reference.

Each volume will contain an introductory chapter detailing the background of the book and its author, important themes, and other helpful information. Then, each section of the book will be expounded as a whole, accompanied by a series of notes on items in the text that need further clarification or more detailed explanation. Appended to the end of each volume will be a bibliographical guide for further study.

Our new series is offered with the prayer that it may be an instrument of authentic renewal and advancement in the worldwide Christian community and a means of commending the faith of the people who lived in biblical times and of those who seek to live by the Bible today.

W. WARD GASQUE

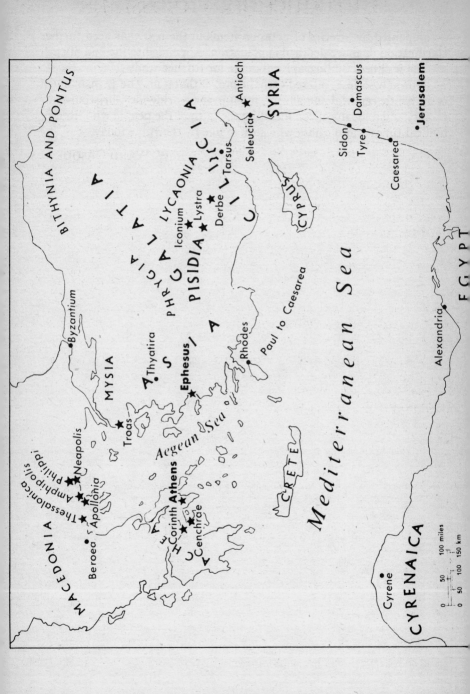

Introduction: Colossians

The City of Colossae

Colossae was a major city situated near the Meander River in the Lycus valley and thus along the main trade route that connected the cities of Phrygia in the east with Ephesus in the west. Historical records indicate that it enjoyed considerable wealth and prestige in ancient times (prior to 400 B.C.). Because of its commercial interests, Colossae had been a significant cosmopolitan city that included diverse religious and cultural elements. The Jewish population was due in part to Antiochus III, who settled about two thousand Jews from Mesopotamia and Babylon in that area around 200 B.C. G. L. Munn observes that "by 62 B.C. the Jews of the Lycus valley were so numerous that the Roman governor forbade the export of currency to pay the temple tax."[1] According to Cicero, there may have been as many as ten thousand Jews living in that area of Phrygia.[2]

Colossae diminished in importance as a city during the Hellenistic and Roman periods. By the time of the Apostle Paul, it was the least important city in the area. Historians record that it was severely devastated by an earthquake in A.D. 61, and unlike its neighboring cities of Laodicea (about ten miles west) and Hierapolis (about sixteen miles northwest), it was never rebuilt. The site was completely abandoned by the eighth century A.D., and to this day no major archaeological work has been carried out on its ruins.

The Church in Colossae

Very little is known about the founding of the Colossian church. The Book of Acts does not specifically record any visit to Colossae by Paul, although scholars such as Bo Reicke have suggested that Paul may have gone to Colossae and other cities in the Lycus valley on his third missionary journey, when he passed through the "region of Galatia and Phrygia" (18:23) and the "interior of the province" on his way to Ephesus (19:1). Reicke takes this to mean the Lycus and Meander valleys, which would have been accessible by the trade route that connected Colossae with Pisidian Antioch.[3]

If this is true, then Paul could be considered the founder of the church. He knows quite a few members of the congregation (4:7–17; Philem.), and those who do not know him personally (2:1) could be recent converts.

The internal evidence of the epistle leads one to conclude that the Colossians first heard the Good News from Epaphras (1:7), who is from Colossae (4:12) and who had become one of Paul's co-workers in the Lycus valley (4:13). Epaphras may have heard Paul teaching in Ephesus, converted to Christianity, and returned home to start a church. According to this reconstruction, Paul was connected with the beginning of the church, but indirectly. The same would be true of other churches that were started as a result of his ministry in Ephesus ("so that all the people who lived in the province of Asia, both Jews and Gentiles, heard the word of the Lord," Acts 19:10).

The False Teaching

The best way to describe the false teaching that was threatening the Colossian church is a syncretistic religious system, that is, a mixture of diverse religious and philosophical components coming from Oriental, Greek, Roman, and Jewish cultures. Phrygia, the area in which Colossae was located, was the home of Cybele, the great mother goddess of fertility. Some descriptions of the features of the Colossian heresy may refer to beliefs and practices of this popular cult.[4]

Since Paul does not deal with the heresy in any systematic way, we are left to reconstruct it on the basis of the words and ideas he uses, as well as from our understanding of the religious systems current in his day. His readers already knew the basic tenets of this teaching, so it was not necessary for Paul to develop it in any detail. The complexity of the system may have led the Christians at Colossae to believe that it was a better solution for their religious hopes and fears than the simple gospel they had heard from Epaphras.

The false teaching had several major components, all interrelated in various ways:

Astrology

In the epistle, Paul warns his readers about the "ruling spirits of the universe" (*stoicheia tou kosmou*, 2:8), "spiritual rulers and authorities" (2:15), and "the worship of angels" (2:18). In ancient thought, the *stoicheia* were the basic or fundamental principles of knowledge and creation, thus making up the totality of the world. Under the influence of Hellenistic syncretism, including Pythagorean philosophy, these "first principles" were elevated to the status of "spirits," personified as cosmic rulers, and, along with all the other astral bodies in the universe, divinized.

One of the basic tenets of astrology is that there is a correspondence between the movements of the gods above and the alterations that take place on earth. People believed that their lives were controlled by these stellar divinities and thus sought to placate them through worship or to defuse their power through sorcery, various rituals, magical rites, and so on. Some of the beliefs and practices that Paul exposes in the epistle are related to astrology. Even the worship of angels may come from the idea that these are powers that control one's destiny (fate) and need to be venerated. Lohse suggests that in some strands of Jewish speculation "the stars themselves were thought of as a distinct class of angels."[5]

Gnosticism

This component of Colossian heresy may explain such references as "worthless deceit of human wisdom" (2:8), "teachings handed down by men" (2:8), "rules about what you eat or drink" (2:16, 20–22), "puffed up by his human way of thinking" (2:18), "false humility" (2:23), and "severe treatment of the body" (2:23).

Gnosticism is the name given to a complex syncretistic religious system in whose teaching knowledge (*gnōsis*) had a crucial place. Since Gnosticism existed in a variety of forms, there is no one unified movement that can properly be called Gnosticism. Much of the scholarly debate today centers around the dating and the doctrines of this heresy that confronted the church throughout its early history.[6]

Traces of Gnostic cosmology, salvation, and ethics can be found in Colossians. The Gnostics accepted the Greek idea of a radical dualism between spirit (God) and matter (the world). They taught that mankind was separated from God by a number of cosmic spheres (usually seven) inhabited and ruled by all sorts of spiritual rulers, principalities, and powers. These are the regions that one must penetrate if one wishes to gain access to heaven.

Salvation, which basically consists of the soul's ascent from earth to heaven, is made possible by *gnōsis*. This saving knowledge is available through such means as doctrinal instruction, ritual, prophecy, sacramental initiation, and self-discovery; it enables an individual to return to the realm of light where the soul becomes reunited with God.

The ethical life of the Gnostics took two major directions. Some moved toward a rigid asceticism. Because they believed that the world was evil, they separated themselves from "matter" in order to avoid further contamination. All the cravings of the body had to be severely restricted. Other Gnostics, however, practiced libertinism, reasoning that since the body already was evil further indulgence in immoral practices would not have any serious consequences. Besides, they felt that they had supernatural *gnōsis* of their "true" nature, so it really did not matter how they lived.

The false teachers in Colossae held to a rigid system of rules and regulations that they felt were necessary to control their behavior. These rules, combined with some forms of Jewish legalism, account for Paul's "manifesto of Christian liberty" in 2:16–23. Basically, he teaches that such dogmas are transitory (2:17), divisive (2:18), enslaving (2:20), temporary (2:22), and useless (2:23). For Paul, these are "manmade rules and teachings" (2:22) and have nothing to do with the true gospel that comes from Christ (2:8).

Mystery Religions

The term *mystery religion* is the name given to a number of beliefs and practices that existed anytime from the eighth century B.C. to the fourth century A.D. They are called mysteries because so much of their teaching and ritual activity was carried on in secrecy.[7]

In Colossians, there may be an allusion to the mysteries in the phrases "the full content of divine nature" (2:9), "special visions," and "false humility" (2:18). Initiates of the mysteries would receive special knowledge and visions of the secrets of the universe. This, in turn, would set them apart from the uninitiated, creating divisions within the society.

Hellenistic Judaism

References to circumcision (2:11), holy days, the new moon festival, the Sabbath (2:16), and the worship of angels (2:18) are definitely Jewish. This is not, however, the orthodox Judaism of Palestine; rather, it is a Judaism that has been thoroughly Hellenized. As such, it forms part of the syncretistic "philosophy" (2:8) that was threatening the Christians at Colossae. Paul does not single out this Jewish element but attacks it along with the entire system.

His solution to the Colossian heresy is found in the application of the Christ hymn (1:15–20), which establishes the pre-eminence of Christ in the universe (cosmically) and in the church (ecclesiastically). Since Christ is superior to every other power in the cosmos (1:15–17; 2:10) and has, in fact, defeated these powers on the cross (2:15), why should believers go on living as if they were still subject to them? They have been set free from these powers by virtue of their union with Christ in baptism (2:20).

Much the same applies to the believers' spiritual life. The path to growth, maturity, and fullness for members within the body comes from their relationship to Christ, the head (2:19), not a return to the enslaving, legalistic rules and regulations that Christ set aside through his death (2:14). The purpose of the exhortations in 3:1 and the following verses is to remind these believers that they need to live out ethically what is theirs theologically because they are members of the body of Christ.

The Purpose of the Letter

If the reason for the writing of Colossians is connected with Epaphras' report to Paul about the false teaching that was threatening the church, then it follows that its purpose is to warn the readers about this heresy and to remind them of the truth of the gospel that they have already received and in which they now live (1:5). Basically, Paul is telling them that Christ has defeated the evil powers by his death on the cross (2:15). This means that the false teaching and enslaving regulations that come from human wisdom and from the ruling spirits of the universe (2:8) have no authority over the believer (2:10); their previous hold over a person's life in the form of an unpaid debt has been canceled (2:14). Paul wants his readers to realize this truth and so reminds them to walk in the light of the traditions that they have received about Christ and the gospel.

This fact accounts for the many references to the truth of the Good News (1:5, 6, 25–27; 2:8, 9, 12, 13) and the admonitions to understand and to live out their hope accordingly (1:9, 10, 12, 23, 28; 2:2, 3, 5–7). The ethical exhortations (3:1ff.) are a further reminder that the Colossians live in union with Christ and under the authority of the exalted Lord.

In Paul's understanding of the gospel there is no room for any kind of exclusivism. His concept of the "mystery" that he has been called to proclaim is that Jews *and* Gentiles, as well as the entire universe, are included in God's plan of redemption (1:20, 25–29). Thus he rejoices that the gospel "is spreading throughout the world" (1:6, 23). Paul's wish is that during—and possibly after—his imprisonment, he may be able to continue his proclamation of the mystery (4:3, 4).

One of the dangers of false teaching in any congregation is that it thwarts God's plan of inclusivism. Those following the "traditions of men" would set themselves up as the enlightened or spiritually elite, believing that their wisdom and legalism make them different from other members in the body of Christ. In opposition to such exclusivism, Paul is inspired to write that believers have already been circumcised in union with Christ (2:11, 12), and as a result of that union, "there is no longer any distinction between Gentiles and Jews" (3:11).[8]

Authorship

Apparently, the Pauline authorship of Colossians was universally accepted until the German scholar E. Meyerhoff questioned it in 1893, largely because of its close dependence upon Ephesians. He was followed by F. C. Baur, who claimed that the heresy described in Colossians could only belong to the second century. Since that time, a number of scholars either hold Colossians to be Pauline or designate it as one of the deutero-Pauline epistles, that is, an epistle written by an author using Paul's name.[9]

The questions of authorship center around the usual categories of vocabulary, style, and theology. Colossians has an unusually high number of *hapax legomena*, that is, it contains thirty-four words that do not appear elsewhere in the NT (New Testament). In addition, there are twenty-eight words that appear in the NT but not in Paul's writings. A number of scholars question whether these could appear unless Colossians were the work of another author.[10]

The style in which the epistle is written is somewhat different from letters that are indisputably Paul's. Scholars have noted that Paul usually deals with theological problems in a vigorous or polemical manner (cf. Galatians, Corinthians, Philippians). In Colossians, the approach is more subdued and less argumentative. The style has a hymnic and liturgical quality about it, and the entire epistle uses a considerable amount of traditional material, that is, Christian teaching that was common in the early church and used by Paul and other writers of the NT.

In spite of the differences in vocabulary and style, however, nearly all scholars agree that these factors alone cannot decide the question of authorship. Some feel that the "special circumstances of the background and purpose of this letter" account for the differences; others claim that because of the high percentage of non-Pauline, that is, traditional, material in the epistle, it is impossible to make any reliable comparisons with Paul's other letters.[11]

E. Lohse, who firmly believes that Colossians is deutero-Pauline, acknowledges that studies of language and style do not settle the matter. For him, it is its theological teaching that sets Colossians apart from Paul and leads to the conclusion that this epistle is the work of a Pauline school using Paul's letters to address a new challenge in the church.

In his detailed and helpful excursus entitled "The Letter to the Colossians and Pauline Theology," Lohse examines the Christology (teaching of Christ), ecclesiology (teaching of the Church), eschatology (teaching of the end times), and sacramentalism (teaching related to Baptism as a sacrament) of Colossians and concludes that in all these areas there are substantial differences with Paul's theology as reflected in his genuine epistles. True, the historical situation necessitated some new theological formulations, but the differences are too divergent, according to Lohse, for Pauline authorship to be supported.[12]

Not all scholars, however, are convinced that the theology of Colossians is non-Pauline. Some believe that the threat of the false teaching required that Paul state and apply his gospel in different ways but deny that he changed or contradicted it. G. Cannon faults Lohse for neglecting the interrelatedness of these theological categories and failing to see that many of the ideas that he labels deutero-Pauline can be found in Paul's chief letters and in the theological affirmations of the traditional material that Colossians uses.[13]

Another argument in favor of Pauline authorship is the close connection between Colossians and Philemon. Since the Pauline authorship of Philemon is rarely questioned, it would follow that Colossians comes from Paul as well. Both epistles contain Timothy's name (Col. 1:1; Philem. 1) and include greetings from the same people (Col. 4:10–14; Philem. 23, 24). Also, Onesimus, the subject of the letter of Philemon, is mentioned as being a member of the group in Colossae (4:9).

Although all contrary evidence needs to be evaluated carefully, it seems reasonable to conclude with G. Cannon "that the author of Colossians was Paul the apostle and that he wrote to the churches of the Lycus valley to warn them about a teaching which advocated practices which would put them in a pre-Christian situation and which contradicted the teachings which they had received about Christ in the Gospel and in baptismal instruction."[14]

Origin

If Colossians was not written by Paul, then it must be the product of the Pauline school that probably was connected with Ephesus.[15] However, if

Paul is the author, then it belongs to one of the "captivity epistles." There are three places of origin that normally are proposed—Rome, Caesarea, and Ephesus.

Rome

The traditional view reconstructed from the Book of Acts is that Paul wrote his captivity epistles while in prison in Rome (Acts 28:16–31; see also Eusebius' *Church History* 11.22.1, which identifies the place of Paul's imprisonment in Col. 4:10 as Rome). The relative freedom that Paul enjoyed in prison and the fellowship of his co-workers make Rome a likely place. Also, it is quite possible that Onesimus, the runaway slave, would have sought anonymity in a large city such as Rome.

There are some factors, however, that mitigate against a hasty acceptance of a Roman origin for Colossians. For one thing, the distance between Colossae and Rome is about twelve hundred miles. Would Onesimus have attempted such a long journey with its increased risk of being caught? Also, according to Philemon 22, Paul expects to be released and to visit Colossae. His request that a room be prepared for him gives the impression that he is close enough for this to happen within a very short time. R. P. Martin also notes that a trip from Rome eastward to Colossae would entail a shift in Paul's missionary strategy, which, according to Romans 15:29, meant going west to Spain.[16]

Caesarea

After Paul was arrested in Jerusalem (Acts 21:27 ff.), he spent two years in prison in Caesarea before he was taken to Rome (Acts 23:33–26:32). Bo Reicke, who is one of the main proponents for this view, argues that Caesarea is the most likely place for Colossians to have been written.[17]

There are a number of supporting arguments: First, a number of the friends who accompanied Paul to Jerusalem and who are with him at prison are from Asia (Acts 20:4; 24:23; cf. Col. 4:7–14 and Philem. 23, 24); second, the missionary activity that Paul envisioned when he wrote Colossians and Philemon and the dispatching of these letters to Colossae with Tychicus make sense if from Caesarea; third, Onesimus would have come to Caesarea because he had friends from that area and would then have returned to Colossae with Tychicus. These, together with other considerations, lead Bo Reicke to conclude that "Philemon and Colossians were sent from Caesarea to Colossae ca. A.D. 59."[18]

Ephesus

The arguments for an Ephesian imprisonment of Paul that could have made the writing of such epistles as Colossians possible are largely arguments from silence. Acts does not record any imprisonment in Ephesus. All that one can say is that the struggles that Paul had in Ephesus (Acts 19:23–41) may be reflected in his correspondence with the Corinthians (1 Cor. 4:9–13; 2 Cor. 1:8–10; 4:4–12; 6:4, 5; 11:23–25). The reference to fighting with "wild beasts" in Ephesus (1 Cor. 15:32) could be a metaphorical expression to indicate verbal confrontation with his opponents rather than a physical struggle with animals as in the gladitorial arena. For Bo Reicke, "It is pure imagination to speak of any captivity in Ephesus."[19]

In spite of the lack of direct evidence, a surprisingly large number of scholars favor an Ephesian imprisonment and origin for Colossians. The proximity of Ephesus to Colossae, the likelihood of Paul's co-workers mentioned in Colossians and Philemon being with the apostle in Ephesus, and the gravity of the riot occasioned by Paul's preaching are mentioned as factors that merit consideration. R. P. Martin, for one, has examined most of the current theories and concludes that the Epistle to the Colossians "belongs to that tumultuous period of Paul's life, represented in Acts 19–20, when for a brief space his missionary labours were interrupted by an enforced spell as a *détenu* [prisoner] near Ephesus."[20]

Though all these suggestions about the origin of Colossians have certain strengths and weaknesses, there does not appear to be any *decisive* evidence for departing from the traditional view, Rome. The inconclusiveness about an Ephesian imprisonment, together with the advanced cosmic Christology of Colossians, make it most likely that the epistle originated during a later period of Paul's life (ca. A.D. 60) and from a setting such as Rome.[21]

Notes

1. G. L. Munn, "Introduction to Colossians," *SWJTh* 16 (1973), p. 10.

2. E. Schweizer, *Colossians*, p. 14, quotes Cicero's *Pro-Flacco* 28.

3. Bo Reicke, "The Historical Setting of Colossians," *RevExp* 70 (1973), pp. 429–33.

4. For additional information on the nature of the false teaching and some of the difficult problems of interpretation, see the commentary text and additional notes on 2:8–23.

5. E. Lohse, *Colossians and Philemon*, p. 98.

6. For some helpful sources on Gnosticism see R. M. Grant, *Gnosticism and Early Christianity* (New York: Harper Torchbooks, 1959); H. Jonas, *The Gnostic Religion* (Bos-

ton: Beacon Press, 1958); R. L. McL. Wilson, *Gnosis and the New Testament* (Philadelphia: Fortress, 1968); E. Yamauchi, *Pre-Christian Gnosticism* (Grand Rapids: Eerdmans, 1973).

7. F. Cumont, *Oriental Religion in Roman Paganism* (New York: Dover, 1956).

8. For further insights into inclusivism in Colossians, see George Cannon, *The Use of Traditional Materials in Colossians* (Macon, Georgia: Mercer University Press, 1983), pp. 217–229.

9. On the question of Pauline and non-Pauline authorship, see A. Patzia, "The Deutero-Pauline Hypothesis: An Attempt at Clarification," *EQ* 52 (1980), pp. 27–42; also see disc. in the Introduction to Ephesians.

10. For a detailed listing and analysis of the vocabulary, cf. Lohse's excursus: "The Language and Style of Colossians," in *Colossians and Philemon*, pp. 84–91. Further parallels between Colossians and Ephesians are discussed by J. B. Polhill, "The Relationship between Ephesians and Colossians," *RevExp* 70 (1973), pp. 439–57; and J. Coutts, "The Relationship of Ephesians and Colossians," *NTS* 3–4 (1956–58), pp. 201–7.

11. R. P. Martin, *Colossians and Philemon*, p. 40; Cannon, p. 175.

12. Lohse, *Colossians and Philemon*, pp. 177–83.

13. Cannon, pp. 196–203.

14. Ibid., p. 14. E. Schweizer makes an appropriate comment on this issue when he writes: "Whether the voice of the apostle comes to us directly or through the mouth of his fellow-worker, it is the message that is essential, not the way in which it reaches us" ("Christ in the Letter to the Colossians," *RevExp* 70 [1973], p. 467); in his *Colossians*, Schweizer has some good practical applications as he addresses the topic "The Epistle to the Colossians Today," pp. 298–302.

15. See n. 9.

16. Martin, *Colossians and Philemon*, p. 26.

17. Reicke, "Caesarea, Rome and the Captivity Epistles," in *Apostolic History of the Gospel*, ed. W. W. Gasque and R. P. Martin (Grand Rapids: Eerdmans, 1970), pp. 277–82; Reicke, "The Historical Setting of Colossians," pp. 429–38.

18. Reicke, "The Historical Setting of Colossians," p. 435. For some decisive arguments against this theory, consult Martin, *Colossians and Philemon*, p. 25.

19. Reicke, "The Historical Setting of Colossians," p. 435.

20. Martin, *Colossians and Philemon*, p. 30. For supporters of the Ephesian origin of Colossians, cf. G. S. Duncan, *St. Paul's Ephesian Ministry* (New York: Scribner, 1930); G. S. Duncan, "Were Paul's Imprisonment Epistles Written from Ephesus?" *ExpT* 67 (1955–56), pp. 163–66; B. W. Robinson, "An Ephesian Ministry of Paul," *JBL* 29 (1920), pp. 181–89; D. T. Rowlingson, "Paul's Ephesian Ministry: An Evaluation of the Evidence," *ATR* 32 (1950), pp. 1–7; Schweizer, *Colossians*, pp. 25–26.

21. A variety of views on the authorship, origin, and nature of Colossians can be found in all of the major "introductions" to the New Testament. Cf. also F. F. Bruce, "St. Paul in Rome. 3. The Epistle to the Colossians," *BJRL* 48 (1966), pp. 268–85.

Note: A list of the abbreviations used in the commentary is found at the end of the book (see p. 272). See also For Further Reading (p. 274); full bibliographical references for works referred to in short-form notes within the commentary are supplied there.

Paul's Greetings

From Paul, who by God's will is an apostle of Christ Jesus, and from our brother Timothy—
²To God's people in Colossae, who are our faithful brothers in union with Christ:
May God our Father give you grace and peace.

The opening greeting in this epistle is typical of the way in which Paul has addressed some of the other churches to whom he has written (1 Cor. 1:1–3; 2 Cor. 1:1–2; Phil. 1:1–2; 1 Thess. 1:1–2; 2 Thess. 1:1–2; cf. Eph. 1:1–2). Although the form of these salutations is quite similar to contemporary Greek models, the content is distinctly Christian and, in the case of Colossians, sets forth some statements that are important to the body of the letter.

1:1 / Paul links Timothy with the writing of this letter (**and from our brother Timothy**). This beloved co-worker had won a respected place in Paul's heart and had become a vital cog in all that Paul was attempting to do for Christ (1 Cor. 4:17; 2 Cor. 1:1; Phil. 1:1; 2:19–24; 1 Thess. 1:1; 3:1 ff.; Philem. 1). By including Timothy in this greeting, Paul communicates to the Colossians that he is not alone in his imprisonment and that someone whom they know from his ministry in Asia Minor joins him in this epistle.

Paul uses a phrase that helps to convey the authority of his message: He is an apostle of Christ Jesus **by God's will.** An apostle is one who is regarded as possessing a certain power and authority. Although there is no indication that the Colossians were questioning Paul's apostolic authority, the content of the letter reveals that they were in danger of falling away from the truth of the gospel by turning to false teachings (2:1–8). Consequently, they needed to hear a strong and authoritative message from one of God's messengers.

1:2 / The Colossians are identified in two ways: First, they are **God's people** (lit., "saints," *hagioi*). It was not uncommon for Paul to call Christians saints (1 Cor. 1:2; Phil. 1:1; Eph. 1:1), because he was referring to their status in Christ and not to the degree of holiness that they may have attained (cf. 1:4). As saints, they are a definite class of people who are called out and separated from their former way of life in order to live in and for Christ (1:21 ff.).

Second, they are **faithful brothers in union with Christ**. Here there is some uncertainty whether Paul's use of **faithful** carries the sense of "reliability," or of "belief," that is, is the apostle referring to those who are faithful to the gospel, or is he referring to those who have been joined together by their faith in Christ and who now form a believing community? Given that many of Paul's greetings and thanksgivings foreshadow later pastoral concerns, it is quite possible that he has the readers' steadfastness or faithfulness in mind (1:10, 23; 2:6, 7).

The greeting ends with an appeal for **grace and peace**, which have their source in God the Father. This serves to draw attention to the favor that God freely and undeservedly bestows upon his people and the healthy or peaceable condition of life that they enjoy because of it.

Paul's Prayer of Thanksgiving

We always give thanks to God, the Father of our Lord Jesus Christ, when we pray for you. ⁴For we have heard of your faith in Christ Jesus and of your love for all God's people. ⁵When the true message, the Good News, first came to you, you heard about the hope it offers. So your faith and love are based on what you hope for, which is kept safe for you in heaven. ⁶The gospel keeps bringing blessings and is spreading throughout the world, just as it has among you ever since the day you first heard about the grace of God and came to know it as it really is. ⁷You learned of God's grace from Epaphras, our dear fellow servant, who is Christ's faithful worker on our^a behalf. ⁸He has told us of the love that the Spirit has given you.

a. our, *some manuscripts have* your.

After the greeting, Paul turns to a prayer of thanksgiving for his readers. Even though he has not ministered to them personally (1:6–8; 2:1), he feels that they are very much a part of his pastoral care and concern. Although Paul certainly is genuine in what he says, it does become apparent that his thanksgivings anticipate some of the problems he will deal with later. Thus, for example, he commends them for their "faith," "hope," and "love," (1:5) and yet strongly encourages them to be filled with the knowledge of God's will and to walk worthy of the Lord (1:9); he praises them for the spread and growth of the gospel in their lives (1:6) but nevertheless prays that they will "bear fruit" and "grow" in the knowledge of God (1:10; 2:6). The entire section 1:3–14 is a beautiful example of how Paul combines praise, thanksgiving, and prayer for his readers.

1:3 / Though the use of the plural **we** may mean that Timothy is a part of the prayer, it is more likely an example of the style that Paul employs on other occasions when he freely alternates between "I" and "we" (cf. 2 Cor. 13:7 ff.; 1 Thess. 1:2, 2:13; 3:9; 2 Thess. 1:3; 2:13). The prayer is **to God, the Father of our Lord Jesus Christ**.

In this expanded version of his prayer (cf. shorter forms in Rom. 1:8; 1 Cor. 1:4; Phil. 1:2; 1 Thess. 1:2), Paul draws attention not only to God as Father—a distinctly Christian insight—but to the **Lord** [*kyrios*] **Jesus**

Christ. This emphasis upon Christ's exalted status as Lord certainly would reinforce the idea that Christ is not an inferior deity but one in whom God himself is found (1:15–20).

1:4 / The next two verses introduce the familiar triad of faith, love, and hope. The numerous references to these concepts in the NT (Rom. 5:1–5; 1 Cor. 13:13; Gal. 5:5, 6; Eph. 1:15–18; 4:2–5; 1 Thess. 1:3; 5:8; Heb. 6:10–12; 10:22–24; 1 Pet. 1:3–8, 21, 22) reveal that they were very much a part of early Christian tradition. Here, Paul is not simply listing them haphazardly but is intentionally developing and applying them for his readers. He has heard of their faith in Christ Jesus from Epaphras, the probable founder of the Colossian church (1:7).

Whereas Christ certainly is the content and object of faith, Paul has in mind the realm or the sphere in which their faith operates; that is, they not only *believe* in Christ but they *live* in him as well (later, in 2:11, 12, and in other passages, such as Rom. 6:1–11; 1 Cor. 12:13, and Gal. 3:26–27, the apostle shows how believers have been baptized into [*eis*] Christ and incorporated into his body). The result of a life *in* Christ is a life *for* Christ. Consequently, Paul can compliment the Colossians on their **love for all God's people**. Their faith in Christ was being demonstrated in a love that had spilled over from their immediate congregation to other churches in the surrounding area, such as Laodicea and Hierapolis.

1:5 / **Hope** is the third member of the triad and is introduced as the basis of **faith and love (so your faith and love are based on what you hope for)**. This message of hope, which is such a vital component of the Christian life, came through the preaching of the Good News. Here Paul is emphasizing that the original and **true message** that they received included a word of hope. It is a possession that they had from the beginning and not something that only the false teachers could offer (2:4, 8).

In this verse, Paul combines the *present* and *future* dimensions of hope. It is normal to think of hope only as something to be realized at the end time when Christ shall appear (3:14). True, hope is a possession given by God and **kept safe for you in heaven**. Scripture does teach that believers will inherit or possess God's promises at some future time (Rom. 8:24, 25). But here Paul is placing a much-needed emphasis on the present aspect of hope. He wants to show his readers that hope belongs to the preaching that they originally heard and that they **already possess** this hope by virtue of being in Christ. Hope is the basis of their love and faith and thus assures them of the adequacy of the gospel they have received. This should preclude any desire to supplement the gospel with additional speculation from the false teachers.

1:6 / Here the emphasis continues to be on the truthfulness of the gospel. In 1:5 it was linked with hope; now the association is with the grace of God. From this, one could conclude that Paul is concerned to show that the message of the gospel is true with respect to hope and grace. But more likely he has the entire message in mind. This Good News, in contrast to the false teachings to which the Colossians have been exposed, is a true message.

The truthfulness and power of the gospel has some practical dimensions as well. First of all, it is universal in scope, that is, spreading (lit., "growing") throughout the entire Roman Empire. The gospel of Christ is for everyone (inclusive) and not for a select few (exclusive) as the heretics are teaching (2:8–15). Second, the gospel is bringing blessings (lit., "bearing fruit") to the whole world even as it is to the Christians in Colossae. The true word of God is something that reproduces and grows (cf. the parable of the sower in Mark 4:1–20 and parallels); it does not sprout and then die out quickly (1 Pet. 1:23–25) as the false teaching was prone to do (2:14–15, 19).

In a sense, Paul is establishing some criteria by which the Colossians can counter the claims of the false teachers. With a concern much like the Apostle John, who wrote "test the spirits to see whether they are of God" (1 John 4:1), Paul wants his readers to test the claims of these heretics against the claims of the gospel. Is it God's truth? Is it universal? Does it bear fruit in people's lives? If not, then it cannot be the Good News that they have received. The gospel needs to bear fruit in order for it to be the gospel!

1:7 / Another test is to consider the messenger. Although Paul did not bring the Good News to Colossae himself, he reminds his readers that they heard (**learned**) it **from Epaphras**, one of their own members whom Paul commends as **faithful worker** of **Christ's** (4:12). This brother, who also shared Paul's imprisonment (Philem. 23), is singled out in 4:13 for his faithfulness and diligence on behalf of the Colossian church.

1:8 / Epaphras has brought the news of the situation in Colossae back to Paul. True, they had some major problems and were in danger of falling into heresy. But Epaphras also told Paul of **the love that the Spirit** [had] **given** them. In other words, their conduct in the community is marked by a love that has its source in **the Spirit** (cf. Rom. 15:30; Gal. 5:22).

Additional Notes

1:3 / For helpful insights on the Pauline thanksgivings, see P. Schubert, *Form and Function of the Pauline Thanksgivings*, *BZNW* 20 (Berlin: Alfred Topelmann, 1939); J. L. White, *Form and Function of the Greek Letter: A Study of the Letter Body in the Non-Literary Papyri and in Paul the Apostle*, SBLDS 2 (Missoula, Mont.: Scholars Press, 1972).

1:6 / There is some ambiguity regarding the translation of this verse and the meaning of "truth." Does the **it** (GNB) refer to **the grace of God** or to **the gospel**, i.e., did the Colossians come to know the gospel, or God's grace, **as it really is** (*en alētheia*)? The RSV has "grace of God in truth"; NIV, "God's grace in all truth." From the Greek it appears that "truth" in 1:6 should keep its identification with **the gospel**, as in 1:5 (*en tōi logōi tēs alētheias tou euaggeliou*). The important point, however, is that Paul's message is based on God's truth and is, therefore, correct teaching. For the phrase "truth of the gospel," see Gal. 2:5, 14.

The concept of "truth" that is employed here is not something that is gained by logical analysis or empirical observation, as in Greek or Western thought. Rather, it conveys the idea of *reliability* in what it claims (Schweizer, p. 35). Thus the Colossians, in addition to hearing the truth, came to recognize it as truth—**as it really is**. Paul places emphasis upon *hearing* and *knowing* the Good News.

Paul's Prayer of Intercession

For this reason we have always prayed for you, ever since we heard about you. We ask God to fill you with the knowledge of his will, with all the wisdom and understanding that his Spirit gives. [10]Then you will be able to live as the Lord wants and will always do what pleases him. Your lives will produce all kinds of good deeds, and you will grow in your knowledge of God. [11-12]May you be made strong with all the strength which comes from his glorious power, so that you may be able to endure everything with patience. And with joy give thanks to[b] the Father, who has made you fit to have your share of what God has reserved for his people in the kingdom of light. [13]He rescued us from the power of darkness and brought us safe into the kingdom of his dear son, [14]by whom we are set free, that is, our sins are forgiven.

b. with patience. And with joy give thanks to; *Or* with patience and joy. And give thanks to.

Following the words of thanksgiving (1:3–8), Paul turns to intercession (1:9–11) and lays a foundation for the Christ hymn (1:12–14). As we have noted (Chap. 2), it is characteristic of Paul to pray specifically for the things that he has mentioned in his thanksgivings (note the **for this reason**). Both the thanksgiving and the intercession are good examples of Paul's continued pastoral concern for this congregation (**we have always prayed for you**) even though he does not know most of them personally.

Although 1:9 forms one of the requests, it stands as a heading for the petitions that follow. Paul begins by asking that his readers be filled with the knowledge of God's will, **with all the wisdom and understanding that his Spirit gives**. This is foundational for the apostle because in Biblical thought there is a close relationship between the *knowledge of* and the *doing of* God's will. Those who are being filled in this way will (*a*) have a worthy walk (1:10a), (*b*) have a fruitful life (1:10b), (*c*) experience growth in the knowledge of God (1:10c), and (*d*) be made strong to endure with patience (1:11).

1:9 / The request that God **fill** (lit., "that you might be filled, *plērōma*), suggests that there is some spiritual vacuum that needs to be corrected. It is the same idea expressed in 4:12 with reference to Epaphras, whose concern for the Colossians was that they stand firm, **mature** (*plērōma*) and fully convinced, in complete obedience to God's will.

The filling is to be with the knowledge of God's will and not some type of speculative or intellectual *gnōsis* ("knowledge") so characteristic of the false teachers. **Wisdom** (*sophia*) and **understanding** (*synesis*) likewise are not some abstract intellectual concepts from the Greek world but attributes that God's Spirit gives. As spiritual gifts from God, they serve to accomplish God's purpose for his people to live abundant, fruitful, and obedient lives. Paul's readers need spiritual wisdom to determine God's will for their lives; they need spiritual understanding to apply God's will to specific situations in life.

1:10 / This verse begins with a construction in Greek (an infinitive of purpose) that expresses the result of being filled with the knowledge of God's will. Hence the GNB **then you will be able to**. The first consequence of knowing God's will is to live as the Lord wants. Other translations have "to lead a life worthy of the Lord" (RSV, NIV) or "so that you may walk in a manner worthy of the Lord" (NASB). The main idea is that a Christian's *profession* is to correspond with his or her *confession*.

Second, the believer is to please the Lord fully in all things. Although the Greek word *areskia* has a negative connotation in secular contexts, here it does not mean seeking favor with someone out of selfish interests or for personal advantage. A life that is lived worthy *of* the Lord will be a life worthy *to* the Lord. Thus a constant goal for a Christian is to please the Lord in every way, that is, in all areas of life.

The third result that the apostle envisions is fruitfulness in good works *and* growth in (by?) the knowledge of God. Although some commentators believe that this sentence expresses two separate petitions (fruitfulness *and* growth), it is better to keep the two Greek participles (*karphorountes* and *auxanomenoi*) together. In 1:6, the apostle stated that the gospel was bearing fruit ("bringing blessings") and growing ("spreading") throughout the whole world. Here he is showing that what is true of the gospel in the world should also be true in the lives of the Colossians.

One of the unfortunate distortions in some forms of Christianity is the misunderstanding of the relationship between theology and ethics, that is, between faith and action. Paul has been presenting a concept of wisdom and knowledge that has moral and practical dimensions. The readers need to be preserved from a barren orthodoxy. The faith that they heard and that transformed their lives is to manifest itself in good works that, in turn, will result in fruitfulness and personal growth (for similar concepts, cf. Rom. 7:4; 2 Cor. 9:8; Gal. 5:6; Eph. 2:10; 4:15; 2 Thess. 2:17; 1 Pet. 2:2; 2 Pet. 3:18). A Christian needs to be active in order to grow spiritually; otherwise, stagnation and regression will set in.

The GNB **grow in your knowledge of God** gives the impression that the growth consists in understanding more and more of God—hence similar to "the knowledge of his will" in 1:9. But the Greek lacks the personal pronoun **your**, and since the dative case in Greek expresses means or instrumentality as well as reference, it may be better to translate this phrase with the word "by" or "through." Paul does not mean, therefore, that their growth is *in* the knowledge of God; rather, it is the *result* of their knowledge of God. Moral and spiritual growth comes from knowing and doing the will of God. God requires (**live as the Lord wants**) and enables each believer to live a worthy and fruitful life.

1:11 / This new life is made possible by the power of God. The repetition of the synonyms **strong**, **strength**, and **power**, show how difficult it is to express the fullness of God's power in words. The expressions that Paul uses here are common in early Christian doxologies that praise God for his glory and power (1 Pet. 4:11; 5:11; Jude 25; Rev. 1:6; 5:13). He knows that his readers are going to need perseverance and steadfastness to continue in the will of God and to accomplish all the things for which he has prayed. Only the divine resources of God's mighty and glorious power can fortify them for this task.

The verb "strengthened" is a present participle (*dynamoumenoi*), indicating that this is a continuous activity of God in the believer and not a once-and-for-all experience. Endurance (*hypomonē*) is that lasting quality that enables one to continue toward a goal. It describes the athlete in Hebrews 12:1 who runs the race to completion or the Christian who patiently bears fruit (Luke 8:15). The Greek word *makrothymia*, often translated as "patience" or "long-suffering," is that quality of self-restraint that enables a person to withstand opposition without retaliation.

1:12 / **And with joy give thanks**: The GNB footnote to this text gives some indication of the difficulty commentators have with the placement of the word **joy**. In the Greek text **with joy** (*meta charas*) is part of 1:11. Hence the idea would be for believers to endure joyfully—a thought similar to Jesus' words in Matthew 5:11–12. Endurance, patience, and joy belong to the fruit of the Spirit (Gal. 5:22–23), and Paul may be calling upon the Colossians to manifest these specific graces in their lives.

The alternative is to connect **joy** with "thanksgiving," as in the GNB (for a similar joining of these two concepts, cf. Phil. 1:4; 4:4–6; 1 Thess. 5:16–18; 1 Pet. 1:8; 4:13). Paul is developing a hymn of thanksgiving (1:12–20) and consequently directs his readers to express his thanks **with joy . . . to the Father**.

The concepts Paul mentions in the following verses are especially appropriate to the situation at Colossae. This church was in danger of turning away from the truth of the gospel (1:5) to "teachings handed down by men" . . . "and not from Christ" (2:8). Since so much of this teaching falsified and depreciated the person and work of Christ, Paul sets out to correct their Christology and does so in the form of a thanksgiving (1:12–14) and a hymn to Christ (1:15–20).

There are several reasons why Paul's readers can rejoice with thanksgiving: First of all, they have an inheritance. The imagery behind this verse probably comes from God's dealing with the people of Israel when he led them out of bondage in Egypt into a portion of their inheritance in the promised land of Canaan (Exod. 6:8). But the new Israel—the church—also has received an inheritance. The reading **your share of what God has reserved for his people** translates an awkward Greek phrase that appears literally as "unto the portion/share which consists in the lot/inheritance" (grammatically, a genitive of apposition that identifies the noun and the word it modifies as the same thing).

Since God has provided the inheritance, he also qualifies or authorizes (*hikanōsanti*) those who obtain it. And all this has already happened to these believers. God has prepared them for their inheritance; they already are God's **people in the kingdom of light**.

People is a translation of *hagioi* (lit., "the separated ones"), normally translated "saints" (RSV, NIV, NASB). The unusual phrase **kingdom of light** is somewhat ambiguous and has received a variety of interpretations. Some commentators take **light** as the *means* by which a Christian qualifies for the inheritance. Others base their understanding on such NT passages as 2 Corinthians 4:6, Ephesians 5:8, and 1 Peter 2:9, where light is used as a metaphor for new life. And a few believe that **light** is analogous in meaning to the "in heaven" of 1:5 or that the author is making a contrast to the "power of darkness" of 1:14 that he anticipates. The saints have been delivered from darkness and live in the domain of light.

E. Lohse draws upon passages from the Dead Sea Scrolls that describe the human "lot" in terms of darkness or light. In this literature, however, the "holy ones" (saints) are the angels and not the people of God.

It is possible that in this context Paul may be thinking of some of the heretical teaching that included the worship of angels (2:18) and the veneration of angelic powers (2:8, 20). If so, his message to the Colossians is that they are joint heirs with the angels (saints) in the realm of light. There is no need to strive for something that they already possess.

1:13 / The second reason for thanksgiving is their deliverance from darkness and their transference to the Kingdom of Christ. Darkness, in the NT, is a metaphor for evil, and those in darkness are without God and live under the rule of Satan, the evil one (Matt. 6:13). Paul, as a messenger of the Good News, was himself told: "You are to open their [the Gentiles'] eyes and turn them from the darkness to the light and from the power of Satan to God, so that through their faith in me they will have their sins forgiven and receive their place among God's chosen people" (Acts 26:18). Christians are described as those who at one time lived in darkness but in Christ have become people of light (Eph. 5:8; 1 Pet. 2:9; 1 John 1:5–10). In this passage of Colossians, Paul reminds his readers that they have been rescued from **the power of darkness**.

The positive side of God's action is that **he brought us safe** (lit., "transferred") into **the kingdom of his dear Son**. The idea expressed by **kingdom** is that of a "rule" and is used as a counterpart to **power**. In other words, as the realm of darkness had a certain power, the transference is to the rule (power, authority) of God's **dear Son** (lit., "Beloved Son," as used at the baptism and transfiguration, Mark 1:11; 9:7, and parallels; cf. also Eph. 1:6). The Colossians have been rescued from the sphere of darkness dominated by evil powers and transferred into the realm of the victorious Son of God.

The phrase **kingdom of his dear Son** or the "Kingdom of Christ," is not common in the NT. Perhaps the apostle uses this expression to emphasize the *present* reality and sphere of their possession in Christ rather than the more common "Kingdom of God," which has a connotation of the future (1 Cor. 6:9; 15:50; Gal. 5:21; 2 Tim. 4:1, 18). Or, Paul simply may be preparing the way for the Christ hymn that follows. At any rate, it serves to remind the readers that they are no longer subject to evil forces; they have been delivered from these powers and are reminded to live victoriously in the power of Christ (3:1–4).

1:14 / The third reason for rejoicing is the forgiveness of sins. Here the subject of the actions is no longer God, as in 1:12–13, but Christ. He is the agent of redemption and the means by which **our sins are forgiven**. The

GNB **by whom we are set free** beautifully captures the essential meaning of redemption as liberation, that is, freedom from the bondage of the evil powers of darkness. The forgiveness of sins is an accompanying result of redemption and not a separate act of Christ as may have been taught by the false teachers.

It would be natural for the Colossians to ask Paul when or where all of this took place in their lives. When has God acted so decisively for us by forgiving our sins and making us children of light? The answer, according to the NT, is in baptism (see note on 1:14).

Additional Notes

1:9 / E. Lohse, (p. 24), has a detailed listing of the words and phrases in 1:3-8 that recur in 1:9-11. He provides some excellent background material to this passage, particularly from the OT and the Dead Sea Scrolls, where the idea is developed that "the will of God demands an obedience that is visible in one's actions" (p. 25). Wisdom and knowledge are gifts of God received through the Spirit. The same is true in the NT, which teaches that to *know* God's will is to *do* God's will (Matt. 7:21; Luke 12:47; 2 Tim. 2:15; Heb. 10:36).

1:10 / On knowledge (*epignōsis*), see J. A. Robinson's extended note in his commentary *St. Paul's Epistle to the Ephesians*, pp. 248-54.

1:12 / See H. Foerster, "*klēroō*," *TDNT*, vol. 3, pp. 758-85. For Lohse's comment on angels, see pp. 35-6 of his commentary. Schweizer thinks that "angels" is unlikely, because *hagioi* is used to describe members of the community (1:2, 4, 26; 3:12).

1:14 / The baptismal language and teaching of Colossians and Ephesians will be brought out in the course of the commentary. On the baptismal motifs of Col. 1:12-14, consult Cannon, pp. 16-19. Cannon's conclusion on these verses is that their confessional nature strongly suggests that Paul was using traditional material connected with the sacrament of baptism.

4

The Hymn to Christ

COLOSSIANS 1:15–20

Christ is the visible likeness of the invisible God. He is the first-born Son, superior to all created things. [16]For through him God created everything in heaven and on earth, the seen and the unseen things, including spiritual powers, lords, rulers, and authorities. God created the whole universe through him and from him. [17]Christ existed before all things, and in union with him all things have their proper place. [18]He is the head of his body, the church; he is the source of the body's life. He is the first-born Son, who was raised from death, in order that he alone might have the first place in all things. [19]For it was by God's own decision that the Son has in himself the full nature of God. [20]Through the Son, then, God decided to bring the whole universe back to himself. God made peace through his Son's death on the cross and so brought back to himself all things, both on earth and in heaven.

Scholars are virtually unanimous in their opinion that verses 15–20 constitute a hymn. And since the existence of hymns in the early church was common (Phil. 2:5–11; Col. 4:16; Eph. 5:19), it is not difficult to believe that this is a carefully written poem intended to convey a specific self-contained message about Christ to the readers at Colossae.

Paul has already alluded to the work of Christ with respect to deliverance and the forgiveness of sins (1:13, 14). In the hymn he continues to draw attention to the person and work of Christ in cosmic and soteriological (pertaining to salvation) terms. Later, in 1:12–13, he shows the readers that the purpose of their reconciliation was to lead a moral and obedient life under the lordship of Jesus Christ.

Whereas most scholars agree on the hymnic nature of these verses, there is less unanimity surrounding such issues as the structure, author, source, and meaning and purpose of the passage.

The Structure of the Hymn

These verses have been arranged poetically in a number of ways. According to some reconstructions of the Greek text, the GNB translation would read as follows:

Strophe I
1:15—Christ is the visible likeness of the invisible God.
He is the first-born Son, superior to all created things.
1:16—For through him God created everything in heaven and on earth, (the seen and the unseen things,
including spiritual powers, lords, rulers, and authorities.
God created the whole universe through him and for him).

Strophe II
1:17—Christ existed before all things,
and in union with him all things have their proper place.
1:18a—He is the head of his body (the church);

Strophe III
1:18b–He is the source of the body's life.
He is the first-born Son, who was raised from death,
(in order that he alone might have the first place in all things).
1:19—For it was by God's own decision
that the Son has in himself the full nature of God.
1:20—Through the Son, then, God decided
to bring the whole universe back to himself.
(God made peace through his Son's death on the cross)
and so brought back to himself all things,
both on earth and in heaven.

The Author of the Hymn

If Paul is considered to be the author of the epistle, then why are there so many questions about the authorship of this specific hymn? The reasons for this are varied and complex, but they center around the fact that (a) the passage contains many words and phrases not found elsewhere in Paul's writings and (b) it was not uncommon for Paul to incorporate previously existing traditional material into his letters. Normally, this included hymns, confessions, creeds, and liturgical materials that were being used by the early church. Where this occurs, Paul could be regarded more as an editor than as the original author.

Most of the Christ hymn in Colossians has come to be regarded as a pre-Pauline composition. Though scholars may disagree on its precise origin, they are quite certain that Paul, in adopting such a hymn, made certain modifications to it in order to apply it to the specific situation at Colossae. (The phrases in parentheses in the reconstruction just given reflect the additions, i.e., interpolations, that Paul *may* have made from the original hymn. The meaning and purpose of these interpolations will be dealt with later in the chapter.)

The Source of the Hymn

A number of sources for the hymn have been suggested. Some scholars have analyzed the content of the hymn from the OT and believe that it has its origin in some type of Rabinical Judaism. Others have come to appreciate its Gnostic background and thus reconstruct the meaning on ideas and language familiar to the teachings of Gnosticism at the time of Paul. Another group of interpreters sees the hymn originating from the circles of Hellenistic Judaism, which, by the first century, had become very syncretistic in its beliefs and practices. Thus it is not uncommon for these authors to refer to Stoic, Gnostic, Hellenistic, and Jewish sources.

The hymn may have had several stages of development: first, as a non-Christian hymn created in the milieu of Greek philosophy and used by such groups as the Stoics and Gnostics; second, as a Christian hymn celebrating the cosmic role of Christ in Hellenistic-Jewish terminology; third, as a Pauline hymn that contains specific additions to correct the erroneous ideas emanating from the false teachers in Colossae.

The Purpose and Meaning of the Hymn

It has been mentioned earlier that Paul's motives for adopting and applying this hymn center around his concern that the Colossians maintain a correct understanding of the person and work of Christ against the false teachings that they have been receiving. They were in danger of falling away from the truth of the gospel to man-made traditions. Paul wants them to remember to follow the Good News as they learned it from Epaphras: "Since you have accepted Christ Jesus as Lord, live in union with him. Keep your roots deep in him, build your lives on him, and become stronger in your faith, as you were taught" (2:6, 7).

The primary purpose of the hymn is to establish the superiority or the pre-eminence of Christ in all things (1:18).

Outline of the Hymn: The Pre-Eminence of Christ
A. Christ's pre-eminence in the cosmos (1:15–17)
 1. The image of the Creator (1:15a)
 2. The agent of creation
   a. of the visible world (1:15b)

1:15 / Christ is the visible likeness of the invisible God. By likeness, Paul does not mean mere resemblance or similarity, because the word used is "image" (*eikōn*). This communicates the idea that Christ participates in and with the nature of God, not merely copying, but visibly manifesting and perfectly revealing God in human form (in 2 Cor. 4:4 Paul talks about "the glory of Christ, who is the exact likeness of God's own being").

The result of the Incarnation is that the invisible God has become visible in the God-man, Jesus Christ. The Apostle John, in a different context, records statements that Christ made: "The Father and I are one" (10:30), and "Whosoever has seen me has seen the Father" (14:9). Such a claim could not be made for any angel or spiritual power. Christ's sovereignty is attested to by his personal and unique relationship to God.

By bearing the image of God in this way, Christ stands apart from the created order as **the first-born Son**, superior to all creation. The phrase **first-born** (*prototokos*) has often been taken in a temporal sense, implying that Christ is the first one to be created and thus belongs to the created order. Apparently the false teachers at Colossae had relegated Christ to the status of a created being. This heresy has a long history, for it was championed by the Arians in the fourth century A.D. and continues to be perpetuated by the Jehovah's Witnesses today.

Paul does not mean that Christ belongs to creation in a temporal way. The issue here is primacy of function, not priority in time. Since Christ participates in the act of creation, he stands over and beyond the created world as the agent by which everything came into existence.

1:16 / After establishing Christ's superiority in the created order, Paul moves on to the invisible world of heavenly and earthly beings. The "all created things" (1:15) is expanded by the phrase that Christ **created everything in heaven and on earth**. The Greek uses two prepositions that aid in the understanding of the action intended: God created the whole universe **through** (*dia*) and **for** (*eis*) **him**. In other words, Christ is both the *agent* and the *goal* of creation. He must not be relegated to the same inferior position as other spiritual powers. All of creation finds its goal in Christ alone. The use of the perfect tense of "created" (*ektisthē*) shows that what has taken place in God's creative activity continues to be effective into the present.

One gets the impression that Paul is taking great pains to avoid any misunderstanding on this matter. He already has emphasized that **everything**, that is, **the whole universe** was created by Christ. Now he amplifies this by the terms **heaven** and **earth** and **the seen and the unseen things**. This includes all **spiritual powers, lords, rulers, and authorities**.

These terms represent a view and classification of **spiritual powers** that was current in the first century. People believed that the world was inhabited by all sorts of alien powers that were a threat to human beings (Rom. 8:38; 1 Cor. 15:24; Eph. 1:21; 6:12; 1 Pet. 3:22). The fact that the reference to these powers is a probable interpolation by Paul into the hymn suggests that these powers were given undue prominence by the false teachers. Paul's point is that these powers are subject to Christ's superiority since they were created *by* and **for** him. He is Lord over all these powers (2:10, 15).

1:17 / The phrase **he existed before all things** serves to reaffirm some of the things that Paul has already said about Christ. But the new thought is that, in union with Christ, all things have **their proper place**. The Greek word *synestēken* that is used here connotes preservation or coherence (RSV, "hold together"). Thus the Lord who creates the universe also sustains it.

1:18 / From cosmic sovereignty, Paul moves on to discuss Christ's preeminence in the church by using the head-body imagery. He has convincingly established Christ's lordship over the world; now he establishes Christ's lordship in the church.

If **the church** can be regarded as a Pauline interpolation, then an earlier version of the hymn must have proclaimed Christ as head of the body only (the GNB inserts **his**, which is not in the Greek. It probably does so because the church is identified as his—Christ's—body). There is much speculation as to the source of the head-body metaphor in Paul's writings. Some scholars are attracted to the idea of "corporate personality" in which all of humanity is considered to be "in Adam." The counterpart in the NT is that, since all Christians are "in Christ"—that is, the church—they can be regarded as the body of Christ. Most scholars, however, believe that the idea comes from Hellenistic conceptions of the cosmic body.

In several Greek sources, including the writings of Plato, the Stoics, and

Philo, there are numerous mythological conceptions of the universe as a body that is governed by a "head." Here, the cosmos is filled by the deity and consequently viewed as the body of the deity over which there is "Wisdom" or "Logos" as its head. The common belief was that, just as man's physical body needs direction and guidance from the head, so the body of the cosmos needs a head such as Logos or Wisdom as a unifying principle.

What the Greeks attributed to Wisdom or Logos for headship, the early church attributed to Christ. He, in other words, is the divine Logos (cf. John's prologue in 1:1–3) who governs the body (*sōma*) of the cosmos. It is quite possible that a Christian version of this hymn initially celebrated Christ's headship over the cosmos. The new development in Colossians is that Paul interprets **body** not as cosmos but as **church**. In other words, although Christ is **head** of the whole world, only the **church** is **his body**.

The identification of **the church** as the **body** of Christ over which Christ is the head in Colossians (1:18, 24) and Ephesians (1:22, 23; 4:15, 16) is not the same as the description of the "body" in Romans and 1 Corinthians. In these two epistles (Rom. 12:1–8; 1 Cor. 12:4–31), Paul uses the concept of the church as the body of Christ and emphasizes the mutual relationships and obligations that exist among its members by virtue of their spiritual gifts. Here the "head" is simply mentioned along with the other members of the body (1 Cor. 12:14–26). Only in Colossians and Ephesians is Christ designated as **head** over **the church**. The reason for this surely lies in Paul's intention to proclaim the lordship of Christ over all things. He wants the Colossians to know that the church is the place where Christ exercises his sovereignty over the cosmos.

This Lord is the **source** (lit., "beginning") of the body's life, vitalizing and energizing it by virtue of his resurrection. Paul utilizes the phrase **first-born Son** for the second time (cf. 1:15) in order to re-emphasize the priority of Christ. The final result of this is Christ's absolute pre-eminence (**in order that he alone might have the first place in all things**).

1:19 / Paul goes on to say that, according to God's decision, **the Son has in himself the full nature of God**. This translation gives no indication of two significant problems connected with the translation and interpretation of this verse.

The first problem is with the meaning of "fullness" (*plērōma*). In 2:9, *plērōma* is equated with all of God's nature as it dwells in Christ ("for the full content of divine nature lives in Christ, in his humanity"). On this basis one is justified in giving it the same meaning as in 1:19 rather than seeing it in some Gnostic way in which *plērōma* is regarded as the totality or fullness of aeons emanating from God and filling the space between heaven and earth. Nevertheless, one aspect of the false teaching in Colossae was that it gave undue prominence to those supernatural powers that filled the universe by regarding them as intermediaries between God and the world. Paul corrects this by affirming that the full nature of God dwells in Christ exclusively.

The second issue centers around the subject of "pleased." The Greek literally reads "because in him (Christ) was pleased all the fullness to dwell." At least three possibilities have been suggested: (*a*) to make Christ the subject, thus giving the meaning that he (Christ) was pleased that all the fullness of God should dwell in him; (*b*) to make *plēroma* the subject, resulting in a translation adopted by the RSV ("for in him all the fulness was pleased to dwell"); and (*c*) to regard God as the subject. Hence the GNB **for it was by God's own decision**, that is, God's good pleasure (cf. NIV: "for God was pleased to have all his fulness dwell in him").

The main argument against this third view is the introduction of God as the subject in a hymn that concentrates on Christ (God has not been mentioned since 1:15). But the Greek text does permit it, and the meaning has support elsewhere in Scripture (cf. Christ's baptism and transfiguration). These technicalities, however, should not detract from the essential truth that Paul wishes to stress, namely, that Christ is the dwelling place (*katoikesai*, "to take up residence") of God. As such, another factor of Christ's sovereignty is established.

1:20 / A final tribute is given to Christ as the agent of reconciliation. God was pleased that his fullness should dwell in his Son (1:19). Now, through the Son, **God decided to bring the whole universe back to himself** (i.e., to reconcile). Reconciliation implies some existing estrangement or hostility that needed to be corrected (1:12, 22; Eph. 2:16). The **all things** that are reconciled is clarified by the phrase **on earth and in heaven**. In other words, it is not just the church (humanity) that has been reconciled; the reconciliation wrought by Christ extends to the entire cosmic order. By doing this, Paul shows the Colossians that every part of the universe is included in the reconciling work of Christ. His love has no limits!

One needs to be careful not to push this language to the extreme. Some have understood it very broadly and believe that humanity and all spiritual powers—including the evil angels—are at peace with God. But such a teaching needs to be interpreted in the light of everything Paul, and indeed the entire NT, says about such doctrines as reconciliation and salvation. The main point Paul makes is that everything has been brought into harmony *through* Christ.

The third Pauline interpolation in this hymn includes the phrase **God made peace through his Son's death on the cross** (cf. Rom. 5:1 ff.). This serves to localize reconciliation in a historical act, accomplished by the shedding of Christ's blood on the cross. Paul will have no part of some cosmic drama that may have been perpetuated by the false teachers.

There is some question regarding **himself**. The RSV and NIV are ambiguous enough that one may take it to mean either God *or* Christ. The same construction (*eis auton*) is used in 1:16, where Christ is the object. The GNB is probably correct in interpreting the verse to mean that reconciliation is to God (**God . . . brought back to himself all things**). Thus reconciliation is *through* Christ but *to* God!

Additional Notes

1:15 / See H. Kleinknecht, "*eikōn*," *TDNT*, vol. 2, pp. 389–90.

1:16 / See W. Michaelis, "*prōtos*," *TDNT*, vol. 6, pp. 865–82; Schweizer, *Colossians*, has a good section on the history of interpretation of this problem, pp. 250–52.

1:18 / "The [Greeks] all thought that the universe was something like a giant body ruled by the gods or, as more and more pagan Greeks would express it in the time of the New Testament, by a god or a supreme power or a universal spirit. There are some who had already used the figure of God as the head of the body, the universe. A Jewish philosopher contemporary of Jesus, Philo of Alexandria, had already spoken of the logos (which means word and/or mind and/or spirit of God) being the head of the universe. Thus, everybody understood that Christ could be the head of the world" (Schweizer, "Christ in the Letter to the Colossians," p. 460).

On "body," see Schweizer, "*sōma*," *TDNT*, vol. 7, pp. 1024–94; M. Barth, "Head, Body, Fulness," *Eph. 1–3*, pp. 183–210; F. F. Bruce discounts a Greek influence on Paul's theology with respect to these concepts in his commentary (pp. 200–5).

1:19 / On "fullness," G. Delling, "*plērēs, plēroō*," *TDNT*, vol. 6, pp. 283–311; Lohse, pp. 52–59; P. D. Overfield, " 'Pleroma': A Study in Content and Context," *NTS* 25 (1979), pp. 384–96; J. A. Robinson, *Ephesians*, pp. 87–89.

1:20 / Barclay lists four different theories on the interpretation of "reconciliation" in this verse: (1) the angels needed reconciliation and redemption because they were under sin; (2) according to Origen, even the devil and his angels would be reconciled in the end; (3) the phrase just emphasizes completeness; and (4) the angels were reconciled to God but not to man (*The Letters to Philippians, Colossians, Thessalonians*, pp. 148–49).

5

The Application of the Hymn to the Colossians

At one time you were far away from God and were his enemies because of the evil things you did and thought. ²²But now, by means of the physical death of his Son, God has made you his friends, in order to bring you, holy, pure, and faultless, into his presence. ²³You must, of course, continue faithful on a firm and sure foundation, and must not allow yourselves to be shaken from the hope you gained when you heard the gospel. It is of this gospel that I, Paul, became a servant—this gospel which has been preached to everybody in the world.

1:21 / In the verses following the Christ hymn (1:21–23), Paul resumes the same kind of pastoral concern so evident in his thanksgiving and prayer (1:3–19). He reminds his readers that the cosmic and ecclesiastical reconciliation that he has just described in the hymn is true for them as well (**at one time you** . . . **"but now"** . . . **"God has made you"**). They have been made acceptable to God and now are challenged to continue in the truth that they have been taught.

A good way to appreciate what God has done is to remember what one was before God's grace was experienced personally (cf. 1:26; 3:7; Rom. 6:22; 11:30; 1 Cor. 6:11). Hence Paul reminds them that in their pre-Christian state they were **far away** from God, and as such, they were God's **enemies**. This enmity manifested itself in an evil manner of life and thought. This stands as quite a contrast to their Christian walk (described in 1:10).

1:22 / But a great change has taken place in their lives because God has acted decisively in Christ. Paul picks up the key word *reconciliation* from the hymn (1:20) and reminds them that God has made them his **friends** (reconciled) **by means of the physical death of his Son**. Both the hymn and this verse emphasize the personal and historical act of Christ. Perhaps the false teachers had either denied or minimized the reality of

Christ's incarnation and death. The emphasis on Christ's physical death may also be a polemic against those who included the angels in the work of reconciliation but who, in contrast to Christ, do not have a body.

Reconciliation has a moral direction to it as well. The GNB captures the Greek (*parastēsai*), which expresses purpose (**in order to bring you, holy, pure, and faultless, into his presence**). Some commentators believe that the terminology used here has sacrificial or cultic meaning (cf. Heb. 9:14; 1 Pet. 1:19). However, the main idea appears to be judicial, that is, those who have been reconciled to God are acquitted of all charges; they are holy, pure, and faultless when they stand before him (Eph. 5:27; Jude 24).

The Good News for the Colossians is that all of this is true for them *now*. This *is* their standing before God because it is his gift to them through Christ. Nevertheless, there is a future aspect in all of this because the "already" and the "not yet" are so characteristic of Paul's writings. What Christians possess now they will have in full at the final Parousia of Christ.

1:23 / Lest his readers entertain any idea that their status in Christ can be treated with indifference, Paul emphatically reminds them of an important condition that needs to be kept in mind: **You must, of course, continue faithful on a firm and sure foundation**. Salvation, although a free gift from God, must be kept. Thus those who have received Christ are admonished to abide or to persevere in Christ (John 8:31; 15:4–7; Acts 14:22; Rom. 11:22; 2 John 9).

To counter the threat of their eroding faith and shifting hope, Paul draws upon some building metaphors that, as elsewhere in Scripture, portray strength, endurance, and security (Matt. 7:24–27; 1 Cor. 3:10–15; Eph. 2:19–22; 1 Pet. 2:4–10). They can only have such a **firm and sure foundation** by following in the faith and hope of the gospel that initially was proclaimed to them as well as to the whole world.

With these themes of faith, hope, and the universality of the gospel, Paul returns full circle to ideas expressed in his opening thanksgiving (1:3–8). There, his concern was that the Colossians see this as evidence for the truth of the Good News; here, he admonishes them to apply this truth to their lives continually.

Paul closes this section by stating that he is related personally to this gospel as a servant (*diakonos*). By doing this, he shows his commitment to the message that the Colossians have heard as well as his identity with his co-workers Epaphras and Tychicus who likewise are servants of the gospel (1:7; 4:7). The statement also serves as a transition to the following verses where Paul outlines his ministry to the church.

Additional Notes

E. Schweizer summarizes the hymnic nature of this passage rather well when he writes: "It is no longer a matter for dispute that we have in these verses a hymn which has been taken over by the author. The prerequisites for this are present, as far as form is concerned; there is a certain rhythm in the construction both as a whole and in detail. There is also a portrayal of Christ, self-contained and surpassing anything that might be expected in the context; and again, there is the customary opening by means of the relative pronoun. More importantly, the distinctive characteristics of the style of the author of the Epistle are not found here, although they otherwise appear throughout the letter, while a plethora of unusual concepts also appear. Above all, however, one cannot help but notice the theological difference between the hymn itself and the commentary which the author of the Epistle provides" (pp. 55–56).

On the reconstruction of the strophic divisions of the hymn as presented by such scholars as E. Norden, J. M. Robinson, and E. Schweizer, see G. Cannon, pp. 19–23. R. P. Martin divides the passage into three parts: Strophe I (1:15–16); Strophe II (1:17–18a); Strophe III (1:18b–20), pp. 55–56. See also Martin's *Reconciliation*, pp. 111–26.

For a recent presentation of the hymnic material in the NT, see G. Cannon, pp. 6–9, esp. n. 17, for bibliographical sources. For Cannon's discussion of 1:15–20, see pp. 19–37. Lohse lists twenty-three significant studies on the hymn (pp. 41–46). Other helpful sources include W. McCown, "The Hymnic Structure of Colossians 1:15–20," *EQ* 51 (1979), pp. 156–62; E. Schweizer, pp. 55–88; E. Schweizer, "The Church as the Missionary Body of Christ," *NTS* 8 (1961), pp. 1–11; E. Schweizer, "Christ in the Letter to the Colossians," pp. 455–62. On the baptismal nature of the hymn, E. Käsemann, "A Primitive Christian Baptismal Liturgy," in *Essays on New Testament Themes*, SBT 41 (London: SCM, 1964), pp. 154–59.

1:21 / The Greek word *apallotrioō* ("alienated, estranged") occurs only here and in Eph. 2:12; 4:18. The use of the perfect tense (*apēllotriōmenous*) emphasizes that their alienation (**you were far away**) was a continuous state of being.

1:22 / Anyone using the Greek text will discover a number of variant readings on the idea of reconciliation, showing the struggle that translators have had with this verse. The GNB, along with other English translations, accepts the active "he reconciled" rather than the passive "you (plural) were reconciled."

1:23 / The phrase **preached to everybody in the world** (cf. 1:6) is not to be taken literally unless it refers to the Roman Empire. Rather, this is a polemical statement to show the inclusiveness of the gospel as opposed to the exclusivism of the false teaching.

6

Paul's Personal Suffering

And now I am happy about my sufferings for you, for by means of my physical sufferings I am helping to	complete what still remains of Christ's sufferings on behalf of his body, the church.

1:24 / Paul begins his discussion by referring to his **physical sufferings** on behalf of the Colossian church. The fact that he is in prison may be uppermost in his mind (4:18), although there may be a general reference to other afflictions that he has experienced throughout his ministry as an apostle of Jesus Christ (2 Cor. 1:4, 6, 8; 2:4; 6:4; 7:4; 8:2; Phil. 1:17). The "rejoicing" does not come because Paul is undergoing trial or persecution. Paul is happy because his **sufferings** are for the believers at Colossae. In this, as well as in such passages as Romans 5:3, 8:38 ff., the apostle captures the spirit of Jesus' words in Matthew 5:10–12, where happiness and persecution are linked together (cf. 1 Pet. 4:13).

In other passages, Paul indicates that his **sufferings** (afflictions) can be understood in a number of ways: They are a consequence of the Christian life and serve to further the gospel (2 Cor. 6:4; Phil. 1:17, 18, 24; 3:10); they enable one to comfort others who are experiencing distress (2 Cor. 1:4, 5); they serve to keep one humble (2 Cor. 12:10); and they are a preparation for future glory (2 Cor. 4:17). The apostle Peter indicates that trials serve as a refining process for faith (1 Pet. 1:6, 7), and James mentions that they produce steadfastness (1:3, 4).

The major difficulty in this verse is how to understand Paul's statement that **by means of my physical sufferings I am helping to complete what still remains of Christ's sufferings on behalf of his body, the church**. This is different than suffering *for* Christ (Phil. 1:29) or even sharing *in* Christ's suffering (Phil. 3:10). Paul understands that his suffering somehow *completes* what is lacking in Christ's afflictions for the church.

A number of interpretations have been suggested for this verse: One view, notably the Roman Catholic, sees a certain deficiency in Christ's suffering for the redemption of the church and believes that Paul's sufferings, as well as the suffering of saints and martyrs, can supplement or complete what was lacking in Christ.

But this view has come under attack for several reasons. Scripture simply does not support the idea that Christ's suffering on behalf of the church, that is, his reconciling work through the atonement, is incomplete in any way. He is the perfect sacrifice for sins, and no one can add to his finished work. Indeed, it would be foolish and contradictory for Paul to imply such an interpretation in a context in which he has just finished emphasizing the sovereignty of Christ in all things. Besides, the Greek word used here for suffering (*thlipsis*) is not used in the NT with reference to Christ's atoning death.

A second interpretation acknowledges the perfection and completion of Christ's death and concedes that no amount of human suffering can add anything to that. Emphasis, therefore, is given to the edificatory nature of the sufferings that Christians endure for the building up of the church, the body of Christ. In other words, the church is built up by the sacrifices, afflictions, or sufferings of Christians everywhere. Certainly there is some truth to this, and it may imply what Paul means by suffering for Christ's sake (Phil. 1:29). However, this hardly does justice to the idea of completing what still remains of **Christ's sufferings on behalf of his body**.

A third and rather detailed interpretation looks for a solution in Jewish and early Christian apocalyptic literature. E. Lohse, for example, believes that the phrase "what is lacking in Christ's afflictions" is equivalent to the concept of "a definite measure for the last days." Here it was believed (cf. also Matt. 24; Mark 13:5–27) that the return of God's anointed, the Messiah, would be preceded by a period of time when God's people would be called upon to suffer the "woes of the Messiah." Some commentators suggest that Paul sees himself as a martyr whose sufferings contribute to completing this period that awaits the return of the Messiah. Paul, therefore, suffers as a servant of the gospel and on behalf of Christ's body, the church.

It is quite possible that Jewish apocalyptic thought serves as a background for Paul's ideas on suffering. But whereas the Jews continued to wait for the Messianic kingdom, the early Christians believed that the eschatological kingdom was inaugurated in the life and ministry of Jesus who suffered vicariously for his people.

A fourth view places Paul's statement within the context of the mystical union that the apostle has with Christ. Here reference is made to Paul's communion (fellowship) in Christ's death and resurrection (Rom.

6:3–11; 2 Cor. 4:10–14; Phil. 3:10) or to Acts 9:4, where Paul's persecution of the church is equivalent to persecuting Christ himself ("Saul, Saul, Why do you persecute me?"). Paul's sufferings for the church, therefore, could be viewed as the sufferings of Christ himself, but through a member of his mystical body.

Some writers employ the term *the corporate Christ,* by which they mean that the sufferings of the church, or individual members of it, are one with the sufferings of Christ. In other words, the afflictions of the church are also Christ's afflictions. Paul's suffering for the church completes Christ's personal suffering.

After the death, resurrection, and exaltation of Jesus, the Christian community believed that they were called upon to suffer just like their Lord, although their suffering had no redemptive efficacy. Scripture is full of references that show that they were to expect various trials, tribulations, and persecutions (Matt. 5:10–12; 20:23; John 15:20; Acts 9:16; Rom. 8:17; 2 Cor. 6:4; Phil. 1:29; 2 Tim. 1:12; 4:5; James 1:2; 1 Pet. 1:6; 2:21; 3:14; 4:1, 13, 16; 5:10; Rev. 2:10).

With the development of Paul's mysticism, that is, his teaching of incorporation into Christ through baptism (Rom. 6:1–10; Col. 2:11, 12; Gal. 3:26–28), the followers of Christ came to believe that their sufferings and the sufferings of Christ were one. It could be that by the statement in 1:24 Paul sees the afflictions that he is suffering in his flesh as the afflictions of Christ (cf. 2 Cor. 1:5; 4:10; Phil. 3:10; 1 Pet. 4:13, for helpful parallels). Paul believes that he is helping to complete what the Messiah began for the church but will not be completed until his return.

One other interpretation understands the phrase "what is lacking in the sufferings of Christ" (RSV) to refer to a deficiency *in Paul* and not in Christ. Paul realizes that his desire to share in Christ's sufferings and to become like his Lord in death is a continuing process (Phil. 3:10). He sees his suffering as a means by which he personally is enabled to reproduce more and more of Christ's Passion in his life. The suffering that the church endures is, therefore, for *its* completion and not toward anything lacking in Christ (see note).

Additional Notes

1:24 / For additional material on some of these interpretations, see R. Yates, "Notes on Colossians 1:24," *EQ* 42 (1970), pp. 88–102; on suffering, H. Schlier, "*thlibō*," *TDNT*, vol. 3, pp. 139–48. E. Schweizer, p. 98, lists a number of German sources on the suffering of Paul. Also helpful is F. Hauck's article "*koinos*" ("fellowship"), *TDNT*, vol. 3, pp. 789–809, esp. pp. 806–7, where he discusses the fellowship that the believer enjoys with Christ.

Lohse's view on the "woes of the Messiah" is discussed in his commentary, pp. 69–72. R. P. Martin adopts this interpretation of 1:24 when he states: "Paul takes over this notion and bends it to his purpose. In his life of service to the Gentile churches he is called upon to represent his people as a martyr figure and to perform a vicarious ministry (2 Cor. 1:6); and in this way he completes the still deficient tally of sufferings which God's new Israel had to endure before the end of the age" (p. 70).

The last interpretation suggested has the support of a number of authors. As early as 1958, E. Hoskyns and N. Davey stated: "This does not mean that there was something lacking in Christ's suffering, but that there was something lacking in St. Paul's. He desires that his body may be, as it were, the arena where the obedience to God may be as wholly displayed as it had been in the passion of Jesus Christ" (*The Riddle of the New Testament* [London: Faber & Faber, 1958], p. 158).

Similar statements are made by L. P. Trudinger, "Further Brief Note on Colossians 1:24," *EQ* 45 (1973), pp. 36–38; and W. F. Flemington, "On the Interpretation of Colossians 1:24," in *Suffering and Martyrdom in the New Testament* (Cambridge: Cambridge University Press, 1981), pp. 84–90. Flemington's ideas are clearly summarized in this quotation: "The defect that St. Paul is contemplating lies not in the afflictions of Christ as such, but rather in the afflictions of Christ as they are reflected and reproduced in the life and behavior of Paul his apostle. St. Paul strives continually to live *en Christōi*, but he knows that in his life there is, as it were, an unpaid balance that needs to be made up before the reproduction of Christ's sufferings in Paul's person is complete. Paul rejoices because in all that he is suffering on behalf of the Colossians he is reducing his unpaid balance, he is making the reproduction a little more like the perfect original" (pp. 87–88).

7

Paul's Proclamation
of the Mystery

COLOSSIANS 1:25-29

And I have been made a servant of the church by God, who gave me this task to perform for your good. It is the task of fully proclaiming his message, [26]which is the secret he hid through all past ages from all mankind but has now revealed to his people. [27]God's plan is to make known his secret to his people, this rich and glorious secret which he has for all peoples. And the secret is that Christ is in you, which means that you will share in the glory of God. [28]So we preach Christ to everyone. With all possible wisdom we warn and teach them in order to bring each one into God's presence as a mature individual in union with Christ. [29]To get this done I toil and struggle, using the mighty strength which Christ supplies and which is at work in me.

1:25 / In this verse Paul continues to affirm his personal role in the events that he is describing: first, "I" became a servant of the gospel (1:23); then "I" am happy about my suffering for you (1:24); now **I have been made a servant of the church by God** on your behalf (1:25). **Task** is a translation of the Greek word *oikonomia*, which has the meaning of "management, stewardship, or commission to an office" (1 Cor. 9:17). Paul reminds his readers that his commission is by divine appointment and that they are included in his ministry, which is the task of fully proclaiming the gospel.

Fully should not be taken to imply that the previous proclamation of the Good News from Epaphras was somehow deficient or incomplete. Paul probably has the scope of the gospel in mind (Rom. 15:19). He already has alluded to the universality and the growth of the gospel (1:16); now he claims that God has appointed him to share in that task as well. The word of God will be fulfilled when it has been preached throughout "the world" (1:23). However, given the situation at Colossae, it is not impossible that Paul is thinking of the content of the Good News. Both the NIV ("to present you the word of God in its fulness") and the NEB ("to deliver God's message in full") understand it this way.

1:26 / The word of God that Paul has been called to proclaim is identified as **the secret** that God **hid through all past ages from all mankind**. The word **secret** is a translation of *mystērion*, which is used in Greek literature to convey the idea of something secret, mysterious, and unknown. The Greek "mystery religions," for example, were given their name because they performed secret rites on those who were initiates (the *mystēs*).

This term *mystery* is used rather extensively in the NT (twenty-seven times in all, twenty of which occur in Paul), and so its meaning must be determined by the context. Here, as in 2:2, Ephesians 1:9; 3:3, 4, 9; 6:19, and Romans 16:25–26, it refers to an aspect of the gospel that had previously been hidden but now, according to the good pleasure of God, has been **revealed to his people**.

1:27 / Paul leaves his readers in some suspense before disclosing the content of this mystery. **God's plan**, he begins, is to make known his rich and glorious secret which he has for all of mankind. And that secret, he goes on to clarify, is that by virtue of their incorporation into Christ his readers will share in the glory of God. The gospel, in other words, initiates a process that proceeds toward a goal that is yet to be fully realized. The content of the mystery is expanded in Ephesians, where the author shows that God's plan was to include the Gentiles in his plan of salvation so that they, along with the Jews, are members of his body (Eph. 2:11–22; 3:2–12).

It is possible to translate the Greek *en* to read Christ *among* you rather than Christ *in* you. If so, the emphasis is upon the preaching of Christ in their midst rather than Christ dwelling within their hearts. But though this may fit the context, it is also true that the Colossians personally share in this mystery by virtue of the indwelling Christ. The mystery is that Christ is both in and among them. They are members of Christ's body here and now; nevertheless, there is an eschatological ring to this concept because their hope is directed toward the glorious future.

1:28 / Now that the nature of the mystery is revealed, Paul adds some specifics to his own commission. By changing the "I" (1:23, 24, 25) to *we*, he accomplished two things: First, he includes his co-workers, particularly Epaphras and Tychicus, who served the Colossian church; second, he sets the true messengers of the secret apart from the false ones who have been invading the church with a different gospel.

Paul's task included the proclamation of Christ to **everyone**. Since this follows so closely after the clarification of the mystery, Paul must mean that his message is the content of the mystery, that is, Christ is in you, the hope of glory. To proclaim Christ is equivalent to proclaiming the gospel (1 Cor. 9:14) or the word of God (Acts 13:5; 17:13).

Besides proclamation, there is instruction: **With all possible wisdom we warn and teach them**. *Nouthetountes* is a pedagogical term used for training, disciplining, and warning (Rom. 15:14; 1 Thess. 5:12, 14). Paul must have found it necessary to protect the community from drifting away from the truth. The teaching is with all possible wisdom, implying, as in 1:9, a practical application to his instruction and not some speculative or esoteric knowledge.

The wisdom that Paul shares with his readers has a definite practical and ethical direction (cf. 1:6, 9); its goal is to bring each member **into God's presence as a mature individual in union with Christ** (cf. 4:12). Two important truths stand out in contrast to the teaching of the false teachers. First, the gospel is for **everyone**; it is a universal message available to all, not only to a special group of initiates. Second, the goal is maturity in Christ (**a mature individual in union with Christ**). The Gnostics stressed the perfection (*teleios*) of those who claimed to be filled with some special wisdom or power. Paul's goal, however, in preaching, admonishing, and teaching was to lead his readers into a mature spiritual life in Christ (cf. Eph. 4:13, 14).

1:29 / Even though Paul was not personally responsible for bringing the gospel to Colossae, he stresses that he labors for this Christian community. **To get this done**, that is, proclaiming the mystery, demands intense desire and hard work (**I toil** (*kopiō*) **and struggle** (*agōnizomenos*). Devoting such intensity to his task would be impossible without the enabling strength that Christ provides.

Additional Note

1:26, 27 / Some helpful information on "secret" (mystery) can be found in G. Bornkamm, "*mystērion*," *TDNT*, vol. 4, pp. 802–28; W. P. Bowers, "A Note on Colossians 1:27a," in G. Hawthorne, ed., *Current Issues in Biblical Patristic Interpretation* (Grand Rapids: Eerdmans, 1975), pp. 110–14; Lohse, pp. 74–75. For additional discussion, see Chapter 3 on Ephesians.

Paul's Concern
for the Churches

COLOSSIANS 2:1–5

Let me tell you how hard I have worked for you and for the people in Laodicea and for all others who do not know me personally. ²I do this in order that they may be filled with courage and may be drawn together in love, and so have the full wealth of assurance which true understanding brings. In this way they will know God's secret, which is Christ himself.ᶜ ³He is the key that opens all the hidden treasures of God's wisdom and knowledge.

⁴I tell you, then, do not let anyone deceive you with false arguments, no matter how good they seem to be. ⁵For even though I am absent in body, yet I am with you in spirit, and I am glad as I see the resolute firmness with which you stand together in your faith in Christ.

c. God's secret, which is Christ himself; *some manuscripts have* God's secret; *others have* the secret of God the Father of Christ; *others have* the secret of the God and Father, and of Christ.

2:1 / In the following verses (2:1–5) Paul elaborates upon his ministry as a servant of Christ. With the exception of 1:24, the previous section (1:24–29) describes a more general or universal situation: Paul suffers on behalf of the entire church; he is a servant of God who proclaims the "mystery" to all men; and he teaches in order that everyone may become a mature person in Jesus Christ. But the toil and agony that characterized his ministry to all the Gentiles is particularly evident in his relationship to the Colossians and the other congregations in the Lycus valley.

Paul has worked as hard—literally, agonized (1:29)—for those whom he has never seen as for those to whom he has personally ministered. But he does not develop an inflated ego; nor does he sink into self-pity. He simply ties his labor in with the specific goals that he has sought to accomplish.

2:2 / Paul's ultimate goal is to encourage his readers (**that they may be filled with courage**). **Courage** is a good translation of the Greek *para-klēsis* because Paul desires that they be strengthened or fortified inwardly in order to face the opposition. It also conveys the idea of warning and consolation, both of which were necessary in this situation.

But how does one gain such inner courage? Paul's answer is that it comes from unity in love and full knowledge in the mystery of Christ. The congregation will be filled with courage as they are **drawn together** (*symbibasthentes*) **in love**. In other words, love is the principle that unites them as the people of God and enables them to face the enemy courageously. This courage also comes from conviction of truth (**the full wealth of assurance which true understanding brings**). There is no room for doubt here, since the word *plērophoria* means "full assurance," or "complete understanding." The object of this conviction is none other than **God's secret, which is Christ himself**. The thoughts that Paul develops here are very similar to Ephesians 3:17–21, which mention inner strengthening, love, understanding, and maturity.

2:3 / This verse is the bottom line to the thoughts that Paul has been developing about the mystery. The mystery ("secret") is Christ (2:2) and ultimately, **he is the key that opens all the hidden treasures of God's wisdom and knowledge**. Paul already has established the pre-eminence of Christ by showing that·he is the supreme and complete revelation of God (1:15–20). It is not surprising, therefore, that Christ embodies *all* of God's wisdom and knowledge as well. There is no need for the Colossians to look beyond Christ; there is no purpose in pursuing other systems of thought; there is no value in secret initiations. Christ is all and in him are all things!

2:4 / Up to this point it has been suggested that most of Paul's language and thoughts need to be interpreted within the context of the heresy that is threatening the church. Here, however, there is the first direct reference to the activity of these false teachers, who, apparently, were very skilled with words. The Greek uses two very colorful words to describe their devious methods: first, they use very persuasive language (*pithanologia*, lit., "pithy speech"); second, they have the ability to deceive, delude, or to seductively charm (*paralogizomai*) their victims. This necessitates Paul's strong warning to the Colossians: **Do not let anyone deceive you with false arguments, no matter how good they seem to be**.

2:5 / Paul, although personally unknown by and physically separated from the church, is with them *in spirit*. By *spirit* he probably means more than his nonphysical parts such as thoughts, heart, or mind. He is with them because of their common faith in Christ; to be in Christ is to be in the Spirit—the Spirit of God (Rom. 8:9 ff.).

The spiritual presence of Paul with this congregation is so real that he actually speaks of seeing them. And what Paul sees causes him to rejoice, for they have not yet succumbed to the false teaching. His prayers and his labor have not been in vain; the Colossians stand firmly together in their faith in Christ.

Additional Note

2:3 / Schweizer makes a good point that knowing Christ is never finished once and for all: "Revelation can only occur when one hears again and again afresh. Indeed, the point thus articulated is that Christ is sufficient, and that there are no other mysteries important for salvation besides or in addition to him. On the one hand, it is the case, then, that the whole revelation of God takes place once and for all in Christ, and one need no longer seek knowledge anywhere else, as some of those in Colossae were obviously trying to do. On the other hand, however, one can never appropriate such knowledge once and for all; rather, one must discover it again and again afresh, by allowing it to be given by Christ" (p. 118).

9

A Summons to Steadfastness

COLOSSIANS 2:6–7

Since you have accepted Christ Jesus as Lord, live in union with him. ⁷Keep your roots deep in him, build your lives on him, and become stronger in your faith, as you were taught. And be filled with thanksgiving.

2:6 / The Greek text begins with a "therefore," indicating that what the apostle is about to say is linked with his preceding discussion on the content of the mystery which is *Christ himself*. As someone has said, "Whenever you see a *therefore* in Scripture, go back to see what it is there for!"

To stand firm does not mean to stand still. Paul is aware that the best defense is a good offense. Consequently, he admonishes his readers to continue on in their faith. By receiving the Good News they **have accepted Christ Jesus as Lord**. But that past event has an abiding significance upon their lives because they are to live in union with him—literally, to "walk with Christ." By stating this, Paul reinforces a theme common in his writings, namely, the relation between theology and ethics (3:1 ff.; Eph. 4–5). Those who have **accepted Christ** are to live in Christ; or, those who are in Christ (the indicative of the Christian life) are to become what they are (the imperative of the Christian life).

2:7 / Paul amplifies what it means to live in union with Christ by utilizing the images of planting and building. The GNB **keep your roots deep in him**—or any English translation for that matter—does not quite capture all the significance of the Greek tenses that are employed. For "rooted," Paul uses the perfect tense, which, in Greek, describes a present state that is the result of some past action. Here the meaning that the perfect passive conveys is equivalent to "having been rooted."

For the building metaphor, Paul uses the present tense, which describes continuous action. The building up of their life in Christ (*epoiko-domoumenoi*) and the establishing (*bebaioumenoi*) of their faith is an ongoing process that is only possible because they are already rooted in the

34

Lord. Hence the imperative tone in the GNB: **Build your lives on him, and become stronger in your faith**.

Some commentators suggest that the reference to "the faith" should be understood as "by your faith" (an instrumental dative) or "with respect to your faith" (a dative of reference). If the former, then the idea is that they are being built up by means of their faith—faith is the instrument of their growth. If the latter, then Paul desires that the Colossians grow in their faith (so GNB, RSV, NIV). Perhaps it may be wrong to make such a fine distinction, because as one grows in Christ one is established both *in* and *by* faith.

The **as you were taught** is a specific reference to the Good News that the Colossians heard and have come to know as the truth of God (1:6). Paul is on the verge of exposing the heresy, and he wants his readers to know that their growth in Christ depends upon following the gospel as orginally delivered to them (1:5–8; 2:6), not some secondary traditions of the false teachers (2:8).

And be filled with thanksgiving: Paul has already mentioned thanksgiving (1:3, 12) and will do so again in 3:15 and 4:2. This phrase surely ties in with his previous admonition to walk in the Lord (2:6). In other words, the Christian life is to be characterized by gratitude to God.

Christian Versus Human Tradition

See to it, then, that no once enslaves you by means of the worthless deceit of human wisdom, which comes from the teachings handed down by men and from the ruling spirits of the universe, and not from Christ. ⁹For the full content of divine nature lives in Christ, in his humanity, ¹⁰and you have been given full life in union with him. He is supreme over every spiritual ruler and authority.

2:8 / Earlier, the readers were cautioned about some of the methods employed by the false teachers (2:4). Now, in a stern warning (**see to it, then**), he exposes this heresy even further. First, its effect is to enslave its victims. The word *sylagōgeo* describes the action of one kidnapping or plundering and then making off with the catch as a prize. It is an appropriate way of portraying the malicious and seductive nature of the heresy.

Second, **it is worthless deceit of human wisdom** (RSV: "philosophy and empty deceit"; NIV: "hollow and deceptive philosophy"). This is the only time that the word *philosophia* occurs in the NT, so it must have been a special feature of this hersey. Paul is not objecting to the study of philosophy (lit., "one who loves wisdom"), because in the Hellenistic world religious communities offered their teaching as philosophy. His concern is with those who have turned the pursuit of wisdom into a "philosophistry" characterized by empty and deceitful practices. This teaching is **worthless** because it does not contain the truth; it is **deceitful** because it captivates people and prevents them from seeing the truth.

Third, these teachings are human and not divine in origin. The teaching according to Christ is Paul's reference to the word of truth, the gospel, which came to the Colossians directly through Epaphras (1:5–7) and indirectly through Paul as God's appointed servant (1:24, 25). The false teachers cannot make such a claim, because their doctrines come from human sources and from **the ruling spirits of the universe** (*stoicheia tou* *kosmou*, lit., "elements of the universe." Most English translations add the word **spirits** to the phrase and come out with "elemental spirits of the universe" (RSV), "elementary principles of the world" (NASB), or "basic principles of this world" (NIV). In Heb. 5:12, the NEB translates the phrase as "the ABC of God's oracles".

As the additional notes will show, there is a wide variety of scholarly opinion as to the meaning of these concepts in the NT (Col. 2:8, 20; Gal. 4:3). The term *stoicheion* is used to indicate something basic or rudimentary, such as the fundamental principles of learning (the ABCs), or the elements from which the world was created (earth, air, fire, and water). These "principles" *may* have been elevated to the level of spirits or angels in the Hellenistic world.

Stoicheion also designates the heavenly bodies that in some cases were personified and worshiped. The control that these elemental spirits had over human beings (fate) could only be broken by correct knowledge (*gnōsis*) and/or ritual, usually in the form of magic or ascetic practices (cf. 2:20–23). But these *stoicheia* could also be the source of wisdom or knowledge and in this way provided the substance of the false message that Paul deals with in the subsequent verses (2:16–19) and exposes as being contrary to the gospel of Christ.

2:9 / In this verse Paul returns to a theme already developed in the Christ hymn (1:15–20) and re-emphasizes that the Colossians do not need any additional source of revelation or authority for their spiritual life. Christ is not simply another of the spiritual forces that makes up the fullness (*plērōma*) of the universe (cf. 1:19). He is superior to all others because he alone is God incarnate and the whole fullness of deity is found in him.

2:10 / But there is more to this wonderful message: The one who is the fullness of the Godhead is likewise the fullness of each believer. The community is fulfilled in him. The Colossians do not need to look beyond Christ for their understanding of the universe; nor do they need to supplement him in their personal lives, because those who are "in Christ" participate in his fullness *now* (the Greek present tense *este*, "you are"). In other words, there is nothing lacking in their relationship to God. Paul ends by reasserting (cf. 1:15–20) Christ's pre-eminence over all alien powers (**he is supreme over every spiritual ruler and authority**). There is no need, therefore, to pay homage to them!

Additional Notes

2:8 / For some comments on the false teaching at Colossae see the Introduction. Nearly every major commentary has a discussion on the heresy as well as on the meaning of *stoicheia tou kosmou*: for example, Lohse, "The Elements of the Universe" (pp. 96–99), and "The Teaching of the Philosophy" (pp. 127–31); Martin, pp. 80–100; Schweizer, "Excursus: The Colossian Philosophy (2:8)," in his commentary, pp. 125–70.

Additional and more technical studies include "*stoicheia*," in W. F. Arndt and F. W. Gingrich, *A Greek-English Lexicon of the New Testament*, 2d ed. (Chicago: University of Chicago Press, 1979), pp. 768–69; A. J. Bandstra, *The Law and the Elements of the World: An Exegetical Study in Aspects of Paul's Teaching* (Kampen: J. H. Kok, 1964); G. R. Beasley-Murray, "The Second Chapter of Colossians," *RevExp* 70 (1973), pp. 469–79; E. Burton, "The Elements of the Universe," in his *Critical and Exegetical Commentary on the Epistle to the Galatians* (Edinburgh: T & T Clark, 1921), pp. 510–18; G. Delling, "*stoicheō*" *TDNT*, vol. 7, pp. 666–87; C. A. Evans, "The Colossian Mystics," *Biblica* 63 (1982), pp. 188–205. A volume listed in For Further Reading, F. Francis and W. Meeks, eds., *Conflict at Colossae*, contains the following articles: "The Colossian Heresy," by J. B. Lightfoot; "The Isis Initiation in Apuleius and Related Initiatory Rites," by M. Dibelius; "The Heresy of Colossians," by G. Bornkamm; "Paul's Adversaries in Colossae," by S. Lyonnet; "Humility and Angelic Worship in Col. 2:18," by F. O. Francis; and "The Background of *EMBATEUEIN* (Col. 2:18) in Legal Papyri and Oracle Inscriptions," by F. O. Francis. Cf. Also M. D. Hooker, "Were There False Teachers in Colossae?" in *Christ and the Spirit in the New Testament*, ed. B. Lindars and S. S. Smalley (Cambridge: Cambridge University Press, 1973), pp. 315–31; Schweizer, "Christ in the Letter to the Colossians," esp. pp. 451–55; for other contributions by Schweizer, as well as additional foreign sources, see his *Colossians*, pp. 121, 311. A unique but helpful interpretation of the *stoicheia* is provided by W. Wink in "The Elements of the Universe in Biblical and Scientific Perspective," *Zygon* 13 (1978), pp. 225–48.

There continues to be debate whether *stoicheia tou kosmou* should be translated as "elements of the universe" or "elemental *spirits* of the universe." According to Schweizer, the designation "elements" does not include the stars and astrological spirits "until the second century A.D. Further, these elements are never adduced in the New Testament lists of powers and authorities, not even in Colossians (1:16; 2:10). Our starting point must be the fact that there is no contemporary evidence for the meaning of 'elemental spirits' or 'stars.' The power which they wield, by binding men to the 'world' through ascetic 'regulations' (vv. 20 f.), is, then, probably comparable to the power belonging to the commandments of the law, which are certainly not demons either" (p. 128).

W. Wink goes through the history of research on the *stoicheia* but concludes that prior to the third century A.D. there is no evidence that they were regarded as personal beings or fallen angels or that they were divinized in any form. The meaning of the term can only be determined from the context, which varies in the NT. For example, the constituent elements of the physical universe (2 Pet. 3:10, 12), philosophical presuppositions (Col. 2:8), religious laws and practices (Col. 2:20; Gal. 4:3, 9), or the rudimentary or first principles (Heb. 5:12).

11

The True Circumcision
and Its Effects

COLOSSIANS 2:11–15

In union with Christ you were circumcised, not with the circumcision that is made by men, but with the circumcision made by Christ, which consists of being freed from the power of this sinful self. [12]For when you were baptized, you were buried with Christ, and in baptism you were also raised with Christ through your faith in the active power of God, who raised him from death. [13]You were at one time spiritually dead because of your sins and because you were Gentiles without the Law. But God has now brought you to life with Christ. God forgave us all our sins; [14]he canceled the unfavorable record of our debts with its binding rules and did away with it completely by nailing it to the cross. [15]And on that cross Christ freed himself from the power of the spiritual rulers and authorities,[d] he made a public spectacle of them by leading them as captives in his victory procession.

d. Christ freed himself from the power of the spiritual rulers and authorities; or Christ stripped the spiritual rulers and authorities of their power.

2:11 / It already has been noted that the doctrine of baptism has a significant place in this epistle (see note on 1:14). In this section (2:11–15), Paul turns to baptism as a way of explaining the means and the results of the believers' union with Christ. With the exception of the language on circumcision, the thoughts are similar to those developed in Romans 6:1–11 and Galatians 3:27–28. It is quite possible that the peculiar beliefs and practices of the Colossian false teachers necessitated this clarification on circumcision and its relation to new life in Christ through baptism.

By insisting that the Colossians already have been circumcised, Paul diffuses any claim for the continuation of this rite in the community. But their circumcision, he clarifies, **is not with the circumcision that is made by men**, literally, "not from human hands." As Gentiles, they have no need to undergo a cultic rite that was practiced by the Jewish people as a sign of membership in the covenant. Nor should they subject themselves to any initiation rites of the false teachers that degrade the body and the flesh.

Believers are circumcised **with the circumcision made by Christ**.

This had nothing to do with the circumcision of Jesus as a Jewish boy (Luke 2:21). Rather, Paul is referring to a circumcision that belongs to Christ and that Christ performs when believers are united to him in baptism. Paul's main point is to contrast physical (outer) and spiritual (inner) circumcision. To experience the circumcision of Christ is nothing other than being buried and raised with him in baptism through faith.

The essence of this spiritual circumcision **consists of being freed from the power of this sinful self** (lit., "putting off the body of flesh"). Christ, in other words, liberates individuals from their unregenerate nature ("body of sin," Rom. 6:6; "body of death," Rom. 7:24). Paul develops similar ideas when he talks about the "old man" that is "put off" in baptism (Rom. 6:6; Eph. 4:22; Col. 3:9, 10) or the crucifixion of fleshly passions and desires (Gal. 2:20; 5:24).

What a tremendous message of liberation and victory this is for a congregation being seduced by a group of false teachers still enslaved to cosmic powers and authorities and seeking to free themselves through useless rituals and ascetic practices (2:16–23)! The Colossians needed to remember that Christ defeated (*apekdysis*, "putting off," "stripping," "disarming") these spiritual rulers in his death and triumphed over them in his resurrection (2:15). This victory, Paul reminds his readers, is theirs because they have been circumcised with **the circumcision made by Christ**, for by union with him in baptism by faith he frees humanity from the powers of evil.

2:12 / Since the "circumcision of Christ" is baptism, then this verse should be viewed as an elaboration of that truth rather than as an introduction of some new ideas. The Greek text begins with the passive participle *syntaphentes*, which is translated "having been buried." The GNB correctly implies this continuity of thought in its translation. The RSV "and you were buried" wrongly gives the impression that burial with Christ in baptism is a different experience.

The similarity of ideas in Colossians 2:11–15, Romans 6:1–11, Galatians 3:26–27, and Ephesians 2:1–10 suggests that these passages were part of standard baptismal instruction in the early church. There are, to be sure, some different nuances and applications necessitated by the context of each epistle. But basically, they teach (*a*) that baptism is a faith-baptism, that is, it is for believers who put their faith in Christ, (*b*) that it is a participation in Christ's death and resurrection, and (*c*) that it has ethical implications because in it the believer receives new life from Christ.

The imagery of burial (death) and resurrection (new life) comes from the NT practice of immersion—the believer was literally lowered into the water. Burial symbolized death to the old life, and the emergence from the water symbolized the new or resurrected life in Christ. Thus, in a very profound way, baptism outwardly symbolizes or dramatizes the inner experience of the forgiveness of sins.

All this should not lead to the conclusion that baptism is only a *symbol* of some prior experience such as repentance or conversion. Since the baptism of the NT is a faith-baptism, it is not uncommon to find forgiveness, regeneration, and justification linked with this rite (John 3:5; Acts 2:38; 22:16; 1 Cor. 6:11; Titus 3:5; 1 Pet. 3:18–21). In other words, baptism, when accompanied by faith, has a sacramental as well as a symbolical function. God, by his Spirit, has chosen to make something happen in baptism. Baptism is both the expression (symbol) *and* the vehicle (means, conveyance) of God's grace. It declares as well as effects one's union with Christ's death and resurrection (cf. Rom. 6:1–10); it is an initiation into Christ's body, the church (1 Cor. 12:13); it is God's way of stamping the believer with his seal of ownership (Eph. 1:13; 4:30).

As the believers in Colossae were **buried with Christ**, Paul likewise affirms that they were also **raised with Christ** in baptism (**in baptism**, rather than "in him" is the proper translation of the Greek relative pronoun *ho*). This resurrection in Christ is nothing other than new life in Christ (Rom. 6:1–11) made possible through faith. Paul presents Christ's resurrection as the supreme manifestation of God's power. And those who have been raised with Christ have been raised through faith in that divine power.

It is significant that the action that is described in verses 11–12 is in the past tense (the Greek aorist): "you were circumcised" (*perietmēthēte*); "you were buried" (*syntaphentes*); "you were also raised" (*synegērthēte*). In other words, these are realities that these believers already possess by virtue of their union with Christ in baptism. There is no need to look for any additional spiritual experience to supplement their faith. The false teaching has nothing to offer that is not already theirs in Christ.

2:13 / The new life that these believers now possess in Christ is contrasted to what they were before their baptism. Basically, they were spiritually dead (cf. Eph. 2:1). This spiritual death manifested itself morally by their **sins** (*paraptōma*, "trespasses") as well as religiously by their separation from God as **Gentiles without the Law**.

It is helpful to know that the Greek word behind the phrase **Gentiles without the Law** is *akrobustia* (uncircumcision). Thus, by way of a contrast, there is a connection with verse 11, where Paul talked about their "spiritual circumcision" (cf. Eph. 2:11, 12). The continuity with verse 13 is shown in the fact that **God has now brought you to life with Christ**. As Christ was raised from the dead by the power of God, the believer, who is in Christ through baptism, has been raised (1:12) and brought to life (1:13).

The Greek text also illustrates how carefully Paul wishes to emphasize their union with Christ. The word for life ($z\overline{o}e$) is prefixed with the preposition *syn* (*synezōopoiēsen*). This preposition is repeated with the pronoun "him" (*syn autoi*), leaving no doubt that their resurrection and quickening to new life is God's action in Christ alone.

This new life in Christ has resulted in a radical change in their moral life. Before, they were **spiritually dead**; now, they are spiritually alive (**God forgave us all our sins**). The change from **you** to **us** probably indicates that Paul is using traditional material familiar to the early church (note Matt. 6:12 in the Lord's Prayer: "Forgive us the wrongs that we have done"). This "forgiveness" also has taken place in the past (the Greek aorist tense). Hence, there is no need to look beyond their experience with Christ to other alternatives.

2:14 / Here Paul begins his elaboration upon the meaning of forgiveness in terms that are particularly applicable to the situation. His main point is that forgiveness of sins means victory over alien powers and freedom from legalistic practices. Again, all the action is described in the aorist (past) tense: He "forgave" (*charisamenos*), "canceled" (*exaleipsas*), "nailed" (*proselōsas*), "freed" (*apekdusamenos*), and he "triumphed" (*thriambeusas*) over these powers by "leading them as captives in his victory procession."

In discussing the nature of forgiveness, Paul refers to a hand-written certificate of indebtedness, similar to a bond or I.O.U. (Greek, *cheirographon*). Scholars are divided on the meaning of this term and the proper interpretation of the entire phrase, **the unfavorable record of our debts with its binding rules**. Some of the suggestions include (*a*) the Law of Moses, (*b*) the covenant between Adam and the Devil, (*c*) a certificate of debt, such as an I.O.U., from mankind to God, (*d*) a heavenly book on which God recorded human sins, or (*e*) Christ himself.

A significant number of interpreters understand this either to be a reference to the Jewish Law—thus God's regulations—or to the man-made traditions of the false teachers that resulted in transgressions. In either case, human beings were unable to keep to these precepts, so they stood as a written code (certificate) against humanity until Christ canceled it by his death.

Either interpretation makes good sense for a number of reasons: first, there are examples in contemporary Judaism in which the Law was applied this way; second, it fits the context of this passage in which Paul is dealing with specific legalistic practices that worked against individuals unless they were kept; third, it helps to explain the occurrence of other terms in the verse, such as **he canceled** and the **binding rules** (*tois dogmasin*). Although the exact meaning of Paul's phrases cannot be traced with certainty, it is clear that his main point is to emphasize the decisive and complete way Christ's death on the cross took care of mankind's indebtedness to God.

2:15 / The negative aspect of Christ's work on the cross is the cancellation of the bond of indebtedness; the positive side is Christ's triumph over the evil powers. Here, on the cross, **Christ freed himself from the power of the spiritual rulers and authorities**. The GNB translation indicates that these evil powers were in some kind of conflict with Christ and that by his work on the cross he decisively liberated himself from their power.

Paul describes this conquest in imagery of a victorious general leading his captives home in some kind of victory procession in which their defeat would be proclaimed publically. Similarly, Christ's defeat of these evil powers has meant that they have been made a **public spectacle**, for he leads them **as captives in his victory procession**. One of the Greek words used (*parrēsia*) shows that this is done "fearlessly" or with "confidence." In other words, Christ, as conqueror, leads his captives openly and with a bold confidence in his victory over them.

Verse 15 also repeats an emphasis that has been seen throughout the epistle, namely, that in Christ alone, by virtue of his work on the cross, the evil rulers no longer have control over the believer. The readers would remember 1:13, where Paul said that they have been rescued from the power of darkness and brought safely into the kingdom of his dear Son. All those who have been baptized into Christ and made alive with him (2:12) participate in his victory over evil.

Additional Notes

2:11 / G. R. Beasley-Murray carries this imagery of circumcision even further: "In this context 'putting (or stripping) off the body of flesh' is most plausibly contrasted with the minor operation in circumcision: bluntly it appears to say that instead of stripping off a little piece of flesh, as in circumcision, the Christian has stripped off his whole body of flesh, and this happened because Christ was 'circumcised,' that is, killed on the cross; the Christian shares so completely in that event, it is as if he himself had suffered that appalling bloody death" ("The Second Chapter of Colossians," *RevExp* 70 [1973], p. 474).

2:12 / Beasley-Murray's comment on the symbolic sacramental nature of baptism in the early church speaks to this point: "In such a setting baptism is less a testimony to a faith previously received than a declaration of a faith here and now embraced, an embodiment of conversion to Christ, and a submission to him who is able to save. In such a milieu it is not surprising that the spiritual realities of conversion and baptism are merged together, for in that context they do fall together" ("The Second Chapter of Colossians," p. 476).

On Paul's emphasis on resurrection in baptism, it should be noted that, in Romans, the resurrection is spoken of as future ("we shall be one with him by being raised to life as he was," 6:5). This (cf. also 2 Cor. 4:14; 2 Tim. 2:11) could be a correction to a certain element in the Gentile church that thought that the resurrection was completed in baptism (2 Tim. 2:18). In Colossians, Paul's emphasis is upon the present reality of the resurrected life in Christ because the false teachers were claiming that the soul was still in the process of ascending to heaven (Schweizer, pp. 144–45).

2:14 / A good description of some of these views is provided by W. Carr in his article, "Two Notes on Colossians (1. Col. 2:14; 2. Col. 2:18)," *JTS* 24 (1973), pp. 492–500. Carr's conclusion is that the dogmas (**binding rules**) are not God's regulations but "those decisions of men which issue in transgressions" or "the autograph of our self-condemnation in all its detail" (p. 496).

For reference with respect to Jewish and Hellenistic literature, see Lohse, pp. 108–9; Martin, pp. 83–85. Martin is attracted to a view that takes the *cheirographon* as a book of works kept by God in which all of humanity's sins are recorded. Although the record is used by the evil spirits to accuse men and women of their fleshly and unspiritual condition, it ceases to be binding, because Christ has destroyed its effectiveness by his death on the cross. It appears, however, that such a view may concede too much. Would Paul not fall into the heretic's trap by acknowledging the existence of something so preposterous as such a list? For another view, cf. O. A. Blanchette, "Does the Cheirographon of Col. 2:14 Represent Christ Himself?" *CBQ* 23 (1961), pp. 306–12.

2:15 / The footnote in the GNB indicates that there are some difficulties connected with this verse: *apekdysamenos* is an aorist middle participle, literally meaning "having stripped (freed) himself." The GNB takes this as a middle in its translation, implying that Christ freed himself from the evil forces that attacked him. It is possible, however, to take the verb in an active sense from the deponent verb *apekdyomai*, making God the subject. Thus, "God stripped the evil powers of their dignity and authority" (see Lohse, pp. 111–12; Martin, pp. 86–88; F. F. Bruce, pp. 239–40; T. K. Abbott, pp. 258–61).

12

A Manifesto of Christian Liberty

COLOSSIANS 2:16–23

So let no one make rules about what you eat or drink or about holy days or the New Moon Festival or the Sabbath. [17]All such things are only a shadow of things in the future; the reality is Christ. [18]Do not allow yourselves to be condemned by anyone who claims to be superior because of special visions and who insists on false humility and the worship of angels. For no reason at all, such a person is all puffed up by his human way of thinking [19]and has stopped holding on to Christ, who is the head of the body. Under Christ's control the whole body is nourished and held together by its joints and ligaments, and it grows as God wants it to grow.

[20]You have died with Christ and are set free from the ruling spirits of the universe. Why, then, do you live as though you belonged to this world? Why do you obey such rules as [21]"Don't handle this," "Don't taste that," "Don't touch the other"? [22]All these refer to things which become useless once they are used; they are only man-made rules and teachings. [23]Of course such rules appear to be based on wisdom in their forced worship of angels, and false humility, and severe treatment of the body; but they have no real value in controlling physical passions.

2:16 / Christ's defeat of these evil powers forms the basis for Paul's polemic in this section. The **so** ("therefore" in RSV, NIV) refers back to the work of Christ and his victory over those spiritual rulers and authorities that were thought to exercise power over the Christian. Christ has freed these believers, and they must guard that freedom by resisting all attempts from the false teachers to subject them to another set of legalistic rules and regulations.

This entire passage is somewhat difficult to interpret. First, Paul uses slogans and phrases that were employed by the false teachers. Though these would have been familiar to the Colossians, they are difficult for the modern reader to understand. Second, in spite of such specific references to the beliefs and practices of the false teachers, it is impossible to identify the heresy with any precision. Some of the things that Paul says look very Jewish; others appear more pagan and Hellenistic. A third alternative, and one that attracts the most attention, is that the heresy represents some form of syncretism that combined elements from a number of religious sources (see discussion in the introduction).

Identifying the heresy is not essential for understanding Paul's basic message. He wants to reassure his readers that, by virtue of the person and work of Christ, they have no need to surrender their freedom to legalism (**so, let no one make rules**). The **no one** refers to the person(s)—to anyone—(2:18) attempting to set up as a judge over members of the congregation who do not follow certain laws with respect to food and the observance of religious festivals.

These regulations go far beyond the requirements of the OT, since the food laws that governed the people of the old covenant were set aside by Christ (Mark 7:19) and declared nonbinding upon the Gentiles (Acts 10:9–16; 15:19–29). One gets the distinct impression that the regulations threatening the Colossians were all man-made traditions. People in the ancient world would abstain from certain foods for a variety of reasons (cf. Rom. 14:17, 21; 1 Tim. 4:3).

The Colossians are not to be bound by rules with respect to food (**what you eat or drink**) or the religious calendar (**holy days or the New Moon Festival or the Sabbath**). It is quite possible that these "special days" governed what a person may or may not eat as well. At any rate, Paul declares freedom from all regulations imposed by the false teachers. By submitting to such regulations, the Colossians would be acknowledging the continuing authority of the evil powers over them. They need to remember that in Christ they have been set free from such tyranny (2:20).

2:17 / All these dogmas are **only a shadow of things in the future**. At one time such rules may have served as a transitory "type" or **shadow** of something more permanent to come. But since the age of fulfillment has come in Christ, these rules have no further intrinsic value. Their function in foreshadowing has been surpassed by Christ: He is the **reality**.

The word used for **reality** is *sōma*. On the one hand, it may simply distinguish true **reality** (substance) from appearance (**shadow**). But *sōma* is the same word that Paul uses for the church as the body (*sōma*) of Christ (1:18; 2:19). This fact, along with the corporate identity that exists between Christ and the believer, makes one wonder whether Paul actually has the church as Christ's body in mind. If so, he would be saying that the reality that exists in Christ is likewise shared by members of his body, the church.

2:18 / One of the devastating effects of all false teaching is the division that it creates within the Christian community (cf. 1 Cor. 1–3; 1 John 2:7–11).

When certain individuals, for example, set themselves up as the spiritual elite by claiming special access to visions, revelations, tongues, prophecies, and so forth (1 Cor. 14), they ignore others who cannot make such claims. At Colossae, this took the form of judgment or condemnation: **Do not allow yourselves to be condemned**, Paul warns, **by anyone who claims to be superior because of special visions**. Quite possibly this heresy had some affinity to the mystery religions, in which such visions were received when the initiate performed certain rites or entered (*embateuō*) into the innermost part of the pagan sanctuary.

The reference to the **worship of angels** goes far beyond anything found in Scripture. True, angels were regarded as celestial beings, intercessors, messengers, agents of God, and so forth, but they were never worshiped as a class of spiritual beings. The elevation of them to cosmic powers and the veneration of them as objects of worship must, therefore, belong to this syncretistic heresy. The angels may, in fact, be the principalities, powers, and authorities that Paul mentions throughout the epistle. If so, they would be worshiped for their power as well as for their control over human beings.

The Greek word used for humility is *tapeinophrosunē*, which, on other occasions, is a positive and commendable disposition of character (3:12; Eph. 4:2; Phil. 2:3; 1 Pet. 5:5). Here the context shows that the heretics were guilty of a **false humility** in connection with their worship of angels. The RSV translates it as "self-abasement," indicating the inward and selfish nature of their cultic conduct.

Paul continues his scathing indictment of these perpetrators of deceit: They claim to be spiritually superior because of their visions and cultic practices, but there is no substance to their claim (**such a person is all puffed up . . . for no reason at all**). In other words, it is all vanity and purposeless.

The source of this vanity lies in a **human way of thinking**. The false teachers may have thought that they were in communion with God; they may have believed that they were inspired by the Spirit. But the fact is that their thoughts and actions were of human rather than divine origin. Thus they remain under the control of the flesh (*sarx*). Paul does not mean to imply that the flesh, in itself, is evil; verses 18 and 19 together show that the problem is in putting one's trust or self-confidence in the flesh rather than in Christ.

2:19 / The false teachers have fallen into error because they have stopped holding on to **Christ, who is the head of the body**. Paul already has discussed the headship of Christ as it relates to the cosmos and the church

(1:15–20; 2:10). Here he applies that concept to the problems facing the church by using the analogy of the human body (cf. 1 Cor. 12:12–31; Eph. 4:15–16). Because these false teachers have detached themselves from Christ, they have deprived themselves of the true source of nourishment and unity.

Christ himself is the only true source of life for the church, for under his control the entire body is **nourished** (*epichorēgoumenon*). This is a present participle, indicating that the process of nourishment or support is a continuing one. The same continuing action applies to the unity of the body as well (*symbibazomenon*): Under Christ's control the whole body is **held together by its joints and ligaments** (cf. Eph. 4:16). The function of these anatomical features is to provide the necessary cohesion for the body. But they can only do so if they remain joined to the head.

Under the headship of Christ, the body grows according to God's plan. Literally, the Greek translates into an awkward phrase "it (the church) grows (unto?) the growth of God." The basic meaning, however, is that God provides the pattern for the church's growth; he also is the source of that growth, which is mediated through Christ, the head.

All of what Paul has been saying adds to his indictment of the false teachers for being vain and carnal (2:18). Since they have cut themselves off from the source of nourishment, unity, and growth, it follows that they are undernourished, fragmented, and stagnant. In fact, the imagery can be carried even further, for it leads to this inescapable truth: The one who separates himself from Christ, the head of the church, is cut off from the church, the body of Christ; the one who separates himself from the church is cut off from Christ, the head.

2:20 / One cannot help but notice the repetition of Paul's earlier thoughts in 2:6–23. First, he applies the truths of the Christ hymn to the situation at Colossae (2:6–10); then he explains the effect of the believer's union with Christ in baptism, culminating in victory over all spiritual rulers and authorities (2:11–15). The heretics, however, did not claim that victory in Christ, because they continued to live in bondage to these spiritual powers—a bondage that manifested itself in cultic practices and angel worship.

Now, in verses 20–23, Paul resumes his indictment of the heresy by exposing its nature even further. Anyone practicing this false religion, he claims, is still enslaved to the cosmic powers. They do not live out the fact that at the time of their baptism (2:11, 12) they died with Christ and were set free from the power of the ruling spirits of the universe.

The tragedy is that the false teachers are not living in the victory and freedom that is theirs in Christ. Since you **have died** to these powers, **Why, then**, asks Paul, **do you live as though you belonged to this world**? The Greek word (*dogmatizesthe*) was used in 2:14 and translated as "binding rules." Here, it occurs in the verbal middle form, which carries the idea "why do you *subject yourselves* to dogmas . . . ?" **why do you obey such rules as . . . ?"**

2:21 / The first characteristic of such rules and regulations is that they are enslaving ("**Don't handle this**," "**Don't taste that**," "**Don't touch the other**"). Such prohibitions can make people paranoid and paralyze them in their conduct for fear of sinning. Apparently this heresy had a long list of foods that were religiously unacceptable, that is, unclean (cf. 1 Cor. 8:1; 1 Tim. 4:3). There does not appear to be any deliberate gradation in this list, although "to handle" (*haptō*) can imply taking hold for the purpose of possessing.

2:22 / Second, these rules and taboos are temporary (**all these . . . things . . . become useless once they are used**). Literally translated, the Greek reads: "which things are all for corruption in the using." All these taboos without exception are subject to dissolution (decay). Why, then, stake so much of your life on things that have no enduring consequence, no eternal reality, no lasting effect?

Third, they are human precepts (**man-made rules and teachings**). No doubt this is an allusion back to such passages as 2:8 and 2:17–18, where Paul already has discussed human traditions and regulations. The idea here is very similar to a reference Jesus makes to the Pharisees: "You hypocrites! How right Isaiah was when he prophesied about you! 'These people, says God, honor me with their words, but their heart is really far away from me. It is no use for them to worship me, because they teach man-made rules as though they were my laws!' " (Matt. 15:7–9; cf. Mark 7:7). A similar concern occurs in Titus 1:13–14, where Paul appeals to "healthy faith" instead of to "Jewish legends and to human commandments which come from men who have rejected the truth." The church of Jesus Christ continually needs to be on guard lest human traditions rob its members of their freedom in Christ.

2:23 / Fourth, they are deceptive and useless: The thoughts in this verse are quite similar to those in 2:18, where Paul talked about visions, false humility, and worship of angels. Here, he adds that the rules and regulations **appear to be based on wisdom in their forced worship of angels, and false humility, and severe treatment of the body**. At best, however, all of these requirements are counterfeit, for they can only deliver appearances and impressions. The wisdom, worship, and humility do not serve to bring them closer to God; the ascetic practices have no effect in preventing sins of the flesh. Basically, all such man-made attempts at religion are worthless—**they have no real value in controlling physical passions**.

Additional Notes

2:17 / The grammatical problems of the phrase *to de sōma tou Christou* are discussed by Schweizer, pp. 157–58. Perhaps a nominative (*ton*) originally stood in place of the genitive, thus meaning that in contrast to the "shadow," "the body *is* Christ"; or, to supply words to produce the meaning, that "the body belongs to Christ" or "the body, however, is the body of Christ." In spite of this, "The only point that is not altogether certain is whether it is Christ or the church that is set as reality in contrast to the shadow" (p. 158).

2:18 / The word *embateuō* has been discussed by a number of scholars: W. Carr, "Two Notes on Colossians (1. Col. 2:14; 2. Col. 2:18)," pp. 492–500, gives it the meaning of entering into the sanctuary "of the mind" rather than a sanctuary connected with initiation into one of the mysteries. Consequently, the translation of the verse reads: "Let no one judge you unfit to be a Christian with his personal wishes about religious excess and his haunting the courts of heaven at worship with angels, his so-called visions, puffed up by his private earthly imagination (p. 499). This view comes close to that of Schweizer, who talks about a kind of "religious meditation" in which an individual would receive a vision of God ("Christ in the Letter to the Colossians," p. 454).

For other comments, see F. O. Francis, "The Background of *EMBATEUEIN* (Col. 2:18) in Legal Papyri and Oracle Inscriptions," in *Conflict at Colossae*, pp. 197–207. Francis concludes that *embateuein* does not confirm a type of mystery religion but in the context of Colossians is used as a word for entering into heaven; H. Preisker, "*embateuō*," *TDNT*, vol. 2, pp. 535–36. In the commentaries, Bruce, pp. 248–49, esp. n. 93; Martin, pp. 94–95.

The problem of angel worship is explored by F. O. Francis, "Humility and Angelic Worship in Col. 2:18," in *Conflict at Colossae*, pp. 163–95. He takes the phrase "worship of angels" as a subjective genitive, meaning that it is the angels who worship and not people who worship the angels, as is commonly thought. See also A. R. R. Sheppard, "Pagan Cults of Angels in Roman Asia Minor," *Talanta* 12/13 (1980–82), pp. 77–101.

2:20 / The choice, as Schweizer points out, "is between the 'world' and its elements on the one hand and 'heaven' and the sovereignty of God on the other (p. 166). Much of Schweizer's understanding of the false teaching relates to Gnostic ideas of the soul's ascent to heaven. Consequently, he understands Paul's polemic in this verse accordingly: "Since the Colossians are anxious that they may not, after their death, be able to ascend to that region above, the author stresses the other side of the matter: they have actually been transposed into that region above already, even if this fact is not yet clearly evident. They must therefore no longer allow regulations to be made as though they were still living in the world" (p. 166).

2:23 / The translation and exposition here do not indicate the difficulties commentators have with a text that many describe as "hopelessly obscure." For attempts to clarify its meaning, see B. Hollenback, "Col. 2:23: Which Things Lead to the Fulfillment of the Flesh," *NTS* 25 (1979), pp. 254–61; J. L. Houlden, *Paul's Letters from Prison: Philippians, Colossians, Philemon and Ephesians*, pp. 199–200; Lohse, p. 124–26; Martin, pp. 98–100; Schweizer comments that "the verse is almost impossible to translate" (p. 168).

13

The Ethical Dimensions of the Christian Life

Chapter three begins what normally is called the "ethical section" of the epistle. This follows a general trend in Paul's epistles in which he first deals with the theological issues and then builds his ethics upon that foundation (cf. Rom. 12:1 ff.; Gal. 5:1 ff.; Eph. 4:1 ff.; Phil. 4:1 ff.).

It is quite common to discuss this characteristic as the *indicative* and the *imperative* of Paul's theology. Basically, it is the "you are" and the "you ought" of the Christian life. In some ways this concept comes across as a paradox in Paul's thought. On the one hand, he can say that, by virtue of his or her position in Christ, the believer *is* "dead to sin," "light in the Lord," "a new creature," and so forth. But then on the other hand, Paul says, "Now become what you are," that is, live as if you were dead to sin, light in the Lord, new creatures.

This tension between the indicative and the imperative, of belonging spiritually to the age to come but living temporally in this present age, is a striking feature of Paul's theology (cf. Rom. 6:1–4, 11, 12, 13; 8:9–17; 13:14; 1 Cor. 6:8–11, 19, 20; 2 Cor. 5:17–21; Gal. 5:24, 25; Eph. 4:1–6; 4:22–5:20; Col. 1:9–15; 3:1–4). This third chapter of Colossians illustrates this principle by stating that the believers have "been raised to life with Christ" but then are summoned to set their hearts "on the things that are in heaven" (3:1); they have died with Christ (2:20; 3:3) but are subsequently told to "put to death" certain vices (3:5). The language of "putting off" (3:9; cf. Eph. 4:22) and "putting on" (3:10; Eph. 4:24) carries a similar message.

This relationship between theology and ethics, or the indicative and the imperative, often is developed around the sacrament of baptism (cf. disc. on 2:11–15). This truth becomes obvious when one considers the consequences of dying and rising with Christ. Since baptism is the founding of a new existence, the Christian life must manifest that change by a corresponding ethical life. The true meaning of baptism, in other words, needs to be lived out in the life of each believer.

This close relationship between baptism and ethics accounts for so many of the ethical exhortations in Colossians and Ephesians being associated with the baptismal event. It also is quite natural to find baptismal and ethical language in close proximity, because baptism was the occasion for ethical instruction.

The preceding discussion provides a context for understanding 3:1 ff., because Paul uses the baptismal event as a means of developing an ethical pattern for his readers. From his previous discussion (2:11–15), they would know that he had baptism in mind when he says "you have died" (2:20; 3:3) and "you have been raised to life with Christ" (2:12; 3:1).

Paul discusses the believer's ethical life in a series of relationships that include Christ (3:1–8); the local church (3:9–17); the family (3:18); one's vocation (3:22–4:1); and society in general (4:2–6). Although these sections contain no specific references to the false teaching in the community, there can be no doubt that an understanding of and obedience to these ethical admonitions will fortify the congregation against the false teachings they have heard and assist them to fulfill their mission before God.

Additional Note

For a helpful discussion of this concept, see W. D. Dennison, "Indicative and Imperative: The Basic Structure of Pauline Ethics," *CTJ* 14 (1979), pp. 55–78.

Although general divisions between the theological and the practical nature of the epistles may be helpful, they are somewhat superficial, because Paul frequently combines theological and ethical truths throughout his epistles. Victor P. Furnish, for example, has shown that the ethical instruction in Paul's letters is not restricted to the closing sections (*Theology and Ethics in Paul* [Nashville: Abingdon, 1968]).

14

The Heavenly Life

COLOSSIANS 3:1–4

You have been raised to life with Christ, so set your hearts on the things that are in heaven, where Christ sits on his throne at the right side of God. ²Keep your minds fixed on things there, not on things here on earth. ³For you have died, and your life is hidden with Christ in God. ⁴Your real life is Christ and when he appears, then you too will appear with him and share his glory!

3:1 / As with a number of other "ethical" sections (cf. 3:5; Rom. 12:1; Eph. 4:1), Paul begins with the word "therefore" (*oun*). The GNB **so** has the similar effect of tying Paul's ethical instruction and theological thought together. These believers **have been raised to life with Christ**. On the basis of that fact they are to set their hearts on the **things that are in heaven**. The verb **set** is a strong imperative and is a good translation of *zēteō*, which means to seek, examine, or search something out with the desire to possess. Those "heavenly things" (lit., "the things above"), both there and in 3:2, are not identified. They may be the virtues of the Christian life that Paul commends in 3:12–16 in contrast to the "earthly" things mentioned in 2:20–23 and 3:5–9 (cf. Phil. 3:19).

Heaven, as well as **throne** and "right hand," should not be understood as some geographic place in the cosmos. The language here, as elsewhere (Matt. 6:20; Eph. 1:3; 2:6; 3:10), is figurative rather than literal; it designates a quality of existence, not a place of being. By **heaven**, Paul means that unseen realm of spiritual reality, the eternal world in contrast to a world that is earthly and transitory.

Through baptism into Christ, the believer participates in that spiritual and eternal realm in which Christ has been exalted and enthroned (Eph. 1:20; Phil. 2:9–11). This serves as a reminder to the Colossians that they already share this exaltation with Christ. It is not merely a future inheritance, because "in our union with Christ he raised us up with him to rule with him in the heavenly world" (Eph. 2:6).

3:2–4 / In addition to setting their hearts they are to **keep** their **minds fixed** on heavenly things. To keep one's mind fixed is to be intent and determined to do something (the RSV has "seek" at 3:1 and "set" at 3:2; the NIV uses "set" in both verses). Basically, the message is that, since the Colossians have "set" their minds on heavenly things, they are to **keep** holding on to that perspective and not the things to which they have already died. Since the resemblance to 2:20 is so striking, Paul obviously has those legalistic rituals in mind (2:21–23) as well as the vices enumerated in 3:5–9. This, too, is a good example of the indicative and imperative in Colossians: In 2:20 Paul stated: "You have died with Christ and are set free from . . . "; in 3:3–4, there is a similar development of thought in that something that was hidden is revealed. The new life that the believer receives in Christ is **hidden**, that is, it is a mystery that one cannot fully explain or physically display. But the true nature of that life (**your real life**) will not remain a secret, because it is indissolubly bound to Christ and will be revealed at his return. This interpretation, which takes **life** in the sense of quality or essence, is preferred to the view that looks to the return of Christ as the time when those who are saved and thus belong to God will be identified.

Additional Notes

3:1 / For a helpful discussion on this section, see C. F. D. Moule, "The New Life in Colossians," *RevExp* 70 (1973), pp. 481–93.

3:2 / If Colossians addresses a Gnostic view of the universe, then "heaven" or "the things above" would be understood in a literal or topographical way. In the ascent of the soul the Gnostics hoped to leave behind all earthly or material things in order to return to an existence in heaven (see Schweizer, p. 175).

15

The Vices of the Old Life

You must put to death, then, the earthly desires at work in you, such as sexual immorality, indecency, lust, evil passions, and greed (for greed is a form of idolatry). ⁶Because of such things God's anger will come upon those who do not obey him.ᵉ ⁷At one time you yourselves used to live according to such desires, when your life was dominated by them.

⁸But now you must get rid of all these things: anger, passion, and hateful feelings. No insults or obscene talk must ever come from your lips. ⁹Do not lie to one another, for you have put off the old self with its habits

e. *Some manuscripts do not have* upon those who do not obey him.

3:5 / The imperative tone that characterized 3:1–2 ("set," "keep") is picked up again in 3:5, but this time in a negative way: **You must put to death, then** . . . . This list of prohibitions belongs to a category of vices that are scattered throughout the NT (cf. Matt. 15:19; Mark 7:21, 22; Rom. 1:24, 26, 29–32; 13:13; 1 Cor. 5:10–14; 6:9–10; 2 Cor. 12:20; Gal. 5:19–21; Eph. 4:31; 5:3–5; Col. 3:5, 8; 1 Tim. 1:9, 10; 6:4–5; 2 Tim. 3:2–5; Titus 3:3; 1 Pet. 2:1; 4:3, 4; Jude 8, 16; Rev. 9:20, 21; 21:8; 22:15). Later, in 3:12, Paul mentions a list of virtues that a Christian is to "put on." This, too, belongs to a catalog—of virtues (Matt. 5:3–11; 2 Cor. 6:6, 7; Gal. 5:22, 23; Eph. 6:14–17; Phil. 4:8; Col. 3:12; 1 Tim. 3:2, 3; 6:11; Titus 1:7, 8; James 3:17; 2 Pet. 1:5–7).

Of all the lists of vices and virtues in the NT, the lists in Colossians, Ephesians, and 1 Peter are the most similar. Scholars who have researched these "catalogs" have concluded that the lists that appear in these three epistles belong to a traditional body of instructional material of the early church and would have been passed on to new Christians on the occasion of their baptism. But even though Colossians, Ephesians, and 1 Peter contain a significant amount of baptismal language and theology, they probably were not written solely for that occasion and should not be regarded as baptismal tracts.

The command (imperative) **you must put to death** is a clear reference to the "death" that these believers have already experienced in baptism. They now are called upon to appropriate that death by removing all earthly desires from their life. The Greek uses the term "earthly members" (*ta melē ta epi tēs gēs*) because it was believed that such vices were located in certain parts of the body. In Romans 6:13 Paul uses the same word when he says: "Nor must you surrender any part [*ta melē*] of yourselves to sin, to be used for wicked purposes. Instead, give yourselves to God, as men who have been brought from death to life, and surrender your whole being [*ta melē*] to him to be used for righteous purposes."

The list in this verse includes five vices that are related to sexual sins. As such, they are manifestations of evil desires and are harmful to other people. **Immorality** (*porneia*) includes all kinds of unlawful sexual behavior, including deviations (1 Cor. 5:1, 10; 6:9; 2 Cor. 12:21; Gal. 5:19; 1 Thess. 4:3; Eph. 5:3; 1 Tim. 1:9, 10) such as prostitution and fornication. **Indecency** (*akatharsia*) or "impurity" (RSV, NIV) is almost synonymous with *porneia* and is used in the NT to describe immoral intent as well as the practice of sexual vices.

Lust (*pathos*), in this context, probably implies some kind of sexual passion, that is, passion or lust that leads to sexual sin. Its counterpart, **evil passions** (*epithumian kakēn*), is used for the desire of something that is forbidden but is pursued in order to satisfy one's desires. Galatians 5:16, for example, says "Let the Spirit direct your lives, and do not satisfy the desires [*epithymia*] of the human nature."

The last vice to be mentioned is **greed** (*pleonexia*), or covetousness (RSV), literally, a desire to have more, to appropriate another's possessions. Since the NT has many warnings against this sin (cf. Mark 7:22; Rom. 1:29; 1 Cor. 6:10; Eph. 5:3), it is not clear whether its occurrence here is linked with sexual immorality or with all areas of life. Both ideas could be in the apostle's mind. The parenthesis (**for greed is a form of idolatry**), which is paralleled in Ephesians 5:5, underscores the idea that greed, along with the other vices, is an illicit evil desire (1 Cor. 5:10, 11; 6:9; Gal. 5:20). Greed is idolatry because it leads one to focus attention and affection on things other than God. This can happen in sexual life as well as with material things. The solution to such idolatry has already been given: "Set your hearts . . . keep your minds" on heavenly things! In other words, give Christ pre-eminence in your ethical life as well.

3:6 / Lest anyone minimize the seriousness of these vices, Paul reminds his readers of **God's anger** (cf. the footnote: The GNB rightly omits "sons of disobedience" because of poor textual evidence. Its inclusion probably is due to Eph. 5:6.) God's judgment upon these sins is widely attested throughout Scripture (Rom. 1:18–32; 1 Cor. 5:10, 11; 6:9, 10; 1 Thess. 4:3–6).

3:7 / Before the Colossians became Christians their life was characterized by such evil passions. They already have been reminded that at that time they were "spiritually dead" in their sins (2:13) and lived as though they belonged to the world (2:20; cf. Eph. 2:1–3). Their whole pagan way of life had been one of enslavement to evil *powers* as well as to evil *passions*. Fortunately, a wonderful change has taken place in them in Christ (the indicative); as a result, they are called upon to demonstrate this new life ethically (the imperative).

3:8 / Paul exhorts those who have been raised with Christ to manifest a new attitude toward sin. What was true of sexual sins applies equally to sins of speech: **But now**, that is, as Christians (cf. the "once you were" and the "now you are" in Eph. 2:3, 11–19), **you must get rid of all these things**. The word *apothesthe*, "get rid of" (RSV, "put off, away"), is part of the clothing imagery that Paul uses in connection with the old and the new life. One's sins are like an old garment that is taken off and discarded so that a new one can be put on (2:11; 3:10, 12; Eph. 4:22, 24). Such language accounts for a custom in many churches: candidates for baptism by immersion "put off" their old, ordinary clothes and "put on" white robes to symbolize their new or resurrected life in Christ.

The sins that affect social relationships can be divided into two categories: **Anger** (*orgē*), **passion** (*thumos*), and **hateful feelings** (*kakios*) are sins that can be internalized; they may or may not be expressed in overt action, although either way they clearly are wrong (Matt. 5:22–30). The other sins are those that are verbalized: **No insults** (*blasphēmia*) **or obscene talk** (*aischrologia*) **must ever come from your lips**.

3:9 / Lying, although it may not belong to the list of the other five vices, certainly fits the context as a verbal sin as well as causing grievous damage to personal relationships, particularly within the body of Christ. Here, as in 3:5-8, Paul reminds them that this sin also belonged to their former way of life and has been put off in baptism (cf. Rom. 13:12–14; Gal. 3:27, 28).

Additional Notes

3:5 / One of the most recent discussions on the vices and virtues in the NT, particularly in their application to Colossians, is by G. Cannon, pp. 51–94. Other helpful studies include B. S. Easton, "New Testament Ethical Lists," *JBL* 51 (1932), pp. 1–12; E. Schweizer, "Traditional Ethical Patterns in the Pauline and Post-Pauline Letters and Their Development (Lists of vices and the House-tables)," in *Text and Interpretation: Studies in the New Testament Presented to Matthew Black*, ed. E. Best and R. McL. Wilson (Cambridge: Cambridge University Press, 1979), pp. 195–209.

16

The Virtues of the New Life

and have put on the new self. This is the new being which God, its Creator, is constantly renewing in his own image, in order to bring you to a full knowledge of himself. [11]As a result, there is no longer any distinction between Gentiles and Jews, circumcised and uncircumcised, barbarians, savages, slaves, and free men, but Christ is all, Christ is in all.

[12]You are the people of God; he loved you and chose you for his own. So then, you must clothe yourselves with compassion, kindness, humility, gentleness, and patience. [13]Be tolerant with one another and forgive one another whenever any of you has a complaint against someone else. You must forgive one another just as the Lord has forgiven you. [14]And to all these qualities add love, which binds all things together in perfect unity. [15]The peace that Christ gives is to guide you in the decisions you make; for it is to this peace that God has called you together in the one body. And be thankful.

3:10 / The GNB clarifies that the **new self** is the new being which God, the Creator, **is constantly renewing in his own image**. Behind this verse one can anticipate a serious question that the Colossians must have had concerning their new life in Christ: "How can I live out ethically for Christ what I have become sacramentally in Christ?" Paul himself was well aware of the tension between the indicative and the imperative, between his status in Christ and the process still to be accomplished (Rom. 7). He knew that in this life the believer is continually being called upon to become *in reality* what he or she is *in fact*.

But how, one may ask, is this seemingly impossible task to be accomplished? How can a person make the right choices? Who will give this new self the necessary ability and strength? The answer, says Paul, lies in the activity of God: **God, its Creator, is constantly renewing in his own image** (cf. Rom. 8:29). These words recall Genesis 1:27, which states that originally human beings were created in the image—that is, moral and spiritual likeness—of God and at that point had the ability to choose between good and evil. In the Fall, however, that image was destroyed. But the good news of the gospel is that now, in Christ, God is at work restoring that lost image. This restoration or re-creation is not mankind's work at all; it is not a process of giving up some vices and accepting a few virtues; this **new being** is God's doing! To express this process the Greek uses a present passive participle (*anakainoumenon*) to indicate that renewal is continous (the present) and that it has an outside source (the passive, lit., "the new life which is being renewed").

In light of Paul's christological teaching in the epistle, one may have expected him to refer to a renewal in Christ's image, or to the second Adam, as he does elsewhere in his writings (Rom. 5:12–21; 8:29; 1 Cor. 15:45–49; 2 Cor. 3:18). Perhaps they are one and the same for Paul, since earlier he referred to Christ as "the visible likeness [image] of the invisible God" (1:15). The purpose of this renewal, he adds, is to bring you to a full knowledge of himself. The believers need to become aware of God in order to do his will (cf. 1:9); God's presence in Christ will enable them to make the right moral decisions.

3:11 / At first glance the thoughts in this verse do not appear to fit the context of the ethical life that Paul has been describing. However, the GNB preserves the continuity of thought by the translation **as a result**. In other words, the consequence of being in Christ, of putting off the sins that exploit and divide humanity, of being renewed after the image of God, is the obliteration of all racial (**Gentiles and Jews**), religious (**circumcised and uncircumcised**), cultural (**barbarians, savages**), and social (**slaves, and free men**) distinctions.

The creation of a new humanity (the church as the body of Christ) is one of the wonderful truths of the gospel. Ephesians 2:11–22 is the most extensive commentary on how Christ broke down the "wall" that separated Jews and Gentiles (cf. also Rom. 2:25–29; 4:9–12; Gal. 5:6). Even the maligned slave and the most primitive pagan (Scythian) are unified in Christ. At the foot of the cross the ground is level!

Though Paul is stating a general theological truth in this verse, there is no doubt that he has the Church in Colossae in mind. What is true universally is true locally as well. That congregation probably was a mixture of all kinds and classes of people. However, those distinctions no longer have any significance when it is realized that Christ is everything and that he dwells in all people (**Christ is all, Christ is in all**). Paul had a similar message for the Corinthians (1 Cor. 12:13) and the Galatians (3:26–28).

3:12 / Verses 12–17 are a continuation of Paul's discussion of those who are baptized. He already has dealt with the negative side by showing that those who have died to their old life are to put off those vices that characterized them as pagans. In this section, Paul turns to the positive side by listing a number of virtues that are to characterize their new or resurrected life. The **so then** ("therefore" in Greek) indicates that what follows is linked to the previous ideas on the new self (3:10, 11).

There are several features of this list of virtues that are worth noting: First, as already explained, this list is part of a body of traditional material that was transmitted in the early church (cf. disc. on 3:5). The language "put on" (**clothe yourselves**) shows that this belongs to the context of baptismal instructions. Second, these virtues are very similar to the "fruit of the Spirit" mentioned in Galatians 5:22, 23. Three of the "fruit" (**kindness, humility, patience**) are directly in the list, while "love" and "peace" are picked up in 3:14 and 3:15, respectively.

A third characteristic of these virtues is that they are "godly qualities," which are used to describe either God or Christ. Many references in the NT, for example, talk about the mercy (Rom. 12:1; 2 Cor. 1:3), **kindness** (Rom. 2:4; 11:22; Eph. 2:7), **humility** (Phil. 2:5–11), meekness (2 Cor. 10:1), and long-suffering (Rom. 2:4; 9:22) of God and Jesus. The application of these virtues to the Christian would follow naturally from the call to imitation, union, or likeness with Christ. Believers are to act toward one another as God and Jesus act toward them.

Fourth, these virtues are social in nature, that is, they describe attitudes and actions that are important for healthy personal relationships. As the Christian has emptied (put off) his or her life of harmful and selfish vices, he or she now is instructed to fill (put on) that void with virtues that have the well-being of others as their prime goal. These virtues are lived out in the context of the local church (body, 3:15) where the Colossians are members with each other (3:13, 16). Their relationships with each other, including worship (3:16, 17), should bear witness that they are new people in Christ.

In verse 12, the believers are identified as **the people of God**, literally, the *hagioi*, "saints," "holy ones" (1:2). This was made possible, Paul tells his readers, because of God's love and election. Their status had nothing to do with their own striving; it was God's choosing. All three concepts (saints, love, election) are reminiscent of OT descriptions of Israel but are taken over and applied to the new Israel, the church (cf. 1 Pet. 2:9).

The Colossians are instructed to put on a number of virtues: **Compassion** is a translation of two Greek words, *splagchna* and *oiktirmos*, literally translated as "bowels of mercy" (KJV) because the bowels, or inner viscera, of a person were regarded as the seat of emotions. As such, the term denoted compassion that comes authentically from the heart and that is translated into corresponding action toward another person.

Kindness (*chrēstotēs*), with such corresponding concepts as goodness, generosity, or courtesy, describes an individual whose life and relationship with others is gracious and empathetic—genuinely concerned for the feelings of others. **Humility** (*tapeinophrosunē*), when properly directed (i.e., not false humility), is a spirit of modesty and disregard for status. It is that quality of Christ that best describes his willingness to become incarnate and suffer for mankind (Phil. 2:5–11).

Gentleness (*prautēs*), which appears in the RSV as "meekness," sometimes has been taken as a sign of weakness, particularly by the Greeks. In the NT, however, it is a disposition characterized by gentleness, consideration, and submissiveness—just the opposite of arrogance, rebellion, and violence. **Patience** (*makrothumia*) is a passive virtue, amplified by such additional concepts as endurance (cf. 1:11), forbearance, and steadfastness. In personal relationships, it is the grace of one who may have the right to retaliate but who chooses to exercise patience instead.

3:13 / There are bound to be conflicts (**complaints**) within the church. When this occurs, says Paul, **be tolerant** and **forgive one another**. Tolerance and forgiveness should not be regarded as two additional virtues but rather as explanations of how gentleness and patience are to be exercised in the body. To be tolerant is be patiently forbearing of others with the idea of forgiving them. Paul appeals to his readers' experience of forgiveness in Christ. They are to forgive because of and according to the example of the Lord.

3:14 / **And to all these qualities add love**. Paul still has the list of virtues in mind that the Christian is to "put on." Love is the crown of all these virtues; it is the final outer garment **which binds all things together in perfect unity** (lit., "the bond of perfectness"). The idea here is similar to Ephesians 4:2–3 and 15–16, where love is the manifestation of new life in Christ and what leads to maturity and unity in his body. Such love removes all feelings of anger, hatred, or an unforgiving spirit (cf. Rom. 13:8–10; Gal. 5:14).

3:15 / The peace of Christ has a twofold application. Since it comes from him, it provides an inner peace for each believer; it is to **guide** (lit., *brabyein* means "to arbitrate," "to control"), to guide in the decisions that he or she makes. Those at peace with themselves will be at peace with others; it enables individuals to be united into a single body. The "complaints" (3:13) that members have against each other are settled when Christ's peace rules in their midst. In the context of the indicative and the imperative, the meaning of Paul's admonition could be stated this way: By virtue of being reconciled to God by Christ you *are* at peace (the indicative; cf. Rom. 5:1; Eph. 2:14; Col. 1:20); now live out that peace (the imperative) in your personal and corporate life.

And be thankful: Thanksgiving (cf. 1:12; 2:7), which is basically a response for the grace of God, is mentioned three times in verses 15–17. Thus, rather than a final admonition in the preceding list of virtues, it serves as a summons to articulate that response in corporate worship and everyday living.

The Expressions of True Worship

COLOSSIANS 3:16–17

Christ's message in all its richness must live in your hearts. Teach and instruct one another with all wisdom. Sing psalms, hymns, and sacred songs; sing to God with thanksgiving in your hearts. [17]Everything you do or say, then, should be done in the name of the Lord Jesus, as you give thanks through him to God the Father.

3:16 / Here is a verse loaded with important truths. Paul has just spoken about the peace of Christ that is to rule in the believers' hearts (3:15). Now he turns to another aspect of Christ, namely, **Christ's message**. Literally, this is the "word of Christ," but taken as an objective genitive in Greek it means the words about Christ, that is, the gospel.

The word of Christ is to dwell within the believer and can do so either richly or feebly. Although the gospel certainly is "rich" in meaning, content, and so on, the Greek adverb "richly" definitely is intended to characterize the manner in which Christ's message is to inhabit the believer (thus the RSV and NIV read: "Let the word of Christ dwell in you richly"). **Hearts** is missing in the Greek, but the thought carries over from the previous verse, where peace is to rule in their hearts (their innermost being, whole self).

The indwelling word will manifest itself in two ways: First, the Colossians are exhorted to **teach and instruct one another with all wisdom**. This is a pedagogical process (cf. 1:28) in which all members share responsibility. In light of Paul's ministry as a teacher and Epaphras' as a transmitter of tradition, this verse should not be taken to imply a deficiency in these church leaders.

The second manifestation of the word of Christ is in worship. Considerable research has gone into analyzing the different components mentioned, so it is not unusual for commentators to suggest that **psalms** (*psalmois*) may have their heritage in the Old Testament; **hymns** (*hymnois*) could include psalms but may be more Christians' songs of praise to God or

Christ; **sacred**, literally, "spiritual," **songs** (*ōidais*) may be musical compositions originating from ecstatic utterances under the inspiration of the Holy Spirit (cf. 1 Cor. 14:16).

On the basis of this passage and a similar one in Ephesians 5:19, it is not possible to establish distinctions in any detail, even though there is a certain diversity about the three. It does help one to appreciate both the richness of Christian hymnody even at this early stage of the church's life and the function of music within the context of worship. When such music is grounded in the word of God (i.e., doctrinal in content), it definitely serves a teaching and instructional function within the body.

Singing is to be expressed in a spirit of **thanksgiving**. Music may edify the members of a congregation, but its primary function is to render thanks to God. The word translated **thanksgiving** is *charis*, not the more common *eucharistia*. *Charis* can also mean "grace," and with the inclusion of the article (*en tē chariti*), Paul may be referring to the grace of God. When Christians sing "in the grace," they sing by virtue of the grace of God which is theirs. (The GNB rightly uses **God** rather than "Lord," which has weaker manuscript evidence and probably represents an attempt to harmonize it with Eph. 5:19).

3:17 / Although this verse follows Paul's thoughts on corporate worship, it is intended to be universal in scope. The apostle has been listing a number of virtues and suggesting patterns of conduct that are to regulate life within the community. But it is obvious that he cannot make out a detailed list of vices and virtues to cover every aspect of life. To do so would mean reverting to the type of Pharisaism that Jesus so vehemently condemned in the Gospels, or patterning his gospel after the heretics at Colossae, with all their rules and regulations (2:8–23).

Rather than a directory of rules, Paul leaves an important principle with his readers: Everything they **do or say should be done in the name of the Lord Jesus**. They were baptized into that name and thus stand under the authority of Christ. Their ethical life—in word or deed—is to manifest that fact. In other words, the best testimony of a meaningful baptism is an obedient life.

Finally, **give thanks through him to God the Father**. The Christian lives out his obedience to Christ, not under compulsion as a duty, but in freedom with thanksgiving. What a striking contrast to the enslaving rules and regulations of the false teachers! The Christian's praise is offered to God through Christ. Once again, Paul reminds his readers that Christ is the only mediator to God.

The Household Rules

The GNB entitles this section "Personal Relations in the New Life." Here Paul sets forth a series of reciprocal admonitions that are to govern the relationships between wives and husbands, children and parents, and slaves and masters. This list forms what has come to be known in academic circles as the *Haustafeln*, a German term meaning a list of rules or duties for members of a household. Similar lists to the one in Colossians are found in Ephesians 5:21–6:9 and 1 Peter 2:18–25, 3:1–7. The Pastoral Epistles (1 Tim. 2:8–15; 6:1–10; Titus 2:1–10) deal with the same classes of people but in a less structured and unified way.

The appearance of these "household rules" in so many NT epistles indicates that such instruction was necessary in the early church. People needed to know how their new life in Christ affected their personal relationships in the household as well as in the larger body of Christ. The similarity of these exhortations, particularly in Colossians, Ephesians, and 1 Peter, indicates that they were part of a body of traditional material that was developed and passed on in the churches. The instructions on slavery, for example, are much longer and serve a different function in 1 Peter than in Colossians or Ephesians; 1 Peter has no instruction for masters, whereas in Colossians and Ephesians it is an important part of a reciprocal relationship. The fact that wives and slaves are found in all lists indicates a concern that needed particular clarification.

Since it is obvious that other cultures and societies, such as the Jewish, Greek, and Roman, had rules and regulations governing social and personal relationships, there has been considerable conjecture in scholarly circles regarding the source of these *Haustafeln* in the NT. Some writers are attracted to ideas in Greek philosophy, particularly in the ethics of Stoicism, where there are significant parallels to the NT. Others suppose Jewish influence, drawing attention to ethical patterns and social concerns in Palestinian and Hellenistic Judaism. A few scholars argue for a distinctly Christian origin, believing that these rules can be traced back to the teachings of Jesus, Paul, and other apostles. There is, however, no easy solution to the question of sources, transmission, and final composition. Suffice it to say that by the time of their appearance in the NT they are regarded as authentic and authoritative instructions.

What does all of this mean as far as Colossians is concerned? First, it would be fair to say that Paul is using a body of traditional material dealing with personal relationships and applying them to the church at Colossae. Second, they must serve a specific function within this letter. As an isolated unit (3:18–4:1) one could say that they simply have a domestic or sociological function. But their location in the epistle is not without significance.

At first glance, this section appears to interrupt Paul's ideas on worship (3:16, 17)—a theme that is continued in 4:2–4 with an emphasis on prayer and thanksgiving. However, by placing the *Haustafeln* in the context of worship, Paul wishes to emphasize the need for *order* in the church, particularly among women and slaves. The primary function of these domestic rules, therefore, is ecclesiological (for the church) rather than merely sociological (for society).

The need for "order" at Colossae, as well as in such congregations as Corinth and Ephesus, has to be seen within the cultural and religious context of the first century. First, there were concerns that arose because of the delay of the return of the Lord. The followers of Jesus expected him to return within their lifetime (Mark 9:1; 13:30, and parallels); Paul, likewise, believed that the coming of the Lord was imminent (1 Cor. 15:51–58). When this did not occur, and certain problems arose in the church because of it, he offered some correctives (2 Thess. 2:1–12; cf. also 1 Thess. 4:13–5:11). The Second Epistle of Peter may be one of the best documents in the NT cautioning against an expectation of the Lord's early return. With the Lord, writes Peter, "there is no difference . . . between one day and a thousand years" (3:8).

When it was believed that the Lord's return was imminent, there was no reason to be concerned about rules governing church order. The early church was basically charismatic in nature, that is, it exercised considerable freedom of the Spirit in its life and worship. This fact provides a backdrop for much of Paul's concern for the disorder in the Corinthian church, where certain spiritual gifts were overemphasized and the congregation became fragmented and competitive (1 Cor. 11–14). This manifestation of religious enthusiasm may have been inspired by the prophetic fulfillment of Joel 2:28 ff. (cf. Acts 2:17–21) and influenced by pagan cults in which ecstasy and spiritual excesses abounded. At any rate, the church service is not the place for everybody to do as he or she pleases; things need to be done in an orderly manner, and the welfare of the entire body must be considered.

With the delay of the Lord's return, the need for order in the church became more obvious. The teaching ministry that initially belonged to the twelve apostles and to charismatic leaders such as prophets and teachers (cf. Acts) was enlarged to include appropriately appointed leaders like Paul as well as bishops (*episkopos*, 1 Tim. 3:1–7; Titus 1:7), deacons (*diakonos*, 1 Tim. 3:8–13), and elders (*presbuteros*, Titus 1:5) who were to teach and care for the church of God. There needed to be order in the church with respect to what was said (received tradition) and how things were done (proper offices).

The delay of the Lord also raised questions about the relationship of Christians to society. What is God's will for believers in the world? How are those who are "in the Lord" to walk before those who are not in the body of Christ? These household rules were created as patterns of instruction to answer such questions and to regulate personal relationships with the home, the church, and society. This concern was extended to include instruction regarding relationships to political authorities as well (Rom. 13:1–7; 1 Pet. 2:13–17).

A second factor at work in this section centers around the growing sense of freedom of women and slaves during Paul's time. Unfortunately, more is known about the subjection of women and slaves than about their emancipation. In Jewish culture, for example, women were relegated to a position inferior to that of men. They were denied certain functions in worship; their court in the temple area was outside of the "court of Israel." According to one rabbinic tradition, Jewish men repeated this blessing every morning: "I thank the Lord that he did not make me a Gentile . . . a woman . . . a boor."

Slaves suffered a similar fate in Greek and Roman society. Much secular literature of that period speaks of slaves in derogatory and demeaning terms. A slave was a living tool and, with the exception of the ability to speak, was considered no better than a beast. Their masters had powers of life and death over them, and they could be abandoned when their usefulness was gone. Many were killed at the slightest provocation.

At the same time, there are many examples of humanitarianism and manumission by slave owners. In some cases, slaves were part of the household and had responsible personal and financial positions. Many of them were treated kindly and honorably. However, the existence of the admonitions to the masters in these codes indicates that this relationship needed to be clarified for Christian slaves and masters.

The emancipation of women was more pronounced in the Gentile than in the Jewish culture, which basically was a patriarchal society. Greek and Roman women had rights and privileges that were denied their Jewish counterparts. Undoubtedly there are exceptions, for one can find conflicting reports in secular literature. Attitudes toward the status and role of women varied at different periods and geographical areas— not unlike today. In worship, however, Gentile women had an advantage over Jewish women. Many of the Greek and Roman deities were female (e.g., Isis and Diana), and most religious cults freely admitted women as participants and leaders.

This kind of religious freedom may have contributed to the problems faced in some of the Gentile churches, such as Corinth. Women—as well as men—who had been converted to Christianity would bring some of their previous religious practices into their new faith. But the ecstasy, glossolalia, prophecy, enthusiasm, and so forth sanctioned in some of the pagan cults was not welcomed in Christianity; it did not produce the kind of reverence and order that was necessary for building up the body of Christ.

This background assists one to place into a proper context other statements by Paul concerning women and worship. Paul's responses often are drawn from his Jewish background, in which the role of males was still dominant. Thus his attitude toward women is determined by the order of creation (1 Cor. 11:3; 1 Tim. 2:13), the sin of Eve (1 Tim. 2:14), and subjection as symbolized by the woman's covered head (1 Cor. 11:5–8). Women in the church during Paul's time are instructed to follow these admonitions and not to do anything that will disturb church order or hinder their witness to the world.

Undoubtedly, the most significant note of liberation for women and slaves was sounded in the proclamation of the gospel itself, in which freedom and equality are essential ingredients to new life in Christ. It is in this spirit that Paul writes to the Galatians: "It is through faith that all of you are God's sons in union with Christ Jesus. You were baptized into union with Christ, and so have taken upon yourselves the qualities of Christ himself. So there is no difference between Jews and Gentiles, between slaves and freemen, between men and women; you are all one in union with Christ Jesus" (Gal. 3:26–28). In Christ, all racial, religious, cultural, and social barriers have been removed (cf. disc. on 3:11). How were the slaves and the women in Paul's day to understand and then translate their newly found freedom in Christ into daily life? The household rules are part of the apostolic response to such questions. By including them in his letter to the Colossians, Paul reminds his readers of the need to maintain religious and social order.

Additional Note

There are many valuable studies on the origin, nature and teaching of the "household rules" in the NT. In commentaries, see esp. Lohse, pp. 154–57; Schweizer's excursus, "The Household Rules," pp. 213–30. Other sources include: P. R. Coleman-Norton, "The Apostle Paul and the Roman Law of Slavery," in *Studies in Roman Economic and Social History*, ed. P. R. Coleman-Norton (Princeton: Princeton University Press, 1951), pp. 155–77, G. Hinson, "The Christian Household in Colossians 3:18–4:1," *RevExp* 70 (1973), pp. 495–506; W. Lillie, "The Pauline Housetables," *ExpT* 86 (1975), pp. 179–83; W. Munro, "Col. 3:18–4:1 and Eph. 5:21–6:9: Evidences of a Late Literary Stratum?" *NTS* 18 (1972), pp. 434–47; K. H. Rengstorf, "*doulos*," *TDNT*, vol. 2, pp. 261–80; E. Schweizer, "Traditional Ethical Patterns in the Pauline and post-Pauline Letters and Their Development (Lists of vices and house-tables")," pp. 195–209; T. Wiedemann, *Greek and Roman Slavery* (Baltimore: Johns Hopkins University Press, 1981). For a current bibliography on the literature dealing with the household codes, see Cannon, pp. 119–20, n. 2. Cannon's discussion of these codes and their application to Colossians includes pp. 95–131.

Wife-Husband Relationships

COLOSSIANS 3:18–19

Wives, submit yourselves to your husbands, for that is what you should do as Christians.	[19]Husbands, love your wives and do not be harsh with them.

3:18 / There are two striking features about the following exhortations: First, according to the acceptable cultural patterns of that day, the first party addressed (wives, children, slaves) is subordinate to the second (husbands, parents, masters); second, in all cases, these are reciprocal admonitions—mutual love and mutual submission are the key elements in these relationships.

Wives are to submit themselves (Greek middle form) to their husbands. Obedience, or submission (*hypotasso*), is enjoined on the basis that it is the "Christian" thing to do. In the Greek, the phrase literally reads, "as it is fitting in the Lord." Either way, it means that Christian wives are to acknowledge what is socially acceptable or "proper" with respect to their husbands. Paul simply states this principle and does not debate the rightness of it or seek to interpret its meaning.

There is nothing in *this* verse to suggest that subordination is based on a hierarchical relationship, sometimes inferred from other Scriptures (cf. 1 Cor. 11:3; Eph. 5:23). *Hypotasso*, from which the word *taxis* ("order," as in taxonomy) is derived, is a common word to designate a relationship of mutual submission. Nothing harsh or demeaning is implied (cf. 1 Cor. 15:28 and disc. on Eph. 5:21 ff.).

3:19 / Husbands are to love their wives and not be harsh with them. **Love** (*agapē*) and harshness stand in stark contrast to each other. Lest husbands interpret "obedience" incorrectly, Paul reminds them that theirs is a relationship to be governed by the highest of all loves—a love that avoids any bitterness, resentment, or tyranny, because its supreme aim is the well-being of the other person.

Additional Note

3:19 / L. J. Baggott states it well when he writes that "the rule of love is always better than the love of rule" in *A New Approach to Colossians* (London: Mowbray, 1961), p. 121.

Child-Parent Relationships

Children, it is your Christian duty to obey your parents always, for that is what pleases God.

²¹Parents, do not irritate your children, or they will become discouraged.

3:20 / Children are to obey their parents in all things. **Always** indicates that this is to be a total obedience, governed, as in 3:18, by the fact that this is the right and acceptable thing to do. It is not known whether Paul had Christian parents in mind or what limits he would have placed on obedience contrary to the law of Christ. Since **please** (*euarestos*) is used elsewhere in Scripture as "that which is acceptable and pleasing to the Lord" (Rom. 12:1; 14:18; 2 Cor. 5:9; Eph. 5:10), the implication is that a child's obedience has the same effect.

3:21 / The obedience required of children does not give parents the freedom to abuse them. Hence, parents are not to **irritate** their children, that is, do anything that will provoke or tyrannize them (*erethizō*). The reason for this is to avoid the negative reaction of discouragement. Harsh and provoking treatment of children merely leads to exasperation and misunderstanding. Parents need to restrain their authority; they should deserve rather than demand obedience. As with wives, the subordinated party (the child) is exhorted to be submissive and respectful; as with husbands, the ruling party (the parent) is admonished to be loving and responsible.

Additional Note

3:20 / According to Hinson, "The strong emphasis upon unqualified obedience of children reflects a Jewish attitude and perhaps indicates a synagogal origin" ("The Christian Household in Colossians 3:18–4:1," *RevExp* 70 (1973), p. 499).

Slaves-Masters Relationships

COLOSSIANS 3:22–4:1

Slaves, obey your human masters in all things, not only when they are watching you because you want to gain their approval; but do it with a sincere heart because of your reverence for the Lord. [23]Whatever you do, work at it with all your heart, as though you were working for the Lord and not for men. [24]Remember that the Lord will give you as a reward what he has kept for his people. For Christ is the real Master you serve. [25]And every wrongdoer will be repaid for the wrong things he does, because God judges everyone by the same standard.

[1]Masters, be fair and just in the way you treat your slaves. Remember that you too have a Master in heaven.

Since many slaves became Christians, it should not come as a surprise that they are singled out for some specific instructions in the NT (cf. 1Cor. 7:20–24; Eph. 6:5–8; 1 Tim. 6:1, 2; 1 Pet. 2:18–25). For the majority of them, membership in the church may have been the only time and place they could experience equality and brotherhood. But belonging to Christ did not remove them from the world or lead to their emancipation. Allegiance to the *heavenly* Lord did not mean freedom from their *earthly* lords. They, more than anyone else, needed clarification on the relation of their status in Christ to their lot on earth.

A quick reading of the passages directed to slaves reveals that the writers of the NT did not take a negative attitude toward the practice of slavery in the ancient world; nor did they attempt to abolish it. Several factors may lie behind their approach:

First, Christianity was not a revolutionary movement bent on destroying the existing world order. To do so would have been suicidal, for what effect would a small and powerless group of Christians have had upon the might of Rome? Any attempt at revolution would have been met with severe persecution and martyrdom.

One of the clear messages in the Book of Acts is that Christianity has not engaged in treasonous activity and should, therefore, be regarded as a legal religion within the Roman Empire (Acts 25:8). Believers are admonished to obey their rulers and accept the temporal order even though it may be unsatisfactory in many ways (Rom. 13:1–7; 1 Pet. 2:13–17).

Second, slavery in the ancient world was a necessary evil, although it was human beings who made the institution evil. Greek and Roman society was made up of masses of individuals without the ability or opportunity to work. The economic, social, and monetary systems that regulate modern society were unknown in the first century. Think of the social chaos that would have resulted from setting free millions of slaves. What would these people do, and how would they be fed? Slavery was a means of maintaining peace and order in the empire; the abolition of this institution would have led to political and economic chaos.

All this does not mean that Christianity merely adapted to its environment without a struggle or any concern for social justice. The ministry and teachings of Jesus (Matt. 25:35–40; Luke 4:18, 19), the life of the early church (Acts 6:1–6; 2 Cor. 8:1–4), and the suffering of Christians (1 Peter, Revelation) prove otherwise. Rather than exercise *revolutionary* power, Christians proclaimed a *transforming* power. By their life and message they set a process in motion that eventually culminated in the abolition of slavery, for once slaves and masters regarded themselves as brothers, equally precious in God's sight, such divisions could not continue.

The approach that the church took toward slavery was determined largely by its theology rather than motivated by its safety. Christians believed that God had chosen them and given them an inheritance; they believed that Christ had brought them freedom and that this would be enjoyed fully when the Lord returned to judge the world and reward the saints. And since they had no mandate from God to overthrow the world, they lived peaceably in the assurance that the last days were near. God had promised them a new Spirit, not a new social order.

As confidence in an imminent return of the Lord waned, the slaves— as did most believers—became restless. They must have wondered when their equality and freedom in Christ would become a social reality. If the Lord was not going to come soon, how much longer were they expected to go on living as slaves? These slaves needed some direction for their lives; they needed a higher motive than maintaining the status quo to explain why they must continue in their lowly position in the social order.

This is where this section in the household rules comes in. These rules are attempts at guiding slaves and masters on sensitive and significant issues. The fact that Paul includes such a lengthy exhortation in Colossians indicates it was an issue that had to be emphasized in order to preserve order. He also may have had Philemon and Onesimus in mind, although the specifics of that case are not developed here (cf. Philemon). What Paul does in this section is to place slavery within the scope of

Christ's lordship—a thought not surprising, considering the development of the pre-eminence of Christ throughout the epistle. He who is Lord of the universe is Lord of the church (1:15–20); and that lordship extends to all its members, including the slaves. Under Christ's lordship, Paul mentions a number of significant changes that have taken place with respect to their status:

3:22 / First, slaves have a new *attitude*. At one time they were motivated by a need for recognition and praise from their master. The unusual word *ophthalmodoulia* is a compound of *ophthalmos* ("eye") and *doulos* ("service"). As non-Christians, their service was performed to gain human approval.

As believers, however, their labor is to spring inwardly from the **heart** rather than from outward considerations. They are to realize that their work ultimately is directed toward Christ, not individuals. "Fear" (*phobeomai*), or reverence for the Lord, becomes the motivating principle that enables slaves to perform their daily tasks.

3:23 / Second, slaves have a new *center of reference*. This is implied already in the last phrase of verse 22, which the thoughts of verse 23 serve to amplify somewhat. Paul wants them to understand that, in spite of their position, they are serving Christ and not men. As a result of their relationship to Christ, they have been freed from viewing work as an obligation and performing it methodically and unenthusiastically for human approval. Thus Paul states that they are to work heartily as though they were **working for the Lord and not for men**.

3:24 / Third, they have a new reward. Once again, Paul reminds them of their new center of reference—**for Christ is the real Master you serve**. Undoubtedly there is an allusion here to wages—or rather the lack of them—and the resentment that may have been generated between slaves and masters. In monetary terms, slaves were poor and had little opportunity of receiving an inheritance or improving their lot. Ultimately, their compensation had to come from the Lord.

The **reward** is the same one referred to in 1:12 with respect to the believer's inheritance. This, however, is not something that the slave earns as a result of faithful service, because the believer's inheritance is a gift of God. The slave's motivation is not material gain but "seeking the things that are above," which, in this case, is service to Christ and the reward that he gives.

3:25 / The point of reference in this verse is not clear; does **wrongdoer** refer to the slave or to the slave owner? Since the masters are not addressed formally until the next verse (4:1), it would be easy to assume that they are not the intended target of this rebuke. But given the context of the preceding verse, with its teaching on reward, could it be that the **wrongdoer** is the master who has failed to compensate his slave adequately? Paul advised the slaves, therefore, to remember that God ultimately will judge all wrongdoing (**God judges everyone by the same standard**). If this verse is taken as a reference to masters, then it forms a beautiful link with 4:1, where the ideas of fairness and justice are raised.

There is a sense in which this verse can apply to the slave as well. They have been exhorted to obey in all things (3:22), to work heartily and sincerely (3:22, 23), and to maintain an eternal perspective (3:24). Could Paul mean that any slave who falls short of that ideal will be judged as a **wrongdoer**? Slaves who do their work faithfully will be rewarded by God; slaves who fail in their responsibility can expect God's judgment. God does not show favor to slaves just because of their low estate.

4:1 / Again, Paul does not demand the abolition of slavery. Christian slave owners are not required to terminate a culturally acceptable practice just because they have become Christians. Nevertheless, Christian masters are different people because of their relationship with the Lord. They, too, have a new center of reference and so are called upon to demonstrate fairness and justice toward those who serve them; they too have **a Master in heaven**.

Here the principle of reciprocity is at work: The same transforming power that enables a slave to perceive and to perform his or her tasks differently is at work in the master who no longer treats the slave as a tool but regards him or her as a person, even as a "brother in the Lord" (Philem. 16). When such a relationship exists between master and slave, there will be no problem of disorder in the church.

Additional Notes

Other helpful insights on slavery can be found in the sources listed in the note in Chapter 18. See disc. and bibliography on Eph. 6:5–9.

3:22 / "Fear should certainly not be thought of as the opposite of trust; this is shown by the fact that in Ps. 33(32):18, for example, it is equated with hoping for God's grace. What fear really means is a way of living which is afraid of nothing except of losing this one Lord, in the same way that a person who is in love fears nothing so much as losing the affection of the beloved," (Schweizer, p. 225).

3:25 / It is interesting to note that the phrase "who judges everyone by the same standard" (RSV, "there is no partiality with him" [God]) clearly is applied to masters in Ephesians 6:9, a point in favor of applying it to masters in Colossians as well, unless the author of Ephesians was trying to make a different point. But given the context of Colossians and the need for "order" in all things, it makes sense to see 3:25 as a reference to the slaves. Obedience is the governing principle in the *Haustafeln*, and here it applies to the slaves. Schweizer suggests that "perhaps the question of who is being addressed is deliberately left open because what is said is valid for everyone" (p. 227).

22

Exhortations to Prayer
and Witness

Be persistent in prayer, and keep alert as you pray, giving thanks to God. ³At the same time pray also for us, so that God will give us a good opportunity to preach his message about the secret of Christ. For that is why I am now in prison. ⁴Pray, then, that I may speak, as I should, in such a way as to make it clear.

⁵Be wise in the way you act toward those who are not believers, making good use of every opportunity you have. ⁶Your speech should always be pleasant and interesting, and you should know how to give the right answer to everyone.

4:2 / The opening verse in this section continues the ideas on corporate worship that were developed in 3:16–18. The summons to **be persistent in prayer** is a theme that is repeated a number of times in the NT (Luke 18:1; Acts 1:14; 1:24; 6:4; Rom. 12:12; Eph. 6:18). This idea of persistence is emphasized by the additional exhortation to **keep alert** (*grēgoreō*, "watchfulness"). Thus it is not just the importance of prayer but the manner in which it is offered that is stressed.

This exhortation may be a caution against casualness in prayer. The call to "watchfulness" formed one of the categories of the baptismal (catechetical) instruction that was given to new Christians (cf. Eph. 6:18–20: "Pray . . . keep alert"; 1 Pet. 4:7; "alert . . . pray"; 5:8: "Be alert, be on watch"). Its inclusion in Colossians is another example of traditional material that was taken over and applied to the situation at Colossae.

Prayer is to be offered in thanksgiving. This is the seventh time that thanksgiving is mentioned in the letter (1:3, 12; 2:7; 3:15, 16, 17). Both thanksgiving and prayer are appropriate responses of the Christian and should be exercised by the worshiping community as well as by the individual. It is the pattern that Paul followed in the letter as he thanked God for the Colossians (1:3–8) and then prayed specifically for them (1:9–14).

4:3-4 / From a general admonition on prayer, Paul turns to a personal and specific request that God will give him an opportunity **to preach his message**. The GNB **opportunity** comes from the Greek *thura*, meaning "door," an expression that is used in Scripture as a metaphor for opportunities to witness (1 Cor. 16:9; 2 Cor. 2:12). The content of Paul's message is the unveiling of **the secret of Christ**, something that he already has explained in 1:26 and 2:2 (cf. Eph. 3:3–6, 9).

Paul indicates that he is **in prison**, literally, "in bonds" (*dedemai*, a perfect passive of *deō*), which could imply being chained up as well as locked in (cf. 4:18). His request for an opportunity to preach may imply a desire for personal release (cf. Philem. 22); but Paul often used his imprisonment to share the Good News as well (Acts 28:30) and felt that these circumstances "really helped the progress of the gospel" (Phil. 1:13). This desire is not only for himself, since he includes his co-workers (the plural **us**) such as Timothy (1:1), Epapras (1:7; 4:12), Tychicus (4:7), Onesimus (4:9), and others he mentions in his final greeting (4:7–18). The desire for clarity (*phaneroō*) in his proclamation must not be taken as a second request (NIV), because this "purpose clause" is subordinated to the previous one: Paul simply wants an opportunity to preach the **secret of Christ** clearly.

4:5–6 / In the next two verses Paul provides some guidelines for Christian relationships to unbelievers (cf. 1 Thess. 4:12). He would not sanction any movement of Christianity into private cliques or withdrawal from society. Rather, believers are to give visible (conduct) and verbal (speech) witness to their faith. The apostle seeks to encourage his readers to behave in a way that will authenticate their faith before those **who are not believers** (*tous echō*). The idea behind **opportunity** is the picturesque word *exagorazō*, which means to "buy" or to "redeem" (*agora*, "marketplace"). It is unclear whether Christians are to make the most of **every opportunity** because it was believed the Lord was near, or, in the light of Ephesians 5:16, "because these are bad days." Either way, the emphasis is upon using every available opportunity for Christian witness. This, however, is to be done wisely. Enthusiasm must be accompanied by common sense and tact. Witness without wisdom often produces bad feeling and brings negative results.

4:6 / Paul realizes that the witness of one's life must be accompanied by the spoken word. **Give the right answer to everyone** may refer to answers required as the result of a personal presentation of the Good News (the Greek is "each one individually"), or Paul may envision a situation similar to 1 Peter: "be ready at all times to answer anyone who asks you to explain the hope you have in you" (3:15, 16a; cf. also Matt. 10:19; Mark 13:11; Luke 12:11, 12; 21:4).

Whatever the situation, two qualities of speech are essential: First, it must be **pleasant**. This is a translation of *en chariti*, literally, "in grace," thus "gracious speech" (RSV). The Christian who is in God's grace will demonstrate that fact by the nature of his or her speech. Second, it must be **interesting**. The Greek text uses the phrase "seasoned with salt," which suggests an image of speech that is wholesome, witty, and palatable, just the opposite of words that are insipid, that is, dull and flat.

With this section, the formal and theological aspects of Colossians come to a close. But what remains in the following verses (4:7–18) should not be regarded as mere addenda that have nothing to do with the content of the letter. These greetings and final instructions make two significant contributions to this epistle.

First, they continue to reveal the true personal interest and pastoral heart that Paul has for this congregation. Throughout the letter he has indicated his concern by way of thanksgiving, intercession, agony, and suffering. That spirit continues here: Paul wants the news of Tychicus to "cheer them up" (4:7), and he shows how Epaphras shares the goals that he himself has for this congregation—for their commitment, maturity, and obedience to the gospel.

Second, they provide valuable historical insight on Paul's co-workers and their relationship to the Colossian church. The personal kinship and support that Paul shows for these "fellow servants" is exemplary of his capacity to love people and to recognize the contribution that they make to his life and the Lord's work. These verses, along with Romans 16:1–24, are a helpful commentary on how God used a number of people for the proclamation of the Good News and the building of the church of Jesus Christ.

Additional Notes

Similar exhortations to prayer and witness can be found in Gal. 5:26–6:6; Phil. 4:8–13; 1 Thess. 5:12–22.

4:6 / See W. Nauck, "Salt as a Metaphor in Instructions for Discipleship," *ST* 6 (1952), pp. 165–78.

23

Final Greetings and Instructions

COLOSSIANS 4:7–18

Our dear brother Tychicus, who is a faithful worker and fellow servant in the Lord's work, will give you all the news about me. ⁸That is why I am sending him to you, in order to cheer you up by telling you how all of us are getting along. ⁹With him goes Onesimus, that dear and faithful brother, who belongs to your group. They will tell you everything that is happening here.

¹⁰Aristarchus, who is in prison with me, sends you greetings, and so does Mark, the cousin of Barnabas. (You have already received instructions to welcome Mark if he comes your way.) ¹¹Joshua, also called Justus, sends greetings too. These three are the only Jewish converts who work with me for the Kingdom of God, and they have been a great help to me.

¹²Greetings from Epaphras, another member of your group and a servant of Christ Jesus. He always prays fervently for you, asking God to make you stand firm, as mature and fully convinced Christians, in complete obedience to God's will. ¹³I can personally testify to his hard work for you and for the people in Laodicea and Hierapolis. ¹⁴Luke, our dear doctor, and Demas send you their greetings.

¹⁵Give our best wishes to the brothers in Laodicea and to Nympha and the church that meets in her house.^{f} ¹⁶After you read this letter, make sure that it is read also in the church at Laodicea. At the same time, you are to read the letter that the brothers in Laodicea will send you. ¹⁷And tell Archippus, "Be sure to finish the task you were given in the Lord's service."

¹⁸With my own hand I write this: *Greetings from Paul.* Do not forget my chains!

May God's grace be with you.

f. Nympha . . . her house; *some manuscripts have* Nymphas . . . his house.

4:7–8 / Two of the individuals mentioned in this list are personal emissaries of Paul to the Colossian church. Tychicus is singled out and commended as a **dear . . . brother, faithful worker**, and **fellow servant**. Paul's association with him goes back to Ephesus (Acts 20:4), where it appears Tychicus may have spent some time as a church leader (2 Tim. 4:12; Titus 3:12).

Paul dispatches Tychicus to Colossae as a personal messenger and probably as the bearer of this letter and anticipates that his coming will cheer them up. The word for **cheer** is *parakaleō*, which conveys a sense of encouragement and comfort in this context. As a "paraclete," Tychicus is a personal agent of the Holy Spirit to this congregation (John 14:16, 26; 16:7, 8).

4:9 / **Onesimus**, who is another **dear and faithful brother**, accompanies Tychicus to Colossae for the same reason. For Onesimus, the return to his hometown must have included some mixed emotions, for he is the slave who ran away from his owner, Philemon. The details of this case, however, are dealt with in Paul's personal Letter to Philemon.

4:10–11 / **Aristarchus** (Acts 19:29; 20:4; 27:2), **Mark** (Mark 14:51; Acts 12:12, 25; 13:13; 15:37, 39; 2 Tim. 4:11; Philem. 24), and **Justus** are identified by Paul as **the only Jewish converts who work with me for the Kingdom of God**. One can almost detect a note of pathos in Paul's statement, since he must have expected a larger number of Jewish Christians to become his co-workers. Nevertheless, he is deeply appreciative for the personal assistance that they have given to him. **Help** (*parēgoria*) includes a note of comfort and may best express the feeling of gratitude that Paul has for these three individuals.

The phrase **Kingdom of God** appears to be another way to express the missionary preaching of Paul and his co-workers (cf. Acts 19:8; 28:30, 31), for their goal was to announce that the Kingdom of God has come in Christ, the Messiah. Elsewhere, Paul identifies this "Kingdom of God" as the domain of the righteous (1 Cor. 6:9; Gal. 5:21).

Although Aristarchus is identified as being **in prison** with Paul, there is no way of knowing whether this (cf. Philem. 23) is to be taken literally or metaphorically (i.e, as a prisoner of the Lord or for Christ's sake, cf. Eph. 3:1; 4:1). The historical circumstances of Paul's imprisonment, the use of the term *synaichmalotos* ("fellow prisoner"), and the absence of any qualifying phrases (such as "of the Lord") favor the literal meaning.

Of these three individuals, Mark was the least known to the Colossians. Thus he is identified as the **cousin of Barnabas**—someone with whom they must have been acquainted. Paul reminds the Colossians of previous instructions to receive Mark if he comes their way. Nothing beyond this reference is known about a previous contact with the church on Mark's behalf. Paul may have given the original instruction himself or he may now be simply endorsing an earlier recommendation by someone else.

4:12–13 / **Epaphras**, another **servant of Christ Jesus**, has been identified with the Colossian church from the beginning (1:7), and so the inclusion of his name comes as no surprise. Paul's commendation of this fellow prisoner (Philem. 23) comes out of a long personal relationship that the two have had. Epaphras must have come to Ephesus during Paul's stay in that city (Acts 19) and been converted under Paul's preaching. Paul's stay in Ephesus was rather lengthy (three years, according to Acts 20:31), and it included an extensive teaching ministry ("and every day he held discussions in the lecture hall of Tyrannus. This went on for two years, so that all the people who lived in the province of Asia, both Jews and Gentiles, heard the word of the Lord," Acts 19:9, 10).

Epaphras must have been well schooled in Paul's theology and thus prepared to be a missionary and teacher in his own right. The gospel that he brought to his native town had given birth to the church in Colossae (1:7) as well as to those in the neighboring cities of Laodicea and Hierapolis. The importance of Epaphras as a missionary to the Gentiles should not be overlooked. Perhaps he had come to Rome to get some advice from Paul on how to deal with the heresy that was threatening the church (2:8).

Epaphras' concern for his congregation manifested itself in his prayer life: He did not give birth to the church and then abandon it; rather, states Paul, **He always prays fervently for you**. The concerns of his prayer are quite similar to those that Paul himself has expressed throughout the epistle (cf. 1:9, 11, 23, 28; 2:2, 5–7; 3:1, 2). The qualities of firmness, maturity, conviction, and obedience will enable the Colossians to deal effectively with the heresy that is threatening their faith.

4:14 / Luke and **Demas** also are included in the list of greetings. Luke's association with Paul remained intimate and strong (2 Tim. 4:11); Demas, however, chose a different fate at a later point in his life ("Demas fell in love with this present world and has deserted me," 2 Tim. 4:10).

4:15–16 / These verses provide some interesting information about church life in the first century: First, it is another example of early Christians gathering in homes for their meetings (cf. Acts 12:12; 16:40; Rom. 16:5; 1 Cor. 16:19; Philem. 2). It was not until the late third century that Christians began to meet in places expressly set aside for worship. Paul sends his greeting to such a house congregation in Laodicea, which met in Nympha's home.

Second, it shows that the churches enjoyed fellowship with each other. It does not appear unusual for Paul to request that his greetings in the Colossian letter be conveyed to a neighboring congregation. The same applies to the exchange of correspondence between the congregations at

Colossae and Laodicea. Since Paul's letters could not be duplicated and purchased by members, they were read aloud and, in this case, exchanged as well (cf. 1 Thess. 5:27).

No one has been able to identify this epistle from Laodicea. Some have suggested that it may be the Epistle to the Ephesians or even Philemon. The most obvious explanation is that it is a letter Paul wrote specifically to this congregation but that for some reason was not retained in the Pauline corpus and (apparently) did not survive. Perhaps it disappeared because the church to whom it was written became spiritually anemic ("barely warm") and died (Rev. 3:14–22).

4:17 / **Archippus**, possibly another member in the Colossian church, is given a specific charge by Paul to finish the task that he was given **in the Lord's service**. Since **task** is a translation of *diakonia*, some commentators have wondered whether Archippus' ministry was that of a deacon. There is, however, no way of knowing whether a specific office is meant or just a specific task to be completed. It must have been a significant matter for Paul to single out Archippus in this way, especially since the letter would be read in public for all to hear.

4:18 / It was customary for such writers as Paul (cf. Rom. 16:22) and Peter (1 Pet. 5:14) to employ secretaries (amanuenses) for the composition of their letters. Paul, for example, may have dictated certain ideas or even written down a broad outline that a secretary would complete. The personal signature (**with my own hand I write this: *Greetings from Paul***) would have given the letter a sense of intimacy (cf. 1 Cor. 16:21; Gal. 6:11; 2 Thess. 2:2).

The concluding request is that the Colossians not forget Paul's chains, literally, "remember my bonds." Earlier, he made a similar request for their prayers (4:3). One wonders whether the request comes from a lonely and discouraged apostle, or whether it is to be understood as an indirect affirmation of his entire ministry as a servant and prisoner for Jesus Christ. Since the normal word for prayer (*eucharisteō*) is not used, it seems likely that the phrase is an appeal to remember and respect Paul for who he is and for what he has written.

Finally, the benediction: **May God's grace be with you**. As the letter began (1:2), so it ends, with a prayer for grace. The Colossians needed more than a letter to sustain them in their Christian life. Only God's grace could fortify them against the false teaching and enable them to remain true to the gospel they had received.

Additional Notes

Apart from the major commentaries on this section see G. E. Ladd, "Paul's Friends in Colossians 4:7–16," *RevExp* 70 (1973), pp. 507–14.

4:16 / Although the GNB has decided (correctly so) that Nympha is a woman, it should be noted that there is a textual variant that has changed the gender to masculine, thus reading "Nymphas, *his* house." For suggestions on this verse, see C. P. Anderson, "Who Wrote 'The Epistle from Laodicea'?" *JBL* 85 (1966), pp. 436–40.

Introduction: Philemon

This epistle of Paul's is a rather personal letter to Philemon, a member of the Colossian church and master of the slave Onesimus. Onesimus has run away from his master and somehow made his way to where Paul is in prison. Here he has become Paul's friend and helper. But Paul realizes that Onesimus needs to correct his situation by going back to Philemon where he rightfully belongs. Paul's Letter to Philemon is an attempt to plead Onesimus' case before Philemon, whom he hopes will respond out of love and forgiveness and restore Onesimus not only as a slave but as a beloved brother in Christ.

From the discussion in Colossians, it already has become obvious that Paul's Letter to the Colossians and his Letter to Philemon have a number of things in common: First, they are written from the same place (see Introduction to Colossians); second, they are addressed to the same church, although Philemon is more a personal letter for one of the church members. Onesimus (Col. 4:9) and Archippus (Col. 4:17) belonged to the Colossians church, so it is fairly safe to assume that Philemon lived in Colossae as well; third, both epistles mention similar circumstances of Paul's imprisonment (Col. 4:3, 18; Philem. 1, 13); fourth, the list of personal greetings is almost identical; fifth, both Colossians (1:1) and Philemon (v. 1) name Timothy as cooperating with Paul in writing the letter; sixth, these letters probably were collected and kept as a single piece of Paul's correspondence. Unfortunately, the compilers of the NT did not keep Colossians and Philemon together in the text.

1

Paul's Greetings

From Paul, a prisoner for the sake of Christ Jesus, and from our brother Timothy—
  To our friend and fellow worker Philemon, ²and the church that meets in your house, and our sister Apphia, and our fellow soldier Archippus:
  ³May God our Father and the Lord Jesus Christ give you grace and peace.

1 / Here is a letter **from Paul** who is **a prisoner for the sake of Christ Jesus** (cf. Col. 4:3, 18). On the basis of verses 9 and 10, this definitely is a physical confinement and not a way of speaking metaphorically. Paul's **brother** in Christ, **Timothy**, joins him in the sending of the letter (cf. Col. 1:1) to Philemon, a dear **friend and fellow worker**. Philemon is a dear (*agapētō*, "beloved") friend because he belongs to a community that is characterized by love; he is a fellow worker because he is actively involved in the work of the gospel in Colossae.

2 / One of the ways in which Philemon has demonstrated his love and concern for the gospel is by opening his house for church meetings. The fact that the greeting extends to **the church** and includes Apphia and Archippus makes this epistle more public than private. The content may primarily be directed to Philemon, but the entire matter surrounding Onesimus is a concern to all the church. No special military significance should be attached to the term **fellow soldier** (*systratiōtēs*). This is another metaphor Paul uses to describe one of his colleagues in the ministry. In Philippians 2:25 the same word is used for Epaphroditus as one who "has fought by my side." In the case of Archippus, **fellow soldier** rather than "fellow worker" may be used because he has some special task to fulfill (Col. 4:17).

Not too much is known about **Apphia**, but since she is so closely linked with Philemon, it is possible that she is his wife. However, it does not necessarily follow that Archippus was their son, as some commentators have speculated. John Knox, for example, has attempted to show that Archippus, not Philemon, is the master of Onesimus and that the "task" that Archippus was to finish (Col. 4:17) refers to the way he was to handle Onesimus. The details of this task are outlined in Paul's Letter to Philemon, which, according to Knox, is the "letter from Laodicea" (Col. 4:16). There are too many difficulties, however, with this theory, and who Archippus was, beyond what is said in Colossians and Philemon, remains highly speculative.

3 / The closing part of Paul's salutation is similar to Colossians 1:2 and the way in which Paul addresses other congregations as well. **Grace and peace** are two of the greatest gifts of the Christian life.

Additional Note

2 / John Knox, *Philemon Among the Letters of Paul*. For an evaluation of the ideas presented by Knox, see Lohse, pp. 186–87.

Two helpful English articles on Philemon are E. W. Koch, "Cameo of Koinonia," *Interp* 17 (1963), pp. 183–87; F. F. Church, "Rhetorical Structure and Design in Paul's Letter to Philemon," *HTR* 71 (1978), pp. 17–33.

Paul's Praise for Philemon

Brother Philemon, every time I pray, I mention you and give thanks to my God. ⁵For I hear of your love for all of God's people and the faith you have in the Lord Jesus. ⁶My prayer is that our fellowship with you as believers will bring about a deeper understanding of every blessing which we have in our life in union with Christ. ⁷Your love, dear brother, has brought me great joy and much encouragement! You have cheered the hearts of all of God's people.

4-5 / These verses, which the GNB entitles, "Philemon's Love and Faith," draw attention to the individual Philemon in much the same way that Paul's thanksgiving and prayer in Colossians focused upon the congregation (Col. 1:3–14). Paul's gratitude for Philemon's love for God's people (v. 5) forms the basis of his request in verse 9; Paul affirms his fellowship with Philemon (v. 6) and, on that basis, requests Philemon to act kindly toward Onesimus (v. 17); as Philemon has cheered the hearts of all God's people (v. 7), Paul desires that his own heart be cheered through Philemon's love (v. 20). Here, too, remembrance becomes an occasion for thanksgiving and prayer: **Every time I pray, I mention you and give thanks to my God.**

Paul is grateful because of the positive things that he has heard about Philemon's **love** (*agapē*) and **faith** (*pistis*). Normally, Paul mentions faith first and then shows that Christian love springs from and is nourished by faith in the Lord (Col. 1:4; Eph. 1:15). Literally, the sentence in Greek reads: "I hear of your love and faith which you have to the Lord Jesus and to all the saints." From this, there is no way of knowing toward what **love** and **faith** are each directed.

In the GNB, the sentence is given this translation: **I hear of your love for all of God's people and the faith you have in the Lord Jesus**. The translators arrive at this interpretation because they realize that the Greek sentence probably employs a grammatical structure known as chiasm. The term comes from the Greek letter *chi*, which is written like an *X*. In a sentence, words or phrases are arranged in inverted parallelism. Verse 5, for example, would read:

a. **love**   b. **faith**
b. **in the Lord Jesus**   a. **for all God's people**

Love (a) comes first because Paul is thinking of Philemon's love, both explicitly (vv. 7, 9) and implicitly (vv. 14, 16, 17, 20); (b) **faith** is the source from which love is derived; (b) faith has as its object **the Lord Jesus**; (a) love is directed to (eis) **all of God's people**. This explanation reflects the usual Pauline way of associating faith with the Lord and directing love to God's people.

6 / Since this is the most obscure verse in the epistle, it may help to compare several translations:

Greek—literally, "so as the fellowship (koinōnia) of your faith working may become in full knowledge of every good thing in us for Christ."

RSV—"and I pray that the sharing of your faith may promote the knowledge of all the good that is ours in Christ."

NIV—"I pray that you may be active in sharing your faith, so that you will have a full understanding of every good thing we have in Christ."

GNB—**My prayer is that our fellowship with you as believers will bring about a deeper understanding of every blessing which we have in our life in union with Christ.**

The best way to approximate what this verse means is to see it in the context of the letter as teaching these truths: All Christians share a common faith; faith should be an active faith because it promotes an understanding of the blessings believers have received; the response of faith is for Christ, that is, for his glory; Philemon's recognition of these blessings will cause him to respond appropriately with respect to Onesimus (v. 14).

7 / The theme of Philemon's love (v. 5) is repeated in this verse: **You have cheered the hearts of all of God's people.** Although there is no way of knowing specifically what Philemon has done, the result was a cheering or refreshing (anapauō) of their innermost feelings (**hearts**). Paul is not as eager to describe Philemon's actions as he is to accentuate his spirit; that same spirit of love will determine how he responds to Paul's request regarding Onesimus (cf. v. 20, where the same word is used). The relationship of Paul to Philemon is that of a **brother**. This is a status that Paul, Timothy, Philemon, and even Onesimus (v. 16) enjoy together.

Paul indicates that he personally has benefited from Philemon's love in a vicarious way. In Philemon's love for all God's people, Paul has experienced great **joy** (charis) and **encouragement** (paraklēsis). Paul had a similar feeling of identity with the Corinthian church when things were going well (cf. 2 Cor. 7:4, 7).

Paul's Request for Onesimus

PHILEMON 8–22

For this reason I could be bold enough, as your brother in Christ, to order you to do what should be done. [9]But because I love you, I make a request instead. I do this even though I am Paul, the ambassador of Christ Jesus, and at present also a prisoner for his sake.[a] [10]So I make a request to you on behalf of Onesimus, who is my own son in Christ; for while in prison I have become his spiritual father. [11]At one time he was of no use to you, but now he is useful both to you and to me.

[12]I am sending him back to you now, and with him goes my heart. [13]I would like to keep him here with me, while I am in prison for the gospel's sake, so that he could help me in your place. [14]However, I do not want to force you to help me; rather, I would like for you to do it of your own free will. So I will not do anything unless you agree.

[15]It may be that Onesimus was away from you for a short time so that you might have him back for all time. [16]And now he is not just a slave, but much more than a slave: he is a dear brother in Christ. How much he means to me! And how much more he will mean to you, both as a slave and as a brother in the Lord!

[17]So, if you think of me as your partner, welcome him back just as you would welcome me. [18]If he has done you any wrong or owes you anything, charge it to my account. [19]Here, I will write this with my own hand: *I, Paul, will pay you back.* (I should not have to remind you, of course, that you owe your very self to me.) [20]So, my brother, please do me this favor for the Lord's sake; as a brother in Christ, cheer me up!

[21]I am sure, as I write this, that you will do what I ask—in fact I know that you will do even more. [22]At the same time, get a room ready for me, because I hope that God will answer the prayers of all of you and give me back to you.

a. the ambassador of Christ Jesus, and at present also a prisoner for his sake; *or* an old man, and at present a prisoner for the sake of Christ Jesus.

Now that Paul has sufficiently commended Philemon for his exemplary Christian life, he moves to the heart of his request regarding Onesimus. In one way, Paul gives the impression that he is "shadow boxing," that is, skirting around the real issue and not confronting Philemon directly. But Paul's strategy is determined by two factors: First, he needs to move very carefully and weigh every word. After all, a request to reinstate a runaway slave was quite unusual in the first century. According to Roman law, masters could demand the return of a slave and inflict punishment at their discretion.

Second, Paul wants to avoid any impression of legislating the decision that he wishes Philemon would make. Even if he has the authority to do so, he realizes that "a man convinced against his will is of the same opinion still." Thus Paul will suggest a course of action and appeal to Philemon's Christian standards but leave the ultimate choice to the slave owner.

8–9 / The **for this reason** (*dio*), links the introductory matters of verses 4–7 with the request that follows. On the basis of Philemon's gracious and generous character, Paul feels that as a **brother in Christ** he has a certain relationship with Philemon that gives him the freedom to make this special appeal. In fact, Paul's language is rather strong, and in a sense, must be based upon his apostolic authority, when he claims that he could order Philemon to take the appropriate action. Paul believed that his office as an apostle of Jesus Christ gave him a certain power and required him to make important decisions (cf. 1 Cor. 5:3; 7:6; 9:1; 2 Cor. 12:12). He is **Paul, the ambassador of Christ Jesus, and at present also a prisoner for his sake**. Perhaps his authority is enhanced because he is also suffering imprisonment for Christ's sake.

There is some dispute regarding the translation of the Greek word *presbutēs*. GNB and RSV use **ambassador**, whereas the KJV and NIV use "aged man" or "old man." The only difference between the Greek word for "old man" (*presbutēs*) and "ambassador" (*presbeutēs*) is the letter *e*. Some linguists have suggested that the letter may have been left out inadvertently during the process of copying the letter; others have argued that *presbutēs* occasionally is used in nonbiblical material as "ambassador" or "envoy" and could, therefore, carry that meaning here. The choice of words is important in understanding the spirit of Paul's request.

If the proper word is "old man," then Paul's appeal has an emotional overtone, that is, he approaches Philemon as an old man now a prisoner of Christ Jesus. **Ambassador**, on the other hand, continues to ring of the authority that he has alluded to in the previous verse. Here, the force of his statement is that, although he could decide for Philemon on the basis of his apostolic authority, he will waive that privilege just as he has before (v. 8). He wants Philemon to act out of conviction, not out of compulsion. But he also wants Philemon to know that his request comes from the heart and not the head only (**because I love you, I make a request instead**).

10 / Finally, it appears that Paul is ready to state his request. But no such luck, for the reader is not informed of that until verse 17. All of Paul's comments prior to that show that he approaches Philemon gradually, tactfully, and in deep humility.

Paul calls Onesimus his **own son in Christ** because he has become a member of God's family. Since Paul was instrumental in bringing Onesimus to Christ through his witness, he describes his relationship to Onesimus as that of a spiritual father. He uses this language of father and child on other occasions when he has been responsible for people having become Christians (cf. 1 Cor. 4:15, 17; Gal. 4:19).

By taking the Greek preposition *peri* as "I am asking *for* him," it is possible to believe that Paul desired to retain Onesimus for his own personal use in prison. But although Paul admits the temptation of such a possibility, one can see from verse 15 that his intention all along has been to return Onesimus. His appeal is "for the sake of," or **on behalf of** rather than "for" Onesimus.

11 / The expressions **of no use to you** and **useful** are a play on the name Onesimus, which means "useful." (This was a common name for slaves in the ancient world because of that meaning.) The force of the pun (a play on words) is this: Before (**at one time**) Onesimus was a useless slave to Philemon, perhaps even when he was in Philemon's possession, but more probably as a runaway slave; **but now**, that is, after his conversion to Christ, he has become **useful both to you and to me**. The irony is that Onesimus can only remain useful to Paul if he remains with him in prison and to Philemon if he returns home to Colossae. But either way, he is a changed man. The contrast in his personal life is as dramatic as it is for the Gentiles whose former life of sin often is contrasted with their new life in Christ ("once . . . now": cf. Col. 3:7, 8; Eph. 2:11, 13; 5:8).

12 / Paul's relationship to Onesimus is so close (son and spiritual father) that Onesimus' departure is like losing part of himself. This is a beautiful example of a brotherhood in which social distinctions no longer matter. In Christ, a delinquent Phrygian slave could become a brother with the great apostle to the Gentiles. Nevertheless, Paul cannot let his heart decide for him, for he knows that the only right and legal thing for him to do is to see that Onesimus goes back to Philemon. This action is affirmed by Paul's resolve to send him back to his rightful owner. The Greek construction is an epistolary aorist, which means that even though it is in the past tense the meaning is in the present—hence, **am sending** rather than "have sent."

13 / Once again, Paul indicates that his personal preference would be to keep Onesimus with him in prison. Somehow Paul envisions that, in spite of his imprisonment, Onesimus' service could promote the gospel in some way. **He could help me in your place** suggests that Paul is thinking of some kind of service from Philemon himself. Did Philemon owe Paul something? The only hint at some kind of debt comes in verse 19, where Paul may be reminding Philemon that it was through Paul's ministry that he became a Christian.

14 / Here Paul displays extreme caution in building up his case. He feels a certain right to retain Onesimus on Philemon's behalf, but he wants such a decision to come directly from Philemon (**I will not do anything unless you agree**). The Greek literally reads "your good deed" (*agathon*), which recalls the same use of the word in verse 6, translated "blessings" in the GNB. But anything that Philemon chooses to do must be done willingly. Compulsion, constraint, coercion, necessity, and so forth are not the attitudes out of which a person is to serve Christ. God loves one who gives gladly, "not with regret or out of a sense of duty" (2 Cor. 9:7). Philemon will best reveal his true Christian character when he acts voluntarily.

15 / Up to this point one could interpret the case of Onesimus as a tragedy, for here is a person who has wronged his master, who may have taken something that did not rightfully belong to him, and who capped that wrong by running away as a fugitive to be hunted down. This is how the situation is viewed on the human and earthly level.

Paul, however, sees it differently, for he sees it from the viewpoint of eternity—in other words, from God's providential arrangement of events. Onesimus' action was deliberate; but his departure did not remove him from the sovereignty of God. True, Onesimus was away from Philemon **for a short time**; but the end result is that God so ordered Onesimus' life that Philemon was able to have him back **for all time**. Mankind's failures often become God's opportunities! Here is a case in which a temporary loss was turned into an eternal gain.

16 / The providential and eternal relationship that Paul envisioned in verse 15 is now expanded in words that capture the very heart of the gospel itself. **Now** that Onesimus has become a Christian, **he is not just a slave** (the word **just** is not in the Greek text and should not be supplied as if to demean the person as a slave). Onesimus comes no longer as a slave,

but much more than a slave: he is a dear brother in Christ. The **in Christ**, which also is not in the Greek text, is supplied to indicate that this brotherhood is spiritual and results from the fact that Paul, Onesimus, and Philemon have been united as brothers in Christ. Although this relationship is meaningful to Paul personally, he rightly perceives that Onesimus' new status has a more meaningful application to Philemon, for whom Onesimus is *both* **a slave** and **a brother in the Lord**.

Here is more of that wonderful exchange Paul began talking about in verse 15. Onesimus leaves for a short time and returns forever; he leaves as a slave and returns **as a slave** and **a brother**. Paul does not use this opportunity to abolish slavery, for Onesimus' spiritual position in Christ does not free him from his human obligations to Philemon. In this respect Paul is consistent with the principles that he laid out in Colossians 3:22–4:1. The new relationship that Philemon and Onesimus have to each other is one in which the human and the spiritual overlap.

17 / At long last, the request: **So** (lit., "therefore") . . . **welcome him back just as you would welcome me**. All along Paul has been appealing to Philemon on the force of certain statements, such as Philemon's Christian character (vv. 4–7), Paul's position as an apostle and prisoner (vv. 8–9), Onesimus' newly found faith and usefulness (vv. 10–13), the principle of voluntarism (v. 14), and Christian providence and brotherhood (vv. 15–16). But before the request comes, Paul lays out yet another incentive—namely, that of partnership. When two people are in *koinōnia* they have common interests, feelings, and goals (cf. v. 6). Paul and Philemon certainly had this by virtue of their common faith. Hence Paul is reasoning that, if Philemon really regards him as a partner, there will not be any problem in honoring the request.

But Paul goes one step further, for he identifies himself so closely with Onesimus that he wants Philemon to receive his slave as he would the apostle—**just as you would welcome me**. Partnership in the Lord has broken down all barriers. Paul epitomizes in his life what he has verbalized in his letter.

18 / The **if** should not be taken as setting up a hypothetical case, since Paul knows full well that Onesimus has wronged his master by running away. Paul does not overlook this fact, for he believes that some compensation should be given to Philemon for the losses that he has suffered. Onesimus' debt has been taken by some to imply that Onesimus stole some money or personal possessions from Philemon before he fled. More

probably, Paul has "time" in mind, since Onesimus' absence would have cost Philemon something. Paul is assuming Onesimus' debts because it was customary in those days for the outstanding debts and penalties of a slave to be assumed or paid for by a new owner. Paul, although he is not the new owner, is willing to repay Philemon for any losses—**charge it to my account**!

19 / Paul reaffirms his intention by stating that he will take care of the outstanding debt. The effect of his personal signature is to "seal" what is like a promissory note—an I.O.U.—and to legally bind him to his newly assumed debt. But having done this, Paul effectively negates the force of it by a gentle reminder to Philemon that since he owes Paul so much he should not think of asking for or receiving any remuneration. It was through Paul that Philemon became a Christian, and in the spiritual realm there is no way that outstanding debts can be paid. Paul's statement reminds one of "the parable of the unforgiving servant, in which the Lord faults a servant who was forgiven of a large debt by the king but who, in return, would not forgive a fellow servant a small debt (Matt. 18:21–25).

20 / The intimacy between Paul and Philemon is reinforced by the term **brother** (cf. v. 7). This enables Paul to state quite bluntly that Philemon should honor his request **for the Lord's sake**—literally, "may I have joy, profit, or help from you in the Lord." The Greek word for **favor** is *oni-nēmi*, which closely resembles **Onesimus**, the name of the slave. This similarity has led some interpreters to conclude that Paul is playing on these words for the purpose of requesting Onesimus for himself. If so, the thought that he is expressing could be either, "may I have Onesimus from you," or, "as Onesimus has been profitable to you, you be of benefit to me."

The phrase **cheer me up** recalls a similar expression in verse 7, where Philemon's love "cheered the hearts of all God's people." Here Paul appeals to Philemon's love, but for a personal reason. The acceptance of Onesimus by Philemon would **cheer** his heart. But it is a joy that is unselfish because it is placed in the sphere of the Lord (**in Christ**). Paul will rejoice because he knows that Philemon is responding from the new life that he has experienced in Christ.

21 / Since Paul knows Philemon so well, he is confident that his friend will comply with his request to receive Onesimus. Actually, the words are much stronger than they appear in the translation (**I am sure . . . that**

you will do what I ask), because Paul speaks of a trust or confidence in Philemon's obedience (*hypakoē*)—an obedience based not on Roman law or apostolic command but on the principle of Christian love. Such love leaves Philemon with only one choice, namely, the highest good for his servant and for the apostle.

Paul is confident that Philemon **will do even more**. But what more could he do? Does Paul anticipate that Philemon will turn Onesimus over into Paul's custody, or does he hope that Philemon will grant his slave *complete freedom*? The final decision is left up to the master.

22 / Paul envisions one more exchange that may be possible within the providence of God. This time, it involves himself and the **hope** that he can exchange his imprisonment for freedom. Thus he prays **that God will answer the prayers of all of you and give me back to you**. It is significant to note that the entire congregation is interceding for Paul's release. Such action binds him closer to this church and gives him hope that God will make it possible for him to see all of them.

Paul is so confident about this that he makes a reservation for a room. The early Christians placed considerable emphasis upon hospitality (Rom. 12:13; 1 Tim. 3:2; Titus 1:8; Heb. 13:2; 1 Pet. 4:9), so Paul's request is not unusual. Since Philemon had a home large enough to hold church services, there would be no problem accommodating Paul if and when he returned to Colossae.

Additional Notes

8 / Although unusual, Paul's request is not without precedent. E. Lohse quotes a personal letter from Pliny the Younger in which this Roman official writes to a certain slave master Sabinianus, interceding for an errant but repentant slave (pp. 196–97).

15 / Paul uses what in Greek is called a passive verb: *echōpisthē* literally means "he was separated from" you. On this, R. P. Martin refers to the Hebrew; in that language, the divine passive "is a mode of expression to denote the hidden action of God as the agent responsible for what is done" (p. 166).

Paul's Final Greetings

Epaphras, who is in prison with me for the sake of Christ Jesus, sends you his greetings, 24and so do my fellow workers Mark, Aristarchus, Demas, and Luke. 25May the grace of the Lord Jesus Christ be with you all.

23-25 / These final verses are almost identical to the closing section of Colossians. Paul ends this letter with words familiar from the opening salutation (v. 3). Here the phrase **may the grace of the Lord Jesus Christ be with you all** serves more as a prayer of benediction than a greeting. The RSV and NIV follow the Greek text by including the word "spirit," reading, "May the grace of the Lord Jesus Christ be with your spirit." The GNB takes it to mean "with you," or **with you all** (cf. Gal. 6:18). The **you all** is in the plural (*hymōn*), so Paul intends that this letter be received by the entire congregation.

Additional Note

On these greetings and the personalities mentioned, see disc. on Col. 4:7–17. These lists show the significance of Paul's co-workers for his ministry. E. Lohse has an excellent comparison of the names that occur in Colossians and Philemon in his commentary, pp. 175–77.

Introduction: Ephesians

The title and salutation in the GNB indicates that this is Paul's Letter to the Ephesians ("from Paul . . . to God's people who live in Ephesus" . . .). From its earliest times, this epistle has been regarded as an authentic epistle of the Apostle Paul, written to the church in Ephesus where he spent about three years as a teacher (Acts 19:10; 20:31).

Since the epistle claims to have been written by Paul, it is not unusual to find a number of personal references to himself and the situation to which he is writing. Basically, he identifies himself as an apostle of Jesus Christ by the will of God on their behalf (1:1; 3:1) who, although he is in prison (3:1; 4:1), appeals to his office as one entitled to proclaim the mystery of the gospel to the Gentiles (3:1-9) and to relate to his readers the essence of the Christian life (4:17 ff.).

Although the epistle does not follow the epistolary form of Paul's letters completely (salutation–thanksgiving–prayer–body–ethical exhortations–greetings), it has many verbal, theological, and literary affinities with Paul's thought. At first glance, there appear to be no glaring differences in Ephesians from the picture that we get of Paul and his thought in other books of the NT. The epistle contains such familiar themes as God's sovereignty, resurrection, the Holy Spirit, ethics, and so forth, and even though there are some new theological emphases, they appear to be consistent with Paul's thought.

The external factors surrounding this epistle likewise suggest that its authenticity was not disputed in the early church. It is listed in Marcion's canon of the NT as the epistle to the "Laodiceans" (ca. A.D. 140) and is recognized in the Muratorian canon (A.D. 180) as Paul's work. This is supported by the testimony of the early church fathers of the second century, such as Irenaeus, Clement of Alexandria, and Tertullian. With a few minor exceptions, the consensus of scholarly opinion is that Ephesians was consistently regarded as a Pauline epistle until the age of critical scholarship in the eighteenth century.[1]

The *destination* of the epistle, however, has not received the same unanimity as its Pauline authorship. The phrase, "in Ephesus" (*en Ephesōi*) is missing in the oldest and most reliable manuscripts. This omission is verified by Origen, Tertullian, and Jerome, even though church tradition has associated it with the city of Ephesus.

The reasons why the address was omitted—if there ever was one—and why it became associated with Ephesus are varied and complex. The most popular theory, in part suggested by the general nature of the epistle, claims that it was a circular letter that Paul intended to be read at more than one place. The original manuscript may have had a blank space, and each congregation could have read its own name into that blank.[2] For various reasons—primarily because of Paul's long association with that church and the importance of that congregation in Asia Minor—it became attached to Ephesus. As in other translations (RSV, NIV, NEB), the footnote in the GNB indicates that there is a textual problem at this point.

With the rise of critical Bible scholarship in the eighteenth century, the mood toward Pauline authorship changed dramatically. By adopting a critical methodology and applying its principles to the external and internal study of the epistle, more and more scholars came to the opinion that Ephesians is not authentically Pauline. The end result is that there are two major positions regarding the authorship of Ephesians today: either it is Pauline or non-Pauline.

Scholars who doubt the Pauline authorship of certain epistles (generally 2 Thessalonians, Ephesians, Colossians, and the Pastorals) claim that they were written by a "second," that is, "deutero" Paul. Basically, this necessitates envisioning an individual or a group of Paul's close co-workers who earnestly desired to communicate the message and authority of Paul to succeeding generations. Many scholars see this as a plausible solution to some of the questions related to authorship.

Several things about the deutero-Pauline hypothesis need clarification. First, it is quite possible that the practice of pseudonymity (writing in the name of someone else) in the first century included some of the letters that make up the canon of the NT. Unfortunately, a number of NT scholars look upon this in a negative way. They see it as constituting forgery or fraud and the authors of such pseudonymous materials as nothing but charlatans, imposters, or deceivers. But such is not the case: Anyone writing in Paul's name could have done so out of sincere motives and believed that he would not dishonor God or the apostle or deceive his readers.

Second, a deutero-Paulinist would not be just a compiler, copier, and transmitter of genuine Pauline material. This would make the deutero-Pauline literature nothing more than a mosaic of passages from Paul's epistles. The one writing in Paul's name would have been a theologian in his own right. He would be faithful to Paul but would find it necessary to modify and expand Paul's ideas and apply them to later developments in the church.

A number of Paul's close associates, such as Timothy, Tychicus, and Luke, would be capable of producing this kind of material. It is even possible that Paul may have led some kind of theological school "in the lecture hall of Tyrannus," while he was in Ephesus, where his ideas were presented and continued to be discussed even after his death (Acts 19:9). Some of his pupils could have felt responsible to interpret, reinterpret, and apply their master's theology to new situations in the post-apostolic period. Writing in Paul's name would have given their letters the stamp of apostolic authority, especially where false teaching was threatening the church.

If Ephesians fits into this hypothetical reconstruction, it could be regarded as a continuation of Paul's thought in another generation. It would be an attempt by the author to present a timely reaffirmation of Paul's understanding of "the mystery of Christ" to the Gentiles. Or, as C. L. Mitton puts it: "the author has presented us in Ephesians with a brilliant and comprehensive summary of Paul's main theological emphases, though he has, where necessary, adapted and interpreted them for the needs of a new situation. Published about a generation after Paul's death, it is, as it were, 'Paul's Message for Today.' "[3] R. P. Martin's suggestion that Luke wrote Ephesians is both intriguing and commendable.[4]

Of the factors that raise questions about the Pauline authorship of Ephesians, there is, first of all, the language and style of the epistle. About ninety words and phrases in Ephesians are not used elsewhere in Paul's epistles. This includes such things as "the Devil," "in the heavenlies," and "the beloved" as a title for Christ, as well as other examples.

In addition to vocabulary, there is the matter of the style in which the epistle is written. In contrast to the polemical tone and rapid movement in Paul's chief letters, Ephesians has a poetic or liturgical ring to it. This comes from a number of features, including its long and complex sentences, extensive use of prepositions, joining of synonyms, and so on.

Although most scholars will agree that linguistic and stylistic differences alone do not disprove Pauline authorship, they do find it difficult to conceive of Paul writing Ephesians in this form. Proponents for its authenticity counter by claiming that the language and style can be accounted for by such considerations as Paul's versatility as a writer, changed historical circumstances, and the fact that the epistle is more reflective and liturgical in nature. "Could," writes A. S. Wood, "an imitator have given birth to anything at once so authentic and yet so original? If he rivaled Paul as a spiritual genius, it is strange that the primitive church knew nothing of him."[5]

A second set of questions about Pauline authorship relate to the repetition in Ephesians of Pauline words, phrases, and concepts, especially from Colossians. Approximately one fourth of the vocabulary and one third of the content of Ephesians is paralleled in Colossians, including some verbatim agreement (cf. Eph. 6:21 ff. and Col. 4:7 ff.). Numerous parallels to other Pauline epistles, as well as affinities with 1 Peter, Hebrews, Luke-Acts, and the Gospel of John have been observed, contributing further to the suspicion that the author of Ephesians was borrowing material from some of these letters for his composition rather than creating his own epistle. Some scholars have found more affinities to the writings of Qumran (the Dead Sea Scrolls) and Gnosticism than to the NT. Even more problematic is the claim that certain words and ideas are used differently or take on a different meaning in Ephesians than they have in Paul's genuine letters (church, stewardship, mystery, and fullness, to name a few).

To counter such conclusions, proponents of Pauline authorship believe that the close connection between Ephesians and other Pauline epistles, including Colossians, is accounted for better by Pauline than by non-Pauline authorship. They argue that the apparent differences in usage or meaning of terms does not warrant denying them to Paul. Here D. Guthrie speaks for a number of people when he writes that "the most natural conclusion from the abundance of parallel passages is that the same mind is reflected in Ephesians as in the other Pauline epistles."[6]

A third consideration related to Pauline authorship is that the historical circumstances surrounding the epistle are vague. It is difficult to believe that Paul would be writing to a congregation with whom he spent three years and not include any personal greetings or refer to any local issues. In fact, the author writes as if he and the readers do not know each other (1:13, 15; 3:1; 4:21). Even if Ephesians were a circular letter, one would expect some allusions to personalities or circumstances associated with Paul's missionary activity in that part of Asia Minor. Barth's suggestion that the epistle was written to Gentile converts who came into the church after Paul's ministry in Ephesus is unconvincing.[7]

There are other problems beyond the impersonal nature of the epistle. Historically, the controversy related to Jews and Gentiles in the church that occupied so much of Paul's life appears to be over (cf. Acts 15; Gal. 2). Many scholars feel that Ephesians reflects the situation sometime after Paul when the church was being prepared historically to face the future and to guard itself against the threat of such heresies as Gnosticism.

Unfortunately, the historical factors alone cannot decide the question of authorship. The problems between Jewish and Gentile Christians are difficult to document historically and may have varied from one area of the empire to another. Some authors place considerable emphasis upon the destruction of Jerusalem in A.D. 70, claiming that if the epistle had been written after this period there would have been some specific reference to that fact, especially in the context of 2:11–22.

Fourth, there are some theological issues that raise questions about Pauline authorship. For convenience, they can be discussed according to the following categories:

Cosmology

Ephesians, even more than Colossians, presents a cosmic picture of God's saving activity and the role of Christ. It gives increasing attention to the principalities and powers and how God has defeated them.

Ecclesiology

One of the most significant and noticeable differences from letters that are undeniably Pauline is that the church in Ephesians is universal, not local. The author writes to embrace all believers everywhere, not only those in Ephesus. Here, as in Colossians, the church is defined as the body of Christ, and Christ is related to the body as the head. In Romans and Corinthians the head is not given such distinction but is recognized as another part of the body.

In Ephesians, the church takes on a cosmic function; through it, the angelic rulers and powers in the heavenly world might know God's wisdom, in all its different forms (3:10). This goes far beyond the local function that the church serves in Paul's undisputed epistles. Some, particularly the German scholar E. Käsemann, see Ephesians moving from Christ—which was the center for Paul—to the church as the center. For Käsemann, this is a sure sign of "early Catholicism."[8]

Part of the ecclesiology in Ephesians centers around the prominence and role of the apostles and prophets (2:20; 3:5) in the founding of the church. For some, the veneration of these offices, the structure and function of the ministry (4:11–16), and the acknowledgment of apostolic authority is a sign of a post-Pauline church. These are matters that arose after Paul's lifetime.

Eschatology

In Paul's undisputed epistles one gets the impression that the Parousia is imminent, that is, Christ is about to return. Consequently, much of Paul's theology and ethical instruction is placed within the context of the end times. Ephesians lacks that eschatological urgency and presents more of a realized eschatology by emphasizing the believers' present experience with Christ. Resurrection and exaltation is a status that believers already enjoy in Christ; more attention is given to life in the Spirit now and less to the future; and even though the church maintains a future hope (1:18), the directives in the epistle prepare the believers to live out that hope in the realities of daily life.

This change in eschatological perspective affects how the author prepares his readers to face the future. Thus the mission of the church takes on a new significance: The church becomes the instrument for fulfilling God's purposes in the world, particularly in uniting Jews, Gentiles, and the cosmos (2:21; 3:10; 4:13, 16; 5:27). The ethical exhortations, household rules and so on suggest that the church is to be as concerned about social and community relationships (socioethical) as it is with personal salvation or reconciliation.[9]

Christology

Some scholars feel that Ephesians omits certain crucial elements of Paul's Christology, and presents a different understanding of the person and role of Christ. Missing is Paul's emphasis on Christ's death, the doctrine of justification, and the Parousia; prominent is the resurrected, exalted, and triumphant Christ. According to J. A. Allan, the "in Christ" formula in Ephesians lacks the mysticism that was so characteristic of Paul.[10] Also, reconciliation is not between man and God but socially between Jew and Gentile and cosmically with the spiritual principalities and powers. Certain acts that Paul attributes to God, such as reconciliation (Col. 1:20; 2:13, 14) and the appointment of church officials (1 Cor. 12:28), are, in Ephesians, presented as the work of Christ (2:16; 4:11).

The conclusion to which many scholars have come after analyzing the theological, historical, ecclesiological, and cosmological thought of Ephesians is that it is difficult—if not impossible—to maintain the Pauline authorship of this epistle in the light of these observations. W. G. Kümmel probably represents most scholars who question Paul's authorship when he writes: "In view of this linguistic, literary and theological state of affairs, it cannot seriously be doubted that Ephesians does not come from Paul and is therefore a pseudonymous writing."[11]

The big question, of course, is whether such observations are true and only capable of one conclusion. Could it be that critics of Paul have misunderstood Ephesians and are guilty of utilizing false assumptions and methodologies—thus arriving at false solutions? That this is possible is certainly made evident by the host of serious scholars who believe that the external and internal evidence with respect to Ephesians confirms the traditional conclusion. For them, Ephesians will remain Pauline until it can definitely be proved that it is non-Pauline.

D. Guthrie represents such a conviction when he states: "To maintain that the Paulinist out of his sheer love for Paul and through his own self-effacement composed the letter, attributed it to Paul and found an astonishing and immediate readiness on the part of the Church to recognize it as such is considerably less credible than the simple alternative of regarding it as Paul's own work."[12]

The question of the authorship of Ephesians currently is at an impasse, with reputable scholars on both sides of the issue. Here it needs to be stressed that this matter should not divide scholarship into conservatives and liberals. Rather than looking at the problem as a case of right or wrong, one needs to appreciate that though both sides are sincere in their approach, everybody works out of certain theological presuppositions that affect the approach to an understanding of God's Word and, in this case, the Epistle to the Ephesians.

Above all, one should avoid concluding that deutero-Pauline authorship of Ephesians makes this a false document that, consequently, has no inspiration, validity, or authority for the church today. Once the motives of a deutero-Paulinist are properly understood and appreciated, Ephesians can speak to the church with the same authority as Paul himself. The church retained and canonized the Epistle to the Hebrews, for example, even though its author is anonymous.[13]

Although the matter of authorship has had a negative effect, polarizing scholarship, there have been two striking positive results with respect to studies in Ephesians: First, the detailed linguistic, literary, and theological study of the epistle has led to a new appreciation of its value to the church. A. M. Hunter includes several centuries of thought when he writes: "John Calvin called it his favourite epistle; Coleridge pronounced it 'one of the divinest compositions of man'; Dr John Mackay has said, 'To this book I owe my life,' and C. H. Dodd has named it 'the crown of Paulinism.' "[14]

Beyond such a eulogy, it is not unusual to discover other accolades, namely, "The Queen of the Epistles," "the quintessence of Paulinism," "The Epistle of the Ascension."[15] J. N. Sanders considers this book Paul's spiritual testament to the church, "the final summing up of the apostle's life, work and thought."[16]

Second, new studies on the nature, purpose, and content of the epistle have been produced. Some of the more significant theories include that it is a summary of Paul's theology, a reminder and congratulation, an anti-heretical tract, a liturgical document, a discourse on the unity of the church.

A Summary of Paul's Theology

Though most of these insights do not depend upon Pauline authorship and can be appreciated by everyone, one idea is that Ephesians is a comprehensive summary of Paul's theology or a commendation of Paul's theology to the church of another generation (Beare; Mitton). R. P. Martin, writing in the *Broadman Commentary*, sees the author "gathering a compendium of Paul's teaching on the theme of Christ-in-his-church; and added to this body of teaching a number of liturgical elements (prayers, hymns, and confessions of faith) drawn from the worshiping life of the apostolic communities with which he was himself familiar."[17]

One of the most ingenious and elaborate theories in this regard is by J. Edgar Goodspeed. Vexed by the internal and external problems of Ephesians, Goodspeed suggested that the epistle was written by Onesimus (former slave and later bishop of the Ephesian church) as a cover or introductory letter for the collection of Paul's epistles (corpus) that was made near the end of the first century after the publication of Acts had created a new interest in Paul. For Goodspeed, Ephesians is "a rhapsody on the worth of salvation," "a mosaic of Pauline material," "a Pauline anthology."[18] The strength of Goodspeed's hypothesis lies more in his understanding of the nature of Ephesians than its purpose.

Some of Goodspeed's insights on the linguistic and literary peculiarities in Ephesians paved the way for other studies. Consequently, it is not unusual for scholars to see the epistle as a summary of Paul's thought to a later generation even if it is not some kind of cover letter for the Pauline corpus. The key to the deutero-Pauline hypothesis, however, is that the author is more than just a collector of Pauline ideas from his genuine epistles; he is "an independently acting and judging theologian of Pauline stamp."[19]

A Reminder and Congratulation

The theory that it is a reminder and congratulation is largely promoted by N. A. Dahl, who understands Ephesians to be addressing the problem of disunity in the church. Consequently, the author appeals for unity by calling the churches back to their beginnings and reminding them that they too share in the privileges that God granted to the Jews. Based upon his understanding of the concepts of "once" and "now," in the epistle, Dahl suggests that Ephesians is "a letter of reminder and congratulation, i.e., not so much as some abstract doctrine on the church, but rather as simply reminding us that we do indeed belong to the church, the body of Christ, and asking us to dwell on all that that implies."[20]

The value of Ephesians for Dahl is that, although its original message had a definite historical context, it can be universalized to speak to the church in every generation: "For the letter to the Ephesians is a congratulation for and a reminder of the sum total of what has been given to us."[21]

As such, the letter presents the reader with both a privilege and responsibility: Believers are privileged to have received such a rich inheritance in Christ. This, however, should not lead to spiritual pride or Christian triumphalism, because believers are reminded of the "once you were" of their lives. The "now you are" is the ethical imperative to live out the new life responsibly.

An Antiheretical Tract

The view that it is an antiheretical tract includes a vast array of scholarly opinion on the nature and purpose of Ephesians. Some scholars, such as F. C. Baur, P. Pokorny, H. Schlier, E. Käsemann, H. Conzelmann, and F. Mussner, believe that the epistle can best be understood within the context of first-century Gnosticism.[22] They find Ephesians to contain a large number of Gnostic terms ("knowledge," "fullness," "mystery," "perfection," "body," "new man," "heavenly union," "revelation," "principalities and powers") and concepts (dualism, cosmology, and ethics). These scholars are not suggesting that the author is a Gnostic or that Ephesians is a Gnostic tract; rather, they believe that the author transfers Gnostic language and thought to the church in order to counter this heresy, which was threatening the church. His method is to provide a point of contact with the readers, but in the process he gives these words and concepts new meaning: "Ephesians turns Gnostic language against Gnosticism."[23]

In this process, scholars such as H. Schlier and F. Beare see the author developing a distinct Christian "gnōsis" (a theory of knowledge) that explained such things as a knowledge of God, man, and the world. Schlier went so far as to call Ephesians a meditation on the wisdom of the mystery of Christ—a "*Weisheitsrede* or *Sophiarede*."[24]

All this research has opened up another possibility for understanding the nature and purpose of Ephesians. Unfortunately, not enough is known about first-century Gnosticism to conclude whether or not the author was confronting this heresy directly or just utilizing the language and concepts of his day.[25]

Another group of scholars has sought to explain the origin of Ephesians on the basis of certain parallels to the language and theology of the Dead Sea Scrolls—that body of literature belonging to the Qumran community. So far, the most valuable contributions have come from individuals like K. G. Kuhn, J. Murphy-O'Connor, and F. Mussner.[26]

These scholars have made extensive comparisons between Ephesians and the Dead Sea Scrolls regarding the hymnic and paraenetic (exhortative material) structure; general concepts like cosmology, creation, dualism, evil; and specific parallels, such as the mystery, saints, temple of God, and so forth.[27] Most of these scholars hoped to establish direct literary influence by Qumran on Ephesians. Murphy-O'Connor went so far as to suggest that Ephesians was written by an amanuensis of Paul who had come from the ranks of the Essenes.[28]

Unfortunately, the evidence does not permit one to come to any definite conclusions regarding the literary connections between Ephesians and the Dead Sea Scrolls. The author of this epistle may simply be using expressions that were common in his day and that he and the writers of the scrolls used independently. For Barth, "Eph *in toto* is neither in form nor in substance any more closely related to Qumran than any other key passages in undisputed Pauline writings."[29]

This brief survey is intended to show that Gnostic and Qumran parallels have received considerable attention and serve as a framework out of which a number of scholars seek to explain the epistle. If the author is consciously combating Gnosticism, then Ephesians could be called an anti-Gnostic tract. With respect to the relationship between Ephesians and Qumran, however, it does not appear that the author is addressing a heretical threat to the church. In this case, he may simply belong to the same literary tradition as that of Qumran.

A Liturgical Document

An analysis of the stylistic features of Ephesians has taken a number of scholars in the direction of proposing that this is some kind of liturgical document rather than an epistle. Moffatt, for example, refers to Ephesians as a "homily" rather than a letter.[30] And, on the basis of such stylistic features as the hymnic material, long sentences, the piling up of synonyms, and so forth, Martin calls this an exalted prose-poem ". . . a typical early Christian liturgy."[31] J. Kirby's work on Ephesians led him to conclude that the epistle is a prayer and a discourse thrown into the form of a letter.[32]

Although some hymnic elements of Ephesians were identified quite early by scholars such as M. Dibelius, E. Lohmeyer, and T. Innitzer, the extensiveness and function of hymnic-catechetical-liturgical material in Ephesians had not been explored until recently.[33] Many scholars concur that the utilization of so much traditional material directs Ephesians toward some kind of liturgical function in the church. But just what that function was varies from scholar to scholar.

J. Kirby, for example, claims that the author writes chapters 1–3 in the form of a Jewish *berakah* (blessing), possibly to be used at the celebration of the Eucharist. Beyond that, the epistle incorporates liturgical material from the church of Ephesus, particularly that which was used for the renewal of the covenant to celebrate Pentecost.[34] N. A. Dahl, in a number of his writings, has proposed that Ephesians is a baptismal letter.[35] This theory has found popular acceptance among a number of NT scholars who believe that the epistle can best be understood in a baptismal setting.

References to the baptismal nature of Ephesians will be made throughout the commentary. It is my opinion that even though Ephesians employs a significant amount of baptismal imagery, it was not written as a baptismal tract to be used in celebrating baptism or giving baptismal candidates catechetical instruction; rather, *baptismal language and theology are used to develop the author's theme of unity in the church.*

A number of scholars, among them, C. L. Mitton, do not attempt to identify the purpose of Ephesians with any specific event such as baptism, the Eucharist, or Pentecost. The writer used this liturgical style, according to Mitton, because he has the worshiping congregation in mind; he knows that they will be reading this letter in the context of worship and prayer. Consequently, "he phrased what he wrote in a style suitable for the hearer and the worshipper rather than the private reader. This would lead him to use a declaratory style—what today is often called a liturgical style. It would not be surprising if he incorporated here and there snatches from a familiar hymn or a phrase from a creedal affirmation; but the liturgical style comes not so much from his borrowings as from his awareness of the context in which his writing would be used."[36]

A Discourse on the Unity of the Church

Anyone reading Ephesians will soon become aware that the church (*ekklēsia*) is given considerable attention:

a. It is mentioned nine times (Greek text, 1:22; 3:10, 21; 5:23, 24, 25, 27, 29, 32).

b. It is discussed by means of various metaphors: biological (the body of Christ: 1:22, 23; 2:16; 4:4, 12, 16; 5:23, 30), architectural (the holy temple: 2:20–22; 4:12, 16), and social (the bride: 5:21–33).

c. It has a universal rather than local meaning. Here "church" is the new creation and the universal society consisting of Jews and Gentiles, not the local congregation "in Ephesus." This also is demonstrated by the transcendental status that believers have in the church because of the realized eschatology in the epistle. "The church shared the heavenly life of its exalted Lord even now in this age (1:22; 2:6; 5:27)."[37] It has a message that is valid for all generations, including the principalities and powers (3:10).

d. The church (body) and Christ (head) are united and interdependent rather than the Head simply being one of many members, as in Romans 12:4, 5, and 1 Corinthians 12:12–26. These observations make one aware that the teaching of the church in Ephesians is both important and new. Basically, the creation of this "one new people" shows that God has acted historically to unite mankind and that the church is a witness to God's ultimate plan to unite all things in Christ (1:10, 22, 23; 2:14–16). The church is, as John Stott so perceptively entitled his book, *God's New Society.*

Since the unity of the church has received so much attention in Ephesians, one naturally wonders what historical and theological factors led to that emphasis. One suggestion relates this theme to the problem of Gnosticism, which essentially dehistoricized Christianity into timeless myths. Thus the author seeks to ground the Christian life in the verities of history and show that the church is a historical witness of God's redemptive activity through Christ.

But the focus of scholarly speculation on the occasion and purpose of Ephesians centers more around the problem of Jewish-Gentile relations. Both Jews and Gentiles were becoming Christians, but there were some basic differences in their understanding of the gospel of Jesus Christ.

One opinion sees the theme of unity in Ephesians necessitated by the problem of *Jewish exclusivism* in the early church. Basically, this is the negative attitude on the part of Jewish believers toward the Gentiles who were becoming Christians. Given their adherence to some of the prescriptions in the Law (Torah)—particularly circumcision and Jewish food laws—some Jewish believers felt that Gentiles had to obey these Jewish laws when they became Christians. This was a threat to the gospel that Paul preached and would have made Christianity a sect of Judaism.

This problem of Jewish exclusivism is described and dealt with at the Jerusalem council in Acts 15:1–35 and in Paul's epistles to the Romans and Galatians. The council decided that Paul could evangelize the Gentiles without requiring them to be circumcised or to adhere to Jewish dietary laws (cf. Acts 15:19–29; Gal. 2). The heart of Paul's gospel is marked by inclusivism rather than exclusivism; it is a gospel characterized by faith in Jesus Christ, not works of the Law—that is, circumcision and food laws; both Jews and Gentiles participate in Jesus Christ, and in him there is "neither Jew nor Greek" (Gal. 3:28).

Though the guidelines for Paul's gospel were established at the Jerusalem council, Jewish exclusivism continued, making it necessary to apply these principles in Paul's churches. Consequently, a major theme in Romans is that the Gentiles had as much right to receive salvation from God as did the Jews; they have been grafted into the "olive tree," which, at one time, had been the exclusive right of the Jews (11:13–24).

In Galatians, Paul faces a similar problem of Jewish exclusivism. His answer to the Jews is that the Gentiles are justified before God by virtue of their "faith in Jesus Christ," not by "works of the Law" (2:16). In other words, Gentiles are not required to "live Jewishly" by submitting to circumcision and observing Jewish food laws.[38]

Could it be that the problem of Jewish exclusivism lies behind the writing of Ephesians? Did the religious and social barriers that separated Jews and Gentiles, and that led to Jewish exclusivism, continue to operate in spite of Paul's earlier clarification of the gospel? Is Ephesians a final attempt to destroy Jewish bigotry by reaffirming Paul's universal vision and showing that the essence of the "mystery" is that Jewish and Gentile believers have been united in one body?

Most of the content of Ephesians could be interpreted as a message to Gentile believers that they have no need to feel excluded from God's people. True, at one time their lives were characterized by disobedience and sin (2:1–3); they were called—probably disparagingly—"the uncircumcised by the Jews who call themselves the circumcised" (2:11); they were foreigners who "did not belong to God's chosen people" and as such had no part in the covenants, were without hope and without God (2:12). But the central message of Ephesians is that this is no longer true because in Christ they have been brought near (2:13), and the "Jewish law, with its commandments and rules" (circumcision and dietary restrictions) that separated Jews from Gentiles, has been broken down (2:14, 15).

The end result of God's redemptive activity is the union of Jew and Gentile in the church. This is more than the picture of grafting provided by the imagery of the olive tree in Romans 11:13–24. The union between Jews and Gentiles is not effected by Gentiles becoming Jews but by the creation of a "new people," the church, that includes both Jew and Gentile (2:15; 3:6). Ephesians clearly teaches that the Gentiles have every right to be considered members of the body of Christ.

Another, and more popular approach, is to look at Ephesians from the perspective of *Gentile exclusivism*. H. Chadwick has suggested that the letter was written to correct a spiritual misunderstanding that had arisen within post-Pauline Christianity.[39] Apparently, the Gentile congregations had divorced themselves from the salvation-history of the Jewish Christians and considered themselves a separate spiritual entity. According to Chadwick, Ephesians insists upon the continuity of Gentile Christianity with Judaism and teaches that Jew and Gentile have been united in Christ.

Chadwick's interpretation is similar to the view of E. Käsemann, who believes that the author of Ephesians needs to remind the Gentile Christians of their roots and the historical origin of the gospel because they were despising their Jewish brethren. In this respect, the epistle elaborates upon a theme that is briefly discussed by Paul in Romans 11, namely, the incorporation of Gentiles into Jewish Christianity.[40]

All this, however, does not provide any clue as to what occasioned such strained relations between Jewish and Gentile believers. W. Grundmann attempts to make a historical connection with the migration of Jewish Christians to Asia Minor after the Jewish war and argues that the influx of this Jewish-Christian circle into the predominantly Gentile Christian churches of Asia Minor led to a split that a Pauline pupil sought to bridge in Ephesians with the application of Pauline thoughts about the unity of these two groups.[41]

A more recent theory by K. M. Fischer attempts to locate the problem of a Jewish and Gentile schism in the church within the context of the Roman Jewish war during the years preceding and following the destruction of Jerusalem in A.D. 70.[42] This war threatened the close relationship between Jewish (synagogue) and Gentile (church) believers because the Gentiles felt that they had to disassociate themselves from all forms of Jewish nationalism (the Zealots) so as not to raise suspicions and risk reprisals from the Roman authorities.

The author of Ephesians, according to Fischer, addresses this situation. Whereas Paul had argued for the inclusion of the Gentiles into the church without becoming Jews (Rom. 9–11; Gal. 1–3), "the author of Ephesians uses Paul's name to argue for the inclusion of Jewish Christians in the community without assimilation to the views of the Gentile majority. When Paul had argued for the inclusion of *gentiles qua gentiles*, the author of Ephesians argued for the inclusion of *Jewish Christians qua Jewish Christians*."[43]

Unfortunately, all these views are highly conjectural, and one is forced to agree with W. G. Kümmel that the concrete situation that occasioned "this reworking of the Pauline message by emphasizing the unity of the church comprised of Gentiles and Jews cannot now be perceived."[44] All one can envision is some kind of spiritual crisis in post-Pauline Gentile Christianity that necessitated an emphasis upon the universal church consisting of Jews and Gentiles.

From the perspective of Gentile exclusivism, these Christians were reminded not to disregard their spiritual heritage with Israel. In their pagan state they were separated from the Jews and had no point of contact with God's covenant people (2:11 ff.). But through Christ and in the church, they have become "fellow citizens with God's people, and members of the family of God" (2:19; 3:6). If the Jews had no right to exclude them from the church, then it was equally wrong for them to disregard the Jews!

Perhaps Ephesians has a dual message: A deutero-Paulinist could be extending Paul's vision of a universal and united church that includes the incorporation of the Gentiles while at the same time reminding them that they are part of God's history of salvation. "Ephesians," writes Barth, "more than any other New Testament epistle, will press the point that Gentiles receive no salvation other than the one they share with Israel and receive through the Messiah. It is the salvation first promised and given to this people alone: Israel."[45]

Failure to identify the concrete situation that occasioned the epistle does not, however, detract from the fact that *unity* is its dominant theme. Although some of this has already been mentioned, there are some specific characteristics of Ephesians that make this obvious and by which the author develops this theme:

a. The source of all unity is in the elective will and purpose of God (1:4, 5, 10; 3:11).

b. Christ is the agent by which or through whom this unity is accomplished. According to J. A. Allan, the phrase "in Christ," "in whom," and so on is used thirty-four times in Ephesians.

c. There are twelve occurrences of the word "one" (*hen*) in the Greek text ("the two one," 2:14; "one new man," 2:15; "one body," 2:16; 4:4; "one Spirit," 2:18; 4:4; "one hope," 4:4; "one Lord," 4:5; "one faith," 4:5; "one baptism," 4:5; "one God and Father," 4:6; "each one of us," 4:7; "each part," 4:16; "each one of you," 5:33); also, the force of *ana* in *anakephalaioō* (1:10) is "one by one," bringing separate items into a single whole.

d. The preposition *syn* ("with," "together with") is used with a number of verbs and nouns. In some cases, these words are used in connection with the believers' union with Christ, such as "he brought us to life with Christ" (*synzōopoieō*, 2:5), "he raised us up with him" (*synegeirō*, 2:6), he seated us in the heavenlies (*synkathizō*, 2:6).

The *syn* nouns are also used to describe the fact that the Gentiles "are joined together" (*synarmologeō*, 2:21; 4:16), "held together," (*symbibazō*, 4:16), and "are being built together with all the others [*synoikodomeō*] into a house where God lives through his Spirit" (2:22). Consequently, they are "joint heirs" (*sygklēronomos*, 3:6), "members of the same body" (*syssomos*, 3:6), and partners (*synmetochos*, 3:6). On two occasions there is a negative use of these compound words: The believers are not to become partners (*synmetochos*, 5:7) with immoral people or join together in fellowship (*synkoinōneō*, 5:11) with the heathen.

e. Considerable attention is given to the concept of peace. Apart from the standard greeting (1:2) and farewell (6:23), peace is central to the idea of reconciliation and unity between Jews and Gentiles (2:14, 15, 17) and is essential for maintaining the unity of the body (4:3). Finally, believers are to arm themselves with the "Good News of peace" (6:15).

f. The Greek word for "unity" (*enotēs*) occurs twice in Ephesians (4:3, 13) and nowhere else in the NT.

g. Apart from these specific examples, there are some general observations that appear to accentuate the need and the possibility for unity: The ethical exhortations are given to the church as a means of maintaining the unity and peace that was brought about by Christ (4:1–6); the gifts of the Spirit show that there can be unity and singleness of purpose in the midst of diversity; believers in the body of Christ "put away" those vices that harm interpersonal relationships (4:25); rather than promoting individualism, life in the church is a joyful sharing together in the common elements of worship (5:15–20); and finally, the principle of submission is given, so that the different members of the household can live together in unity, peace, and love (5:21–6:9).

The attention given to this theme has led H. von Soden to view Ephesians as a "hymn of unity."[46] One dimension of that theme is ecclesiological: Jew and Gentile have been brought together into one body, the church. The other dimension is cosmological: The church is a witness to the cosmic powers (3:10) that God's ultimate purpose of bringing all creation together is being accomplished (1:10, 22, 23).

Throughout the epistle the author uses the language and theology of baptism to develop the theme of unity. He considers baptism to be the rite by which one participates in Christ (2:5-10) and thus partakes of all the blessings of God (1:3-14; 2:13 ff.; 5:8 ff.). Furthermore, the appearance of the *one baptism* in 4:5 as one of the foundational principles of the unity of the church demonstrates the importance of this sacrament for the author and his agreement with the tradition of the early church in considering baptism a sacrament of unity (1 Cor. 1:13 ff.; 12:12, 13; Gal. 3:27, 28; Col. 3:10, 11).

The act of baptism is also used to describe the change of status from pagan to believer. The author accentuates this change by contrasting what his readers "once" were (2:1 ff., 11 ff.; 5:8a) and what they have "now" become in Christ (2:4 ff., 13 ff.; 5:8b ff.). This also is in keeping with the view of the early church that interpreted baptism as participation in the events of Christ (indicative) and the beginning of a new ethical life (imperative; cf. Rom. 6:1-11; 2 Cor. 5:17; Col. 3:3; Titus 3:5-7).

Ephesians contains a large amount of paraenetic material (4:1-3; 4:17-5:20; 5:21-6:6) that probably belonged to the common catechetical tradition of the early church. The author uses these exhortations to expound upon the nature of the new life in Christ and to show the unifying effect this ethical action is to have upon all human relationships in the church (4:3, 15, 16, 25-32; 5:31-33).

From the preceding discussion it becomes obvious that the other questions about Ephesians are related to the question of authorship. If Ephesians is written by Paul, the following conclusions are possible:

Origin. Ephesians is one of the "captivity epistles," written while Paul was in prison. The NT records a brief imprisonment in Philippi (Acts 16:19-33), two years in Caesarea (Acts 23:23-26:32), and two years in Rome before the end of Paul's life (Acts 28:16-31).[47]

Although there is no specific mention of an Ephesian imprisonment, Paul's references to the suffering and affliction he experiences in Asia (2 Cor. 1:8-10) and to other imprisonments (2 Cor. 6:5; 11:23) and his statement "I have fought with 'wild beasts' here in Ephesus" (1 Cor. 15:32) have been taken to imply an Ephesian imprisonment of some duration. Though this theory has some appeal, it is basically an argument from silence and depends upon its association with Colossians (cf. Introduction to Colossians). The same can be said for an origin from Caesarea (cf. Introduction to Colossians). If it is seen as a Pauline epistle, there is precious little evidence to overthrow the traditional theory that it was written by Paul during his Roman imprisonment. The style and content make more sense if associated with the final years of Paul.

Date. A Roman origin would date the epistle somewhere between A.D. 62 and A.D. 64; if Ephesus, about A.D. 54–57; if Caesarea, about A.D. 59–61.

Destination. Given the problem regarding the phrase "in Ephesus," the best solution appears to take the epistle as some kind of circular letter that was intended for more than one church but that, in the course of events, became associated with Ephesus.

This identity with Ephesus could be the result of Paul's personal ministry there as well as the significance of that city as a religious center and capital city in Proconsular Asia. The NT references to Ephesus indicate that it held a strategic position for the missionary activity of the early church (Acts 19:10; 1 Tim. 1:3; 2 Tim. 1:18; 4:12; Rev. 1:11; 2:1–7).

While Paul was teaching in Ephesus (in the "hall of Tyrannus," Acts 19:9, 10), Epaphras heard of the gospel and, as a result of his conversion to Christianity, went back to his home in Colossae and started a church there (Col. 1:7; 4:12). Much the same thing may have happened with the seven churches mentioned in Revelation 1–3 and other cities not mentioned in the NT. A. S. Wood observes that "Ephesus was surrounded by 230 independent communities within the Roman province of Asia. If the Christian faith were firmly established in the capital city, it could be spread from the hub to the rim."[48]

If Ephesians is the product of a deutero-Paulinist, then the following conclusions are possible:

Origin. The origin must remain highly conjectural. But given the significance of Ephesus as an evangelistic and teaching center for Paul and his "school," the epistle probably emerged from this location.

Date. The date must be somewhere after Paul's death (ca. A.D. 64) and before the end of the first century. Since there are some "echoes" of Ephesians in Clement's letter to the Corinthians (ca. A.D. 95), it must have been written no later than the early 90s.

Destination. Ephesians is a universal letter intended for a number of Gentile churches in Asia Minor, including the Ephesian congregation.

Conclusion

All the internal and external questions surrounding this epistle should not detract from its essential beauty, value, and complete authority for the church. It just happens that there is a uniqueness or elusiveness about it that makes it difficult to categorize or place within the context of Paul's life. And because it is capable of fitting into more than one historical context, it seems best to regard it as a development of Paul's vision for a universal and unified church consisting of Jewish and Gentile believers.

Notes

1. M. Barth, *Ephesians 1–3*, p. 37; Mitton, *Ephesians*, pp. 2–4. For a helpful article see J. B. Polhill, "An Introduction to Ephesians," *RevExp* 76 (1979), pp. 465–79.

2. For further details on the circular letter theory, see most introductory sections in the major commentaries and D. Guthrie's *New Testament Introduction* (Downers Grove, Ill.: Intervarsity Press, 1971), pp. 510 f. (hereafter cited *Introduction*). Several specialized studies include R. Batey, "The Destination of Ephesians," *JBL* 82 (1963), p. 101. (Batey suggests that during the process of transmission the textual reading *ousin* replaced the original *Hasias*); D. A. Black, "The Peculiarities of Ephesians and the Ephesian Address," *Grace Theological Journal* 2 (1981), pp. 59–73; M. Santer, "The Text of Ephesians I.1," *NTS* 15 (1969), pp. 247–48. E. Best gives a very thorough study of all the evidence in "Ephesians I.i," in *Text and Interpretation*, ed. E. Best and R. McL. Wilson (Cambridge: Cambridge University Press, 1979), pp. 29–41.

3. Mitton, *Ephesians*, p. 11; cf. also Mitton's *The Epistle to the Ephesians: Its Authorship, Origin and Purpose* (Oxford: Clarendon, 1951), pp. 243 ff., for a more complete treatment of his views on the date of Ephesians. For clarification on this view of a later author, see A. Patzia, "The Deutero-Pauline Hypothesis: An Attempt at Clarification," *EQ* 52 (1980), pp. 27–42.

4. R. P. Martin, "An Epistle in Search of a Life-Setting," *ExpT* 79 (1968), pp. 296–302. For comments on Martin's views, cf. D. J. Rowston, "Changes in Biblical Interpretation Today: The Example of Ephesians," *Biblical Theological Bulletin* 9 (1979), pp. 121–25.

5. A. S. Wood, "Ephesians," in *The Expositor's Bible Commentary*, vol. 2, p. 7. For a defense of Pauline authorship on these grounds, see Guthrie, *Introduction*, pp. 491 ff.; Barth, *Ephesians 1–3*, p. 6. The most thorough book in English dealing with all matters of introductory problems in Ephesians is A. van Roon, *The Authenticity of Ephesians, Supplement to NovT*, vol. 39 (Leiden: Brill, 1974). Cf. also J. N. Sanders, "The Case for Pauline Authorship," in *Studies in Ephesians*, ed. F. L. Cross, pp. 9–20.

Much of the debate regarding authorship centers around the similarities between Ephesians, Colossians, and other NT epistles. Useful comparisons can be found in most commentaries; see Abbott, *Ephesians and Colossians*, pp. xxiii–xxix; Foulkes, *Ephesians*, pp. 20–30; Mitton, *Ephesians*, pp. 11–18; Mitton, *The Epistle to the Ephesians*, parts II and III and appendixes; Moule, *Ephesians*, pp. 29–32; Wescott, *Ephesians*, pp. xxv–lx. Two excellent articles are J. Coutts, "The Relationship of Ephesians and Colossians," *NTS* 3–4 (1956–58), pp. 201–7; J. B. Polhill, "The Relationship between Ephesians and Colossians," *RevExp* 70 (1973), pp. 439–50.

6. Guthrie, *Introduction*, p. 497.

7. M. Barth, *Ephesians 1–3*, pp. 3–4.

8. For an explanation of Käsemann's ideas on "Early Catholicism," see Patzia, "The Deutero-Pauline Hypothesis," pp. 30–31.

9. M. Barth, *Ephesians 1–3*, p. 45.

10. J. A. Allan, "The 'In Christ' Formula in Ephesians," *NTS* 5 (1958–59), pp. 54–62.

11. W. G. Kümmel, *Introduction to the New Testament*, 17th ed. (Nashville: Abingdon, 1975), p. 361. See also D. E. Nineham, "The Case Against the Pauline Authorship," in Cross, *Studies in Ephesians*, pp. 21–35. All the issues surrounding the authorship, destination, purpose, and so forth of Ephesians can be frustrating to the reader. H. J. Cadbury recognized this a long time ago in his article, "The Dilemma of Ephesians," *NTS* 5 (1958–59), pp. 91–102.

12. Guthrie, *Introduction*, pp. 507, 508.

13. The value and authority of Ephesians as a deutero-Pauline epistle is discussed by Mitton in his *The Epistle to the Ephesians*, pp. 270–78. He believes that on the analogy of the authorship of the Epistle to the Hebrews an initial loss turns out to be a gain. As a deutero-Pauline letter, Ephesians reveals a new mind and an authoritative voice into the generation of believers that followed Paul.

14. A. M. Hunter, *Introducing the New Testament*, 2d ed. (Philadelphia: Westminster, 1957), p. 120. Other studies that express similar views include N. Alexander, "The Epistle for Today," in *Biblical Studies*, ed. R. J. McKay and J. F. Miller (Philadelphia: Westminster, 1976), pp. 99–118; W. B. Colbe, "The Queen of the Epistles," *SWJTh* 6 (1963), pp. 7–19.

15. W. Barclay, *The Letters to the Galatians and Ephesians*, p. 83; F. F. Bruce, *Ephesians*, p. 11; C. R. Erdman, *The Epistle of Paul to the Ephesians* (Philadelphia: Westminster, 1931), p. 14.

16. J. N. Sanders, "The Case for Pauline Authorship," p. 16.

17. R. P. Martin, "Ephesians," p. 126. See also M. Barth, "Traditions in Ephesians," *NTS* 30 (1984), pp. 3–25.

18. Goodspeed's ideas are presented in *The Meaning of Ephesians* (Chicago: University of Chicago Press, 1933) and *The Key to Ephesians* (Chicago: University of Chicago Press, 1956). For a critique of Goodspeed's hypothesis, see Guthrie, *Introduction*, pp. 512–14; Wood, "Ephesians," p. 112.

19. E. Lohse, "Pauline Theology in the Letter to the Colossians," *NTS* 15 (1969), pp. 211–20.

20. N. A. Dahl, "Interpreting Ephesians: Then and Now," *Theology Digest* 25 (1977), p. 314.

21. Ibid, p. 314.

22. For a long list of scholars with this persuasion, see Barth, *Ephesians 1–3*, pp. 12 ff.

23. Dahl, "Interpreting Ephesians: Then and Now," p. 307.

24. H. Schlier, *Der Brief an die Epheser* (Düsseldorf: Patmos Verlag, 1962), p. 21. For Beare's comments, see his "Ephesians," pp. 674–75.

25. See E. Yamauchi, *Pre-Christian Gnosticism* (Grand Rapids: Eerdmans, 1973).

26. Kuhn, "Der Epheserbrief im Lichte der Qumrantexte," *NTS* 7 (1960–61), pp. 334–46; Murphy-O'Connor, "Who Wrote Ephesians?" *BibTod* 18 (1965), pp. 1201–9; F. Mussner, "Beiträge aus Qumran zum Verständnis des Epheserbriefes," *Neutestamentliche Aufsätze* (Regensburg: Verlag Friedrich Pustet, 1963).

27. See Mitton's summary, *Ephesians*, pp. 18 ff.

28. Murphy-O'Connor, "Who Wrote Ephesians?" "The sometime Essene, now a disciple of the man who wrote I Corinthians 13, had well assimilated the most profound lesson of his master" (p. 1209).

29. Barth, *Ephesians 1–3*, p. 21; cf. also R. A. Culpepper, "Ethical Dualism and Church Discipline: Ephesians 4:25–5:20," *RevExp* 76 (1979), pp. 529–39, for comparisons between Ephesians and Qumran.

30. J. Moffatt, *Introduction to the Literature of the New Testament*, 3d ed. (Edinburgh: T. & T. Clark, 1918), p. 388.

31. R. P. Martin, "Ephesians," p. 128. See also Martin, *Reconciliation*, p. 157.

32. J. Kirby, *Ephesians: Baptism and Pentecost*.

33. One example is J. T. Sanders, "Hymnic Elements in Ephesians 1–3," *ZNW* 56 (1965), pp. 214–32.

34. J. Kirby, *Ephesians: Baptism and Pentecost*, p. 170.

35. N. A. Dahl, "Adresse und Proömium des Epheserbriefes," *TZ* 7 (1951), pp. 241–64; "Bibelstudie über den Epheserbrief," in *Kurze Auslegung des Epheserbriefes* (Göttingen: Vandenhoeck & Ruprecht, 1965), pp. 7–83; "Anamnesis," *Studia Theologica* I (1948), pp. 69–95. For other studies on the liturgical/baptismal nature of Ephesians, see R. R. Williams, "The Pauline Catechesis," in *Studies in Ephesians*, ed. Cross, pp. 89–96; P. Carrington, *The Primitive Christian Catechism* (Cambridge: Cambridge University Press, 1940); E. G. Selwyn, *The First Epistle of St. Peter* (London: Macmillan, 1946); J. Coutts, "Ephesians I.3–14 and I Peter I.3–12," *NTS* 3 (1956–57), pp. 115–27.

36. Mitton, *Ephesians*, p. 30.

37. Martin, "Ephesians," p. 129.

38. See Cannon, pp. 183–96. For some helpful correctives to the usual interpretation of Paul's attitude toward the Law, cf. K. Stendahl, *Paul Among Jews and Gentiles and Other Essays* (Philadelphia: Fortress, 1976); E. P. Sanders, *Paul and Palestinian Judaism: A Comparison of Patterns of Religion* (Philadelphia: Fortress, 1977).

39. H. Chadwick, "Die Absicht des Epheserbriefes," *ZNW* 51 (1960), pp. 145–53; also his "Ephesians," in *Peake's Commentary on the Bible*, ed. M. Black and H. H. Rowley (Edinburgh: Thomas Nelson, 1962), pp. 980 ff.

40. E. Käsemann, "Ephesians and Acts," *Studies in Luke-Acts*, ed. L. E. Keck and J. L. Martyn (Nashville: Abingdon, 1966), pp. 288–97.

41. W. Grundmann, "Die NEPIOI in der Paränese," *NTS* 5 (1958–59), pp. 188–205.

42. See K. M. Fischer, *Tendenz und Absicht des Epheserbriefes* (Göttingen: Vandenhoeck & Ruprecht, 1973).

43. Quoted from C. Roetzel, *The Letters of Paul—Conversations in Context*, 2d ed. (Atlanta: John Knox, 1982), p. 104.

44. Kümmel, *Introduction to the New Testament*, p. 364.

45. Barth, *Ephesians 1–3*, p. 66.

46. H. von Soden, quoted in A. S. Wood, "Ephesians," p. 18.

47. For a discussion on the origin of Colossians, see the "Introduction" to that epistle. Beyond the sources listed there, G. S. Duncan has written *St. Paul's Ephesians Ministry* (New York: Scribner, 1930); additional studies by Duncan on the origin of the captivity epistles can be found in *ExpT* 43 (1931), pp. 7–11; *ExpT* 46 (1935), pp. 293–98. More recently, "Important Hypotheses Reconsidered VI. Were Paul's Imprisonment Epistles Written from Ephesus?" *ExpT* 67 (1955–56), pp. 163–66.

48. Wood, "Ephesians," p. 12.

The Opening Greeting

From Paul, who by God's will is an apostle of Christ Jesus—
 To God's people in Ephesus,[a] who are faithful in their life in union with Christ Jesus:
 [2]May God our Father and the Lord Jesus Christ give you grace and peace.

a. *Some manuscripts do not have* in Ephesus.

1:1 / With the exception of the omission of Timothy, the opening of this greeting is quite similar to Colossians 1:1. The letter claims to be from Paul, **an apostle of Christ Jesus**. This term was one that Paul used frequently to indicate that he was "one who was sent" (*apostellō*, "to send") as a missionary or special envoy of God. It is used of the twelve disciples as well as for others who fulfill an apostolic function, such as Andronicus and Junias (Rom. 16:7). At times, it is applied to Christians who have a very vivid experience of Christ (Acts 1:21, 22; 1 Cor. 9:1). By the time Ephesians was written, it was used primarily for those who were the founders of the Christian church (2:20).

The statement that Paul's apostleship is **by God's will** repeats a theme that Paul emphasizes throughout his epistles: At his commissioning, he and Barnabas are to set apart to do the work to which God has called them (Acts 13:2); to the Romans he writes "as an apostle chosen and called by God" (1:1) with the "privilege of being an apostle" (1:5); to the Galatians he states in no uncertain terms that his call "did not come from man or by means of man, but from Jesus Christ and God the Father" (1:1; cf. also 1:13–16); and though Paul may at times feel unworthy of his calling (1 Cor. 1:9), he affirms that God's grace has made him what he is (1 Cor. 1:10). This awareness of God's initiative in his call kept Paul from boasting about his position; it also legitimized his office as an apostle on occasions when his authority was questioned (cf. Galatians and Corinthians).

The readers are identified, first of all, as **God's people** (lit., "saints"). As such, they are people who are consecrated to God by being separated from sin. Second, they **are faithful in their life in union with Christ Jesus**. By this translation, the GNB gives **faithful** a passive meaning, that is, those who are being faithful or trustworthy. It could also have an active meaning, indicating that these are believers who have put their faith in Christ Jesus. Both meanings, however, are expressed within the body of the letter: God's people are those who have put their faith in Christ (the indicative) and who live out that faith in obedience to the Lord (the imperative).

The text indicates that the letter is addressed to God's people who live **in Ephesus**, although the footnote indicates that there is a textual question concerning the inclusion of the phrase **in Ephesus**. Most likely the destination was omitted in the original manuscript because the epistle was intended to be a universal letter to be circulated among a number of churches (see Introduction).

1:2 / The greeting ends with Paul's usual mention of **grace and peace** (cf. Rom. 1:7; 1 Cor. 1:3; 2 Cor. 1:2; Gal. 1:3; Phil. 1:2; Col. 1:2; 1 Thess. 1:1; 2 Thess. 1:2. Titus 1:4, 1 Tim. 1:2, and 2 Tim. 1:2 include grace, mercy, and peace). *Chairein* was a common word for greeting in the Greek world (Acts 15:23; 23:26; James 1:1). Paul uses *charis*, which to believers has come to mean God's free and unmerited goodness upon mankind.

The Hebrews greeted each other with *shalom*, a common term for "peace" as well as fullness or wholeness of life. The apostle, likewise, is doing more than just greeting his readers with these terms, because grace and peace are gifts of God given through Christ. By bringing these two gifts together, he is urging that his readers enjoy life because of the favor that God freely has bestowed upon them. Both concepts form a very important part of the letter (peace: 2:14, 15, 17; 4:3; 6:15; grace: 2:5, 7, 8; 3:2, 7; 4:7).

One cannot help but notice the significant role attached to Christ in these opening verses. Paul is designated as an apostle of **Christ Jesus**; the believers live their life in union with **Christ Jesus**; and together with God the Father, the **Lord Jesus Christ** bestows the divine gifts of grace and peace upon his people.

In the following discussion it will be noted that Ephesians has a number of stylistic features that make it similar to Colossians. First, it follows the pattern of praise, thanksgiving, and prayer. In Colossians, Paul began by thanking God for his readers (1:3–8) and then praying that God would accomplish certain things in their lives. In Ephesians, there is a similar structure: The epistle begins with a great hymn of praise or thanksgiving to God (1:3–14) and follows up with a long prayer (1:15–2:20) in which the apostle expresses the concern that his readers understand how God has blessed them through Christ.

A second similarity relates to the hymn and its place in the epistle. In Colossians, the ideas of the Christ hymn (1:15–20) were applied again and again throughout the letter. Much the same could be said of Ephesians, for this opening eulogy serves as an excellent preface to the remaining doctrinal section. The idea of redemption is prominent in the phrases dealing with the exaltation of Christ (1:15–22), salvation by faith (2:1–10), the unity between Jew and Gentile (2:11–22), and the revelation of the mystery of Christ (3:1–12).

Third, Ephesians may be divided conveniently into a doctrinal and a practical section, since we find the author providing a theological base (chapters 1–3) and then applying these truths to the Christian life (chapters 4–6). Such divisions, however, should not be taken too rigidly, for one finds ethical exhortations in the midst of doctrinal discussion (e.g., 1:4; 2:10) and doctrinal teaching continued throughout the last chapters (4:1–16; 5:21–6:9).

A Hymn of Praise

EPHESIANS 1:3–14

Let us give thanks to the God and Father of our Lord Jesus Christ! For in our union with Christ he has blessed us by giving us every spiritual blessing in the heavenly world. ⁴Even before the world was made, God had already chosen us to be his through our union with Christ, so that we would be holy and without fault before him.

Because of his love ⁵God[b] had already decided that through Jesus Christ he would make us his sons— that was his pleasure and purpose. ⁶Let us praise God for his glorious grace, for the free gift he gave us in his dear Son! ⁷For by the death of Christ we are set free, that is, our sins are forgiven. How great is the grace of God, ⁸which he gave to us in such large measure!

In all his wisdom and insight ⁹God did what he had purposed, and made known to us the secret plan he had already decided to complete by means of Christ. ¹⁰This plan, which God will complete when the time is right, is to bring all creation together, everything in heaven and on earth, with Christ as head.

¹¹All things are done according to God's plan and decision; and God chose us to be his own people in union with Christ because of his own purpose, based on what he had decided from the very beginning. ¹²Let us, then, who were the first to hope in Christ, praise God's glory!

¹³And you also became God's people when you heard the true message, the Good News that brought you salvation. You believed in Christ, and God put his stamp of ownership on you by giving you the Holy Spirit he had promised. ¹⁴The Spirit is the guarantee that we shall receive what God has promised his people, and this assures us that God will give complete freedom to those who are his. Let us praise his glory!

b. before him. Because of his love God; *or* before him, and to live in love. God

Many great words and phrases have been used to describe the beauty of this opening hymn that praises God for the spiritual blessings he has bestowed upon the believer in Christ. J. Stott, in his commentary (p. 32), quotes a number of authors who use such phrases as "a magnificent gateway," "a golden chain of links," "a kaleidoscope of dazzling lights and shifting colors," a "rhapsodic adoration," a "paean of praise."

Unfortunately, the English translations do not retain the hymnic nature and rhythmic pattern that is discernible in the original language. In the Greek, for example, the entire section of twelve verses is one long sentence. This helps one to appreciate how the author's thoughts keep moving to new heights. Having to divide the section into sentences (RSV and NIV, six; NEB, eight; GNB, thirteen) destroys the continuity of both style and thought.

A number of proposals have been offered with respect to the origin of the hymn. Those who take the Ephesian letter to be genuinely Pauline naturally attribute these verses to the great apostle. Scholars who question Pauline authorship suggest that an author writing in Paul's name (a deutero, or "second" Paul) borrowed terms and phrases from Paul's other epistles and composed a hymn that resembles something that Paul would have written.

The search for origins and models has moved in a number of directions. J. Kirby believes that this passage is modeled after a Jewish *berakah* ("blessing") in which God is praised for his goodness. Others have noted the strong liturgical nature of the passage and have suggested that it belongs to the worshiping community. As such, either it could have a prior and independent existence apart from Ephesians or it could have been written by the author to provide a liturgical piece to be used for church worship and instruction (Mitton, pp. 22–24).

A number of scholars who have tried to explain the origin of Ephesians from a baptismal context have focused their attention on this particular hymnic section. In the hymn, the author utilizes such baptismal terms and concepts as sonship (1:5), redemption (1:7), and sealing (1:13). The most likely explanation for the appearance of these terms is that the writer is drawing upon baptismal theology to thank God for all the blessings of redemption that he has provided through Christ to those who have believed. Since the passage is a hymn, it is quite possible to regard it as a baptismal hymn that may have been part of the worshiping tradition in the early church and that the author took over and incorporated into his redemptive eulogy. The baptismal motifs in this hymn have been so convincing to some scholars that they have concluded that the entire epistle was written as a baptismal tract or at least connected with the celebration of baptism in the church.

From the baptismal nature of this opening hymn, however, it does not necessarily follow that the occasion of this epistle is to instruct the readers on the meaning of their baptism. If this were the purpose, one might expect baptism to be mentioned more explicitly, for as it stands, the word "baptism" occurs only once (4:5). Rather, the author finds the baptismal motifs and language appropriate to describe all the blessings that God has bestowed upon his readers in Christ. The early church understood baptism to be the act in which the believer appropriates in faith the blessings of redemption in Christ. Thus it was sufficient for him to allude to baptism but not to define its meaning directly.

Another noticeable feature of the hymn is the place that it gives to all three members of the trinity. In a broad sense, the work of the Father is described in verses 3–6; the Son, in verses 7–12; and the Holy Spirit, in verses 13–14. But all three persons permeate the entire passage. God is the *source* of all the spiritual blessings that are mentioned throughout the hymn; Christ is the *agent* in whom these blessings are realized for the believer. The name "Christ"—or some form of that name, or the personal pronoun "in him," "in whom," and so on—occurs thirteen times in this passage. All that God has purposed for the believer is fulfilled in Christ. The Holy Spirit is mentioned as the one who *seals* or marks the believer as belonging to Christ. And, since the blessings that are enumerated in this passage are "spiritual," they are given by the "Spirit."

1:3 / **Let us give thanks**: The Greek word behind this phrase is *eulogētos*, which carries the meaning of speaking (*legō*) well or kindly (*eu*) of someone. In this context, the phrase could be expressed as "thanks be," "blessed be," or "praise be" to God. In the NT, the word is used exclusively for God, since he alone is worthy to be blessed; he is blessed because he is the author of all the blessings that he bestows upon the believer in Christ. Since such forms of blessings were common among the Jews, this passage may have a Jewish antecedent.

Thanks is given to **the God and Father of our Lord Jesus Christ** (cf. 1:3; 2 Cor. 1:3; 1 Pet. 1:3). Grammatically, the phrase could read, "God who is the Father of our Lord Jesus Christ." As such, it indicates the unique relationship that God and Christ have to each other. In the context of the NT, believers call God "Father" because of the sonship that is received through Christ (cf. 1:5; Rom. 8:14–17; Gal. 4:6, 7).

He has blessed us: It is important to note that this is in the past (Greek aorist) tense, meaning that the author envisions a time when God acted to provide these blessings rather than anticipating that God will do something in the future. These blessings became a reality for the believers **in our union with Christ**—that is, in baptism.

The nature or essence of the blessing is **spiritual**. Although the word is singular (**every spiritual blessing**) it needs to be understood as a comprehensive phrase: God's blessings are unlimited, and he does not withhold anything from his people. The sphere of these blessings is **the heavenly world**. In other words, the reference is not to material, physical, or temporal blessings: They are not part of one's treasure "where moths and rust destroy, and robbers break in and steal" (Matt. 6:19). As spiritual gifts in the heavenly world, they are imperishable and belong to the eternal order "where moths and rust cannot destroy, and robbers cannot break in and steal" (Matt. 6:20).

The phrase **in the heavenly world** is a translation of the Greek "in the heavenlies" (*en tois epouraniois*). Since it is an adjective without a noun, English translations supply such terms are **world** (GNB), "places" (RSV), or "realms" (NIV). This clarification, however, should not lead one to conclude that Paul has a geographical place or cosmic location in mind somewhere in the universe above the earth. *Heavenlies* is a term signifying the spiritual world, that is, the unseen world of spiritual reality and activity. This is the sphere in which the believers are blessed. The other four occurrences of "heavenly world" in the epistle (1:20; 2:6; 3:10; 6:12) help to express this idea more clearly.

In the ancient world, it was believed that there was a great cosmic struggle between the forces of good and the forces of evil. Generally, the heavens were considered to be the place where this battle between the evil rulers, principalities, powers, and ruling spirits of the universe (*stoicheia tou kosmou*) was being waged. A significant part of the message in Colossians is that these spiritual forces are inferior to Christ in the order of creation (1:16) as well as subject to Christ through his victory on the cross, where Christ "freed himself from the power of the spiritual rulers and authorities . . . and made a public spectacle of them by leading them as captives in his victory procession" (2:15). Ephesians continues these ideas by teaching that, because of Christ's victory over these evil powers, he is exalted to God's right hand "to rule above all heavenly rulers, powers, and lords" (1:20, 21). Furthermore, these powers are learning of God's wisdom through the witness of the church (3:10).

Ephesians teaches that believers are involved in a similar battle: "We are not fighting against human beings, but against the wicked spiritual forces in the heavenly world, the rulers, authorities, and cosmic powers of this dark age" (6:12). But by virtue of their union with Christ, they share in Christ's victory and likewise rule with Christ in the heavenly world (2:6). In fact, all the blessings that are enumerated in this passage are either fulfilled in union with Christ or are mediated through the agency of Christ.

1:4 / The first specific blessing to be mentioned is what has come to be known in theological circles as election or predestination. Basically, this doctrine affirms that God has taken the initiative in the "electing" or "choosing" process. In the OT, God chooses Israel from among all the nations of the earth to be his covenant people (Deut. 4:37; 7:6, 7; Isa. 44:1, 2); in the NT, God chooses people to become members of the new covenant, the church (John 15:16; Rom. 8:29; 9:11; Eph. 1:4, 5; 2 Thess. 2:13; 2 Tim. 1:9; 1 Pet. 1:2); and individuals such as Jeremiah (1:5) and Paul (1 Cor. 15:9–11) believed that even their vocation was destined by God.

Unfortunately, the Christian church has become polarized into theological camps over this doctrine. Some (namely, the Calvinists) have placed all the emphasis upon the sovereign grace of God in matters of salvation; others (namely, the Arminians) have emphasized man's free will in the salvation process. And since the Bible does not attempt to harmonize this apparent paradox, it continues to remain one of the more divisive and speculative "mysteries" of the Christian faith.

When dealing with this issue, one should avoid the extremes in theory and practice that so often characterize adherents of one view or another. Election to salvation does not imply that God, therefore, predestines the rest of mankind to damnation; nor should election lead to spiritual pride among the elect. Election simply affirms that personal faith rests upon the prior work (grace) of God, so that, with respect to salvation, God has taken the initiative to claim a people for himself. An individual is free to choose God only because God has already decided for such a person from eternity. Likewise, election should not lead to spiritual complacency; it is a privilege and responsibility that is unto holiness of life and for good works (1:4; 2:10).

The author indicates that God's intention for the salvation of humanity precedes the creation of the world and the historical process (**before the world was made, God had already chosen us to be his through our union with Christ**). When Paul, a member of the church and a chosen apostle to the Gentiles, reflects upon the doctrine of election, he may be reasoning in the following way: "How did I, a Pharisee and a former persecutor of Christians, get to be what I am? How is it that the Jews—and now the Gentiles—have become part of God's family? Surely it is not because of some national merit or personal attainment through faith or good works! This had to be God's doing. He knew from eternity how he would work in me and in the world; it was not a last-minute decision that the Gentiles were to become heirs of salvation" (3:3). When the apostle writes to the Corinthians about their new being in Christ, for example, he states: "All this is done by God, who through Christ changed us from enemies into his friends" (2 Cor. 5:17–19).

John Stott makes a helpful comment by drawing attention to the relationship of the three pronouns in the phrase "he chose us in him" (RSV). God chose us, even before we were created, to be redeemed through the work of Christ that had not yet taken place (Stott, p. 36). Such, however, is the marvel of God's elective grace toward mankind.

The goal of election is that the believer be **holy and without fault** before God. This phrase is similar to Colossians 1:22 and may be part of the OT sacrificial language that the NT uses on other occasions (cf. 5:27; Heb. 9:14; 1 Pet. 1:19; Jude 24). In some cases, the doctrine of predestination has led to moral license rather than personal holiness. Not a few believers have reasoned that since they are "eternally secure," their ethical life is no longer of concern to God or to other people. Such reasoning, however, is unfortunate, because the believers' standing before God and election (the indicative) is demonstrated by the kind of life that they live ethically (the imperative).

1:5 / It is difficult to know what to do with the phrase **because of his love**. The GNB (as RSV, NIV) takes it to go with verse 5, thereby indicating that God's choosing was motivated by his love. On the basis of this love, God had **already decided that through Jesus Christ he would make us his sons**. But the phrase could be taken with the action described in verse 4, as mankind's love to God rather than God's love to mankind. Thus the meaning would be that believers should be holy and without fault before him in love (*en agapē*). *Agapē* is used elsewhere in Ephesians for Christian love (3:17; 4:2, 15, 16; 5:2). Still, it is very fitting to mention *God's* love so early in the epistle and that this is what motivated him to decide (lit., "foreordain") to redeem humanity: It **was his pleasure and purpose . . . to make us his sons**.

Sonship is the second blessing listed in this passage, and this, too, is a gift mediated **through Jesus Christ**. Paul uses this term in Romans 8:15, 23, 29, and Galatians 4:5 to indicate the special relationship that believers have to God. Here sonship is tied in with God's elective purpose for humanity.

The language of this passage is similar to that in the accounts of Jesus' baptism (Matt. 3:13–17; Mark 1:9–11; Luke 3:21, 22) and transfiguration (Matt. 17:5; Mark 9:7; Luke 9:35). In these Gospel accounts of Christ's baptism, as in Ephesians 1:5 and 6, baptism and sonship are closely related and Christ is given the title "beloved" or **dear Son** (1:6). This similarity of language and ideas (sonship, *huiothesia*; good pleasure, *eudokia*; and beloved, *agapētos*) leads one to infer that this reference to the election and sonship of the Christian may have some connection with the baptism of Jesus. Thus one could say that as Jesus was proclaimed **son** at his baptism, baptism is the event whereby believers obtain their sonship. This thought is quite explicit in the baptismal passage in Galatians 3:26–27 that states that "it is through faith that all of you are God's sons in union with Christ Jesus. You were baptized into union with Christ and now you are clothed, so to speak, with the life of Christ himself."

1:6 / Theology is doxology! In other words, sonship (the indicative) is a summons to praise God for his glorious grace. Literally, from the Greek, the phrase reads, "to the praise of the glory of the grace of him of which he graced us in the beloved." This reading helps one to see how much emphasis the writer puts upon grace (cf. 1:2). It is almost that he is so enraptured by the thought of God's grace that he does not want to let it go. Also, it is a fitting way to end a section devoted to the work of the Father (1:3–6). The fact that almost identical phrases are used in 1:12 ("praise God's glory" and 1:14 ("let us praise his glory") confirms the hymnic nature of this entire section.

1:7 / There is a definite parallel here to Colossians 1:14, where redemption (**we are set free**) and the forgiveness of sins are closely connected. But in Ephesians, the means of redemption is amplified by the phrase **for by the death** (lit, "blood") **of Christ we are set free, that is, our sins are forgiven**. The emphasis here is upon forgiveness, which in turn is followed by the resounding response on the greatness of God's grace. Since sonship takes place through baptism, and since sonship and forgiveness are so closely linked in this passage, one wonders if the author still has the baptismal event in mind when he speaks of the forgiveness of sins.

1:8 / The magnitude of God's grace is amplified in this opening phrase, **which he gave to us in such large measure** (*eperisseusen*). The poetic nature of the Greek makes it difficult to know whether to attach the following words (**in all his wisdom and insight**) with verse 8 or verse 9. Is it *God's* wisdom and insight (GNB, RSV) or is it wisdom and insight that God, through his grace, has lavished upon believers so that they could understand God's will (NIV, NEB)? Given the parallel with Colossians 1:9 and the meaning of verse 9, it seems better to take wisdom and insight as coming from God's grace.

The two terms, **wisdom** (*sophia*) and **insight** (*phronēsis*), though not consistently distinguished in Scripture, generally refer to the knowledge of something, followed by the ability to apply that knowledge or wisdom to a right course of action. God, in other words, has provided the knowledge and ability to know and to do his will.

1:9 / God's gift of wisdom and insight enables the believer to understand God's **secret plan**. In Colossians, that secret plan (mystery) meant that the Gentiles were recipients of the Good News and heirs of salvation (1:26, 27; 2:2; 4:3). Though this thought appears also in Ephesians (cf. 3:3–6), this epistle carries the concept somewhat further with its emphasis upon the church and the unity of mankind. The revelation is part of God's eternal plan (**what he had purposed**) and is something that will be accomplished **by means of Christ**. As in verse 5, God's purpose includes his good pleasure as well (cf. *eudokia* in Luke 2:14; Gal. 1:15). In other words, it pleased God to make his secret plan known and to complete that plan in his Son.

1:10 / The Greek word behind **plan** is *oikonomia*, which is used in the NT as the "management," "stewardship," or "administration" of a household or office (Luke 16:2–4; 1 Cor. 9:17; 1 Pet. 4:10). Here the basic idea appears to be that Christ is the steward through whom God is working out his plan for the world—a plan that is in process and that God **will complete when the time is right** (lit., "in the fullness of time").

God's ultimate plan is to unify all of creation under the headship of Christ. Elsewhere in the epistle, the author talks about bringing the Jews and Gentiles together into one body (2:11, 12; 3:6); here, however, he envisions a global unity. In many ways the words are reminiscent of the Christ hymn in Colossians, in which all things on earth and in heaven are reconciled in Christ (1:20).

It is difficult to know how far one should push this language or attempt to comprehend the scope of the author's ideas. Are **all creation** (*ta panta*) and **heaven** and **earth** just metaphors for universality, or does he mean the unity of heavenly beings (i.e., angels, principalities, powers, spirits, etc.) with human beings? Is he thinking of some kind of cosmic and earthly renewal characteristic of the end times (Matt. 19:28; Rom. 8:18–25; 2 Pet. 3:10–13)? Although one cannot be sure of the details, it is clear that this hymn praises God that ultimately all things will find their place and unity in Christ.

The difficult word *anakephalaiosasthai* is translated appropriately in the GNB **to bring ... together ... with Christ as head**. In secular terms, the word is used for the summation of things, such as adding up numbers in mathematics or concluding an argument in a debate. In today's language, people speak of "the bottom line" in much the same way. Paul uses the term in Romans 13:9 when he indicates that all of the commandments are being "summed up" in the one command of love.

In Ephesians, however, "addition" or "summation" do not quite express the author's thought adequately. To bring everything together **with Christ as head** suggests that all things (human beings, history, and the entire universe) find their focus in Christ. This, essentially, is the content of God's secret plan!

1:11-12 / Up to this point in the hymn (vv. 3-10), the personal pronouns "we" and "us" refer to all Christians, irrespective of national origin. But an important change takes place in the concluding verses of the hymn, where a distinction is made between Jewish and Gentile Christians: In verses 11-12, the "us" with whom the author identifies himself is the Jewish Christians; in verse 13, the "you" definitely refers to the Gentile believers; then the "we" in verse 14 refers to all of God's people—both Jewish and Gentile believers. The distinctions mentioned here will receive further attention in chapter 2 of the epistle, where it is shown *how* Jews and Gentiles were brought together into one body in Christ.

When the author describes God's action upon the Jewish believers, he repeats many of his earlier words and ideas: **All things are done according to God's plan and decision** (cf. 1:5, 9); **because of his own purpose** (1:5); **what he had decided from the very beginning** (1:4). With respect to the Jewish Christians, he wants to emphasize that what has happened to them was not by chance or by human merit but is due entirely to the eternal and elective purposes of God in Christ. All is of God!

The GNB translation indicates that **God chose us to be his own people**. This certainly is an improvement over the RSV, which omits the idea altogether, and the NIV, which puts it in a footnote. The word behind this concept is the verb *klēroō*, which means "to choose," "to appoint by lot." The noun (*klēros*), therefore, would be "the lot," "share," or "portion" that was obtained by lot. The Greek word for "inheritance," "possession," or "property" is the cognate word *klēronomia* (cf. 1:14).

In the Greek text, the word occurs as an aorist passive (*eklērōthēmen*), which is translated literally "we have been chosen" (from the verb *klēroō*). The important question for interpretation is whether the verb should be limited to the action of "choosing" or whether it implies choice with possession, such as God's **own people** (GNB) or "inheritance" (KJV).

Behind this language is the OT concept that Israel was God's "lot" or "chosen people" (Deut. 4:20; 9:29; 32:9; 1 Kings 8:51; Ps. 106:40; Jer. 10:16; Zech. 2:12). Given the context of verse 11 within a hymn that is celebrating God's elective purpose, it seems likely that the author is referring to the Jewish Christians as those whom God has chosen as his **own people**. Now, however, that possession is claimed by virtue of their **union with Christ**.

The gratitude over being God's heritage (**own people**) leads to another doxology (cf. 1:6): **Let us, then, . . . praise God's glory**. The people of the new Israel are summoned to praise God in the same manner that Israel was called as a nation to declare God's glory (Isa. 43:21; Jer. 13:11).

Who are those who were **the first to hope in Christ**? Some commentators, by virtue of the Greek article with Christ, take the reference to be to the Jewish nation and their expectation of "the Christ," that is, the coming Messiah; others see the comment applying to those Jews who believed in Christ and became the first Christians. In priority of time, they preceded the Gentiles with their hope (and faith) in Christ. This latter view appears to fit this context where the contrast between Jewish (1:11–12) and Gentile believers (1:13) is being discussed.

1:13 / Here the author turns to the Gentiles and affirms that they, too, **became God's people**. He then proceeds to outline the steps that were involved in their coming to Christ:

First, they **heard the true message, the Good News**. On some occasion these readers heard the message of the gospel, which resulted in their salvation. In this context, salvation probably signifies inner renewal and all the blessings and privileges available to believers because of their status in Christ (cf. 2:1 ff.) rather than preservation from the wrath of God (cf. Rom. 5:9).

The phraseology of this opening statement is similar to Colossians 1:5 and to the ideas in Romans 10:14 and 17, which show that the proclamation *of* the gospel precedes faith *in* the gospel. A similar sequence takes place during Peter's sermon on the day of Pentecost when he summons those who heard the Good News to repent and be baptized (Acts 2:37 ff.).

Second, they **believed in Christ**, literally, "in whom also having believed." Although the content of belief is not mentioned, it definitely must include the person of Christ ("If you declare with your lips, 'Jesus is Lord,' and believe in your heart that God raised him from the dead, you will be saved," Rom. 10:9) or the Good News that bears witness to him.

Third, **God put his stamp of ownership on you by giving you the Holy Spirit he had promised**. The imagery behind this phrase comes from the ancient custom of sealing (*sphragizō*), in which personal possessions such as animals, household goods, slaves, and so on received a mark or stamp of ownership in much the same way that things are branded or identified today. This act also served to confirm or authenticate what was genuine or false. A seal on a letter or document, for example, declared that it was legally valid. People belonging to religious cults often were sealed with marks that bore the image of their god(s). The Book of Revelation talks about those who have or do not have "the mark of God's seal on their foreheads" (Rev. 9:4; cf. also 7:2–8; 22:4; 2 Tim. 2:19).

In the NT, there are a number of references that indicate that the Holy Spirit is the Christian's seal: In Romans, Paul relates the inner witness of the Spirit to the believer's sonship (8:15, 16; cf. Gal. 4:6), thus affirming that the presence of the Holy Spirit in the believer is a sign that he or she belongs to God. The apostle is even more explicit in 2 Corinthians 1:22, "[God] who has placed his mark of ownership upon us, and who has given the Holy Spirit in our hearts as the guarantee of all that he has in store for us." Ephesians 1:13 confirms this by assuring the believer that the **stamp of ownership** is the possession of the Holy Spirit. It is a visible attestation that one belongs to Christ.

Although Paul connects the giving of the Holy Spirit to the acts of "hearing" the gospel and "believing" in Christ, there are credible reasons to believe that verse 13 has the baptismal event in mind, even though the term is not mentioned explicitly. First, there is an inseparable connection between faith and baptism in the NT. Baptism is believers' baptism, and those who believed in Christ expressed their faith almost immediately in baptism (Acts 2:38, 41; 8:12, 35–38; 9:18; 10:47, 48; 19:5). Faith and baptism went so closely together that they were regarded as *one* act rather than two. Peter, for example, instructs his hearers to repent, that is, to have faith, believe, *and* to be baptized for the forgiveness of sins (2:38). When Paul becomes a Christian, he is told to "get up and be baptized and have your sins washed away by calling on his name" (Acts 22:16). Within the framework of the NT, one was not baptized unless one believed; nor did one believe without being baptized.

Second, the NT connects baptism with the reception of the Holy Spirit. Peter summons his audience to be baptized and receive "God's gift, the Holy Spirit" (Acts 2:38). Paul associates baptism and the Holy Spirit on several occasions in his letters (1 Cor. 6:11; 12:13; Titus 3:5). And when Luke describes some of the major epochs in the life of the early Christian church, he includes faith, baptism, and the reception of the Holy Spirit as essential parts of becoming a Christian, that is, of Christian initiation (Acts 2:38 ff.; 8:12–17; 10:44–48; 19:1–6). There is no need for a "spirit baptism" or a rite of confirmation apart from the reception of the Holy Spirit at the time of water baptism.

On the basis of these observations it appears legitimate to interpret 1:13 within the context of baptism. The aorist participles "having heard" (*akousantes*) and "having believed" (*pisteusantes*), followed by the aorist passive ("you were sealed with the Holy Spirit of promise"), are reminiscent of the faith, baptism, Holy Spirit pattern noted above. The author does not envision a sequence of events separated by a long period of time.

Although the Holy Spirit is the seal (1:13; 4:30; 2 Cor. 1:22), and 1:13 is a strong allusion to baptism, it is by no means certain that sealing is used as a technical term for baptism in Ephesians. The first definite reference to the "seal of baptism" occurs in the second century (ca. A.D. 150) in *The Second Letter of Clement* (7.6; 8.6). From this time onward, *sphragis* is the seal received by all Christians at baptism and thus becomes a term for baptism itself.

The effect of the Holy Spirit is to put his **stamp of ownership** on the believer. As a seal, the Spirit marks one out as belonging to Christ. It is interesting to note that this is virtually the same effect that baptism "into Christ" has. To be baptized into the name or person of Christ is to become Christ's possession, to be placed under the Lord's authority and protection.

1:14 / In addition to ownership, the Holy Spirit is a **guarantee** that believers will receive God's promises. Most commentators suggest that the idea of **guarantee** (*arrabōn*) came into the Greek world from the Phoenicians who, in matters of trade, often would make a deposit or an installment as earnest money with the balance to be paid in full at some later date. Such an act obliged both buyer and seller to complete the transaction. But "the deal" included a sense of "quality" as well, for the person receiving the down payment looked forward to receiving full payment with goods of the same quality (Mitton, pp. 62–63). In the Christian life, the Holy Spirit is a pledge that God will complete his promise to deliver what he **has promised his people**. The statement in 2 Corinthians 5:5 is more specific about this idea: "He gave us his Spirit as the guarantee of all that he has in store for us." In other words, one's present life *in* the Spirit is a foretaste of one's future and eternal life *with* the Spirit!

Beyond "guaranteeing" one's inheritance, the Holy Spirit assures believers **that God will give complete freedom to those who are his**. Included in this translation are the two important theological concepts of redemption (*apolutrōsis*) and possession (*peripoiēsis*). Some commentators (cf. Abbott, p. 24) believe that the context ("our inheritance") requires that possession likewise be "our possession." Thus, believers are redeemed, but await a future time when they will take full possession of their redemption. This view has led to the very ambiguous and inadequate translation in the RSV: "which is the guarantee of our inheritance until we acquire possession of it, to the praise of his glory."

Most commentators—and as a result most English translations, like the GNB—believe the verse to be stressing that God is the agent of redemption (**God will give complete freedom**) and that believers are **his** (God's) "possession" (NIV, NASV), or "his own" (NEB). Although redemption is a present gift, the Holy Spirit assures the believer that ultimately God will redeem completely those who are his; he is a guarantee unto the **complete freedom** (redemption) of God's own people (cf. 1 Pet. 2:9).

These thoughts recall the "already" and the "not yet" of the Christian life. Believers have been given the Holy Spirit, enjoy new life in Christ, have been redeemed, but still await the fulfillment of these blessings at the second Advent. The sealing of the Holy Spirit has an eschatological function that points toward the final day, when their bodies will completely be freed (redeemed) from all the effects of sin. Ephesians 4:30 expands this concept more fully when it states that "the Spirit is God's mark of ownership on you, a guarantee that the day will come when God will set you free." A similar thought on redemption is expressed in Romans 8:23, where Paul discusses the future glory of God's people and God's creation: "We who have the Spirit as the first of God's gifts, we also groan within ourselves as we wait for God to make us his sons and set our whole being free."

This great hymn of praise ends with a repetition of a doxology that has been sounded before. It appears that such praise is called for at places where God's elective purpose and will for humanity is revealed and expanded: 1:3–6 focuses on the plan of the Father and ends with the summons to "praise God for his glorious grace"; 1:7–11 draws attention to the provision of the Son and his work in redemption and the revealing of God's secret plan and likewise ends with a doxology, "Let us . . . praise God's glory"; in 1:13–14 the pledge of the Holy Spirit is presented in relation to the unfolding plan of God. Once again, there is cause to praise God's glory. God's people are to live for God's glory!

Additional Notes

On 1:3–14 cf. J. T. Sanders, *"Hymnic Elements in Ephesians 1–3," ZNW* 56 (1965), pp. 214–32. Other specialized studies include V. A. Bartling, "The Church of God's Eternal Plan: A Study of Ephesians 1:1–14," *Concordia Theological Monthly* 36 (1965), pp. 198–204; J. Coutts, "Ephesians I.3–14 and I Peter I.3–12," pp. 115–27; N. H. Keathley, "To the Praise of His Glory: Ephesians I," *RevExp* 76 (1979), pp. 485–93; P. T. O'Brien, "Ephesians I: An Unusual Introduction to a New Testament Letter," *NTS* 25 (1979), pp. 504–16. O'Brien notes that vv. 3–14 have a "didactic intent," a "paraenetic aim," and an "epistolary function."

The following phrases from vv. 3–14 in the GNB indicate the many variations of the "in Christ" statements:

in our **union with Christ** (v. 3)
through our **union with Christ** (v. 4)
through Jesus Christ (v. 5)
in his dear son (v. 6)
by means of Christ (v. 9)
with Christ as head (v. 10)
in union with Christ (v. 11)
in Christ (v. 12)
in Christ (v. 13)
en hoi ("in him," i.e., Christ, v. 13)

1:3 / Some helpful material on "heavenlies" includes C. C. Caragounis, *The Ephesian Mysterion*, pp. 146–52; J. A. Robinson, *Ephesians*, pp. 20–22; A. T. Lincoln, "Re-Examination of 'The Heavenlies' in Ephesians," *NTS* 19 (1973), pp. 468–83. Lincoln gives a good history of interpretation as well as an examination of H. Odeburg's *The View of the Universe in the Epistle to the Ephesians* (Lund: C. W. K. Gleerup, 1934). He differs with Odeburg by concluding that 3:10 and 6:12 have a "local" rather than a "spiritual" meaning: "In Ephesians then it would not be surprising if *en tois epouraniois* were to have a reference to heaven as a distinct part of the created universe but one which retains its concealing relation to the spiritual world and to God himself, and thus also its aspect of incomprehensibility" (p. 480). See also Lincoln's *Paradise Now and Not Yet: Studies in the Role of the Heavenly Dimension in Paul's Thought with Special Reference to His Eschatology*, SNTSMS, vol. 43 (Cambridge: Cambridge University Press, 1981), esp. pp. 135–68.

1:7 / For the association between baptism and the forgiveness of sins in the NT, cf. Acts 2:38; 22:16; 1 Cor. 6:11; Titus 3:5; 1 Pet. 3:18–21, and the disc. on Col. 2:11–15.

1:10 / The ideas in this verse should not be used to promote a doctrine of "universalism" that teaches that all humanity ultimately will be saved (see Stott, *God's New Society*, pp. 42–45; Caragounis, *The Ephesian Mysterion*, pp. 143 ff.; S.

Hanson, on *anakephalaiosis*, in his *The Unity of the Church in the New Testament*, pp. 123-25.

1:11-12 / On "we" and "you," see D. Jayne, " 'We' and 'You' in Ephesians," *ExpT* 85 (1974), pp. 151-52; R. A. Wilson, " 'We' and 'You' in the Epistle to the Ephesians," *Studia Evangelica* 2 (1964), pp. 676-80.

1:13 / G. Fitzer, "*sphragis*," *TDNT*, vol. 8, pp. 939-53; P. W. Evans, "Sealing as a Term for Baptism," *The Baptist Quarterly* 16 (1955-56), pp. 171-75; J. Ysebaret, *Greek Baptismal Terminology* (Nijmegen: Dekker & Van de Vegt, 1962), pp. 182 ff.

On water and spirit baptism, see G. R. Beasley-Murray, *Baptism in the New Testament* (London: Macmillan, 1962); J. Dunn, *Baptism in the Holy Spirit* (London: SCM, 1970).

1:14 / On the "already" and the "not yet" in Paul's theology, cf. J. D. Hester, *Paul's Concept of Inheritance*. Scottish Journal of Theology Occasional Papers No. 14 (Edinburgh: Oliver & Boyd, 1968), esp. pp. 90-104; D. R. Denton, "Inheritance in Paul and Ephesians," *EQ* 54 (1982), pp. 157-62; P. L. Hammer, "Comparison of *klēronomia* in Paul and in Ephesians," *JBL* 79 (1960), pp. 267-72.

Prayer for Divine Enlightenment

EPHESIANS 1:15–19

For this reason, ever since I heard of your faith in the Lord Jesus and your love for all of God's people, ¹⁶I have not stopped giving thanks to God for you. I remember you in my prayers ¹⁷and ask the God of our Lord Jesus Christ, the glorious Father, to give you the Spirit, who will make you wise and reveal God to you, so that you will know him. ¹⁸I ask that your minds may be opened to see his light, so that you will know what is the hope to which he has called you, how rich are the wonderful blessings he promises his people, ¹⁹and how very great is his power at work in us who believe. This power working in us is the same as the mighty strength

From the context of 1:15–2:10 it appears that these verses form the next major section of Ephesians. The apostle has just finished recalling the spiritual blessings that God, through Christ, has bestowed upon all believers. From this rather universal truth, he turns to something more specific: His thoughts move from doxology to prayer; he reminds his readers that he thanks God for them (vv. 15, 16) and that he prays specifically that they will have the necessary wisdom to understand these blessings in Christ (vv. 17–19).

When the apostle begins talking about Christ, however, he seems to abandon the form of prayer and move into an exposition of God's power as manifested in Christ's resurrection, exaltation, and headship over the church (1:20–23) and as manifested in the new life that he gives to the believer in Christ (2:1–10). In some ways, it is possible to regard 1:20–3:13 as a long doctrinal parenthesis in which the apostle develops his ideas on the unity of Jew and Gentile in the church (2:11, 12) and expounds upon his personal role as a messenger of the Good News (3:1–13). In 3:14–31 he returns to the form of prayer found in 1:15.

1:15 / **For this reason** may refer to all that has been said in 1:3–14 about the blessings of God. But the apostle may have something more specific in mind, because he immediately mentions the faith and love of the readers. No doubt his thoughts and prayers go back to the fact that they, as Gentiles, heard the Good News and became God's people (1:13, 14).

The statement **ever since I heard of your faith in the Lord Jesus** speaks strongly against Ephesus as the destination of the letter, for it is unlikely that Paul would have been so vague and impersonal with people to whom he had ministered for three years (Acts 20:31). This is more what one would expect with Colossians; he does not know that congregation personally and only hears about the church through Epaphras' report (Col. 1:4, 7, 9). But it is remotely possible that he could be referring to a recent report—perhaps from someone like Epaphras—on the progress of their faith. All that he has heard is that God's people who are faithful (1:1) have their faith grounded **in the Lord Jesus**. Faith is given practical expression through their **love for all God's people** (cf. Col. 1:4); or to state it another way, love toward God's people is an outgrowth of their faith in Christ. Love, faith, and hope (1:12, 18) appear in Ephesians and in the Pauline epistles as basic Christian graces (cf. Col. 1:5).

1:16 / The report that the apostle has heard drives him to a prayer of thanksgiving for his readers (**I have not stopped giving thanks to God for you. I remember you in my prayers**). The combination of prayer and thanksgiving, as well as constancy in prayer, are characteristic of Paul (Rom. 1:8-10; Phil. 1:3, 4; 4:6; Eph. 5:19, 20; Col. 1:3; 3:15-17; 4:2; 1 Thess. 1:2; 5:18). In this prayer one notes that the petitions become more specific and relate to a deeper understanding and appropriation of the blessings that the readers already possess by virtue of being in Christ.

1:17 / Prayer is made to **the God of our Lord Jesus Christ, the glorious Father**. Basically, this is a variation of the title of God in 1:3. Christ not only addresses God as his "Father" (Matt. 27:46; Luke 10:21; John 17:1 ff.; 20:17) but reveals him as such (John 14-17). Here that revelation is expanded by the phrase **the glorious Father**. This concept of God received considerable attention in the opening eulogy (1:6, 12, 14) and beyond this verse is mentioned again in 1:18; 3:14, 16, 21. God not only is the Father of glory, "but he is the Father to whom all glory belongs." The glory of God is the full revelation of his attributes, including his majesty and power.

The first request in this prayer is that God will give believers **the Spirit** (lit., "that he may give you a spirit of wisdom and revelation in the knowledge of him [God]"). From the Greek, there is no way of knowing that the Holy Spirit is meant by "spirit" (*pneuma*). Normally, when "the Spirit" is intended, it is preceded by the article *the*. Without the article some manifestation or gift of the Spirit must be intended, such as the spirit of holiness (Rom. 1:4), gentleness (1 Cor. 4:21; Gal. 6:1), truth (John 14:17), or faith (2 Cor. 4:13), for example (Wescott, p. 24). This accounts for the RSV reading of "spirit" with a small *s*.

The readers already have received and been sealed in the Holy Spirit at the time of their baptism. This prayer, therefore, is not for the Holy Spirit itself, but for a "spirit of wisdom and revelation," which is a special gift, manifestation, or application of the Holy Spirit. This giving of the Spirit will make the readers **wise** with respect to their understanding (*epignōsis*) of God. *Epignōsis*, as contrasted to *gnōsis*, which normally has a broad application, is "knowledge" limited to religious and moral things, hence directed toward God or the ways of God in some manner. The following verses will reveal the spiritual direction of this request and how it is illustrated and developed. To know God is to "see his light" (1:18a); enlightenment leads to an understanding of the hope of God's call (1:18b), God's blessing (inheritance, 1:18c), and God's power (1:19), as demonstrated in Christ's resurrection (1:20) and exaltation (1:21–23).

1:18 / **I ask** should not be taken as a second request but as a continuation of the prayer that began in 1:17 (the Greek does not repeat the purpose clause): Enlightenment is the result of knowing God and his will more perfectly. Light and knowledge often are linked together in Scripture. Psalm 119:18, for example, is a form of a petition in which the author asks, "Open my eyes to behold the wondrous things in thy law." In the NT, human beings are often depicted as living in darkness and needing the light of Christ or the light of the gospel to change their lives (cf. John 1:9; Acts 26:18; Eph. 5:8; 1 Pet. 2:9; 1 John 1:7; 2:8 ff.).

This illumination takes place—literally—in "the eyes of your heart" (RSV, NIV). In biblical language, the "heart" is a comprehensive term used for the entire inward self or personality of an individual, including intellect, will, and emotions (Matt. 5:8; Rom. 10:8–10). Unfortunately, the GNB **minds** departs from the text at this point. Being enlightened by the light of God's truth affects one's *entire* inward being.

One of the problems in the interpretation of this verse is the meaning of "enlightenment." In the Greek, *pephōtismenous* is a perfect passive participle that denotes completed action, a present state that has resulted from past action. The tense of the verb here prohibits taking "enlightenment" in a progressive sense—that is, as becoming more and more enlightened. Such an observation leads to an obvious question: When has God acted upon the believer in such a way?

In the NT, the verb *phōtizein* ("to give light," "to illuminate") and the noun *phōtismos* ("enlightenment," "illumination") are used to express the results of spiritual encounter. Christ, for example, is the "real light, the light that comes into the world and shines on all men" (John 1:9). Second Corinthians 4:4 speaks of "the light that comes from the Good News about the glory of Christ," and 4:6 says that "God has made [past tense] his light to shine in our hearts, to bring us the light of the knowledge of God's glory shining in the face of Christ." In 2 Timothy 1:10, the Good News is the means of bringing "life and immortality to light" (*phōtisantos*). Illumination, in other words, comes through the reception of the gospel.

On the basis of what has been said previously about the baptismal nature of Ephesians, is it possible that the author is thinking of baptism as the time when the believer was "enlightened"? It certainly is an appropriate term for baptism inasmuch as those who receive the light of God's word are baptized and in their baptism are given the Holy Spirit and its gift of wisdom and understanding (1:17).

Hebrews and 1 Peter provide some interesting insights on this point. In 1 Peter, an epistle that many scholars associate with baptism, the writer speaks of believers as "God's own people" whom God called "from the darkness into his own marvelous light" (2:9; cf. Eph. 5:8 and the disc. of 5:8–14 as a baptismal liturgy). On two occasions, Hebrews uses "enlightenment" in the past tense: In 6:4 it occurs in the context of teaching about "baptism" (cf. 6:2) and leads the author to ask, "For how can those who abandon their faith be brought back to repent again? They were once in God's light [*phōtisthentas*]; they tasted heaven's gift and received their share of the Holy Spirit." In 10:32 he summons his readers to remember the past, "In those days, after God's light had shone on you [*phōtisthentas*], you suffered many things."

Although the NT speaks of enlightenment in ways unconnected with baptism, Hebrews 6:4 and 10:32, 1 Peter 2:9, and Ephesians 5:8–14 provide some textual evidence to indicate that a connection was made and that "enlightenment" in Ephesians 1:18 could refer to baptism. In the second and third centuries, enlightenment definitely became a technical term for this Christian rite.

The prayer for enlightenment leads to a number of specific requests: first, that the readers will know the **hope** to which God has called them. Hope, here, is not some subjective feeling or personal aspiration such as

"I hope that . . . " or "I hope for . . . " (cf. 1:12). Rather, it is an objective element that belongs to the believer. Elsewhere in Scripture, it is a deposit in heaven (Col. 1:5), Christ in the Christian (Col. 1:27), something "set before" the believer (Heb. 6:18), and the second Advent (Titus 2:13). In this context, the author prays that his readers will have wisdom, understanding and enlightenment to know the full meaning of their call from God (cf. 4:4) and the assurance that their life in Christ and sealing with the Holy Spirit brings.

A second request is that they will know the richness of the **blessings** that God has promised to them. One way to understand this phrase is to see it as a clarification of the **hope** to which God has called his people—that is, that **hope** consists of all the **blessings** (lit., "the inheritance") that God has granted to the believer (cf. 1:14 and Col. 1:12, which must be in the writer's mind). The Greek, however, indicates that this is *God's inheritance* (*tēs klēronomias autou*) and not something that the saints receive, as in 1:14 and Colossians 1:12. As such, the apostle is thinking of the church as God's people—God's inheritance. The prayer would then be for a deeper understanding of what it means to be God's possession. The focus is upon the "state" of the believers as God's people rather than on the details of the blessings that that inheritance includes.

1:19 / A third request is that believers know about the greatness of God's power within them. After the apostle has mentioned "the hope of God's calling" and "the glory of God's inheritance," he is led to contemplate "the power of God" that makes all that possible. Stylistically, the sentences are very poetic (liturgical language) in nature and in the Greek include such synonyms as **power** (*dynamis*), **working** (*energia*), "might" (*kratos*), and **strength** (*ischus*). By this, he simply wishes to emphasize that nothing is impossible for God. The power of God that is at work in the believer is the same power (**mighty strength**) that is manifested in the resurrection, exaltation, and universal dominion of Christ. The author returns to that power at the end of his prayer in 3:20.

Additional Notes

1:15 / The GNB does not indicate that some Greek manuscripts omit the word **love**. The result of this is the unusual and unprecedented expression that faith is toward (*eis*) God's people. The best explanation is that **love** belonged in the original text but was unintentionally omitted in the process of copying the manuscripts (see B. Metzger, *A Textual Commentary on the Greek New Testament* [New York: United Bible Society, 1971], p. 602; also, the explanation in H. C. G.

Moule, *Ephesians*, p. 56). For comments on **God's people** ("saints"), cf. disc. on 1:1 and Col. 1:1.

1:17 / Wescott provides a helpful summary and explanation of "glory" in his *Ephesians*, pp. 187–89. On "knowledge" and "wisdom," cf. disc. on Col. 1:9, 10, and the extended note on *epignōsis* in J. A. Robinson, pp. 249–54.

1:18 / The baptismal nature of 1 Peter is surveyed in R. P. Martin's "The Composition of I Peter in Recent Study," *Vox Evangelica*, 1 (1962), pp. 29–42. See also J. Coutts, "Ephesians I.3–14 and I Peter I.3–12," *NTS* 3(1956–57), pp. 115–27; F. L. Cross, *I Peter: A Pascal Liturgy* (London: Mowbray, 1954); F. W. Beare, *The First Epistle of Peter*, 3d ed. (Oxford: Blackwell's, 1970). The reference for identifying enlightenment and baptism is in Justin's *Apology* I, 61, 65. Additional discussion is in J. Ysebaret, *Greek Baptismal Terminology*, (Nijmegen: Dekker & Van de Vegt, 1962), pp. 157 ff.

4

The Result of
Christ's Enthronement

which he used when he raised Christ from death and seated him at his right side in the heavenly world. ²¹Christ rules there above all heavenly rulers, authorities, powers, and lords; he has a title superior to all titles of authority in this world and in the next. ²²God put all things under Christ's feet and gave him to the church as supreme Lord over all things. ²³The church is Christ's body, the completion of him who himself completes all things everywhere.ᶜ

c. who himself completes all things everywhere; *or* who is himself completely filled with God's fullness.

1:20 / The writers of the NT show that the early church was convinced that the Jesus of Nazareth, who died by crucifixion, also was raised by the power of God and exalted to a position of authority: "Christ Jesus who died, or rather, who was raised to life and is at the right side of God, pleading with him for us" (Rom. 8:34; cf. also Acts 2:32, 33; 3:15; 4:10; 5:30, 31; 10:40; Rom. 4:24; 8:11; 10:9; 1 Cor. 6:14; 15:15; 2 Cor. 4:14; Gal. 1:1; Col. 2:12; 1 Pet. 1:21). They also believed that he was very much alive in their midst through the Holy Spirit.

Although it is common to think of resurrection and exaltation as two separate events, it is helpful to consider them as two different ways of expressing the same theological truth, namely, the power of God over the forces of death. Paul illustrates God's power by stating that it was manifested when he raised Christ from death and seated him at his right side in the heavenly world (cf. also Acts 2:32, 33; Rom. 8:11; Phil. 2:9; 1 Tim. 3:16). Christ's post-Resurrection appearances should be interpreted as periodic earthly visitations and manifestations of the resurrected and exalted Lord during a period of forty days. What Luke is saying in Acts 1:1–11 is that the ascension marked the end of that kind of appearance; henceforth, Christ will manifest himself through the Holy Spirit.

The phrases **seated him at his right side** and **heavenly world** come from Psalm 110:1 ff.; all the honor, dignity, and authority of the enthroned king are now attributed to Christ. These phrases are not to be interpreted literally but understood as metaphorical language used to express Christ's presence with his Father in the invisible world, the sphere of eternal reality. Later, in 2:1–10, the author will apply these statements to the believer as well. The reality of Christ's resurrection and exaltation becomes a sign and pledge of the triumph of the Christian (cf. Rom. 8:11; 2 Cor. 4:14; 1 Pet. 1:21).

1:21 / Christ's heavenly ascension and authority is expressed by stating that he **rules there above all heavenly rulers, authorities, powers, and lords**. The categories that are used here are similar to the lists in Romans 8:38, 1 Corinthians 15:24, Colossians 1:16; 2:15; and 1 Peter 3:22. Such concepts of "heavenly beings" belonged to the ancient world, were expanded during the intertestamental period in the apocryphal literature, and were employed by some authors of the NT to illustrate the spiritual struggle between the forces of good and evil or light and darkness. The exorcism of demons by Jesus, for example, is seen as a sign of his authority and power over demonic forces (cf. Mark's Gospel and disc. on Col. 1:16).

Part of the message of Colossians is that Christ is superior to all evil powers. In the Christ hymn (1:15–20), Paul affirms Christ's sovereignty by stating that these powers are created by Christ and thus are subject to his authority. Later, he shows that, by virtue of Christ's death on the cross, he has triumphed over them and leads them as a victorious captor (2:15). As a result of Christ's supremacy and victory, these evil forces are reduced to a state of impotence and inferiority; they no longer exert any power or influence over the believer who has identified himself with Christ.

Ephesians does not appear to direct any polemic against a false system that was elevating the importance of these spiritual powers. Although some interpreters have argued for a Gnostic background to the epistle (see Introduction), it certainly is not as obvious as it is for Colossians. The closest the author comes is to indicate that the Christian's spiritual battle is "against the wicked spiritual forces in the heavenly world, the rulers, authorities, and cosmic powers of this dark age" (6:12).

In 1:21, these powers are mentioned only in the context of Christ's exaltation. In fact, the verse states that **he has a title superior to all titles of authority** (lit., "above every name that is being named"; cf. Phil. 2:9). Furthermore, this supremacy is so expansive or all-encompassing that it spans both the present and future ages. J. A. Robinson puts these great thoughts together very succinctly when he writes: "Above all that anywhere is, anywhere can be—above all grades of dignity, real or imagined, good or evil, present or to come—the mighty power of God has exalted and enthroned the Christ" (p. 41).

1:22 / The apostle presses on with thoughts of Christ's supremacy, using images characteristic of a royal court where the defeated foes pay homage to their victor: **God put all things under Christ's feet**. This appears to be an obvious quotation from Psalm 110:1 and, as applied to Christ, illustrates his conquest of all spiritual enemies and his authority over them.

Sometimes the readers of the NT find it difficult to interpret and apply such a principle as Christ's sovereignty because it uses ancient cosmological concepts and is stated in mythic and poetic language unfamiliar to modern people. The tendency is either to dismiss such language as irrelevant and nonsensical or to demythologize it.

M. Barth has made an attempt to understand the apostle's thoughts by probing into the history, essence, and function of these spiritual powers. From his study, he concludes that "Paul means by principalities and powers those institutions and structures by which earthly matters and invisible realms are administered, and without which no human life is possible" (*Eph. 1–3*, p. 174). Barth includes such categories as kings, procurators, senators, judges, high priests, and so forth who function in political, financial, juridical, and ecclesiastical offices. C. L. Mitton carries this even further and wonders about substituting for principalities and powers such "evil powers in our contemporary world as racism, nationalism, hate, fear, uncurbed sexual desire, drug addiction, alcoholism, etc. As with 'principalities and powers,' before these the individual feels helpless even though he recognizes their power to destroy the best things in human life" (p. 72).

1:23 / From the ideal of sovereignty the apostle moves to the concept of vital union, which he expresses by the head-body metaphor: **The church is Christ's body**. This idea is unique to the teaching of Ephesians (1:23; 5:23) and Colossians (1:18, 24; 2:19) and goes beyond Paul's idea on the church in Romans and Corinthians, where "head" is mentioned along with other members of the body (1 Cor. 12:14–26). Christ is not a part of the body, such as the head or the foot, but rather the whole of which the various members are parts (1 Cor. 12:12). In Romans and Corinthians, Christ equals the body; but in Ephesians and Colossians, the church equals the body, and Christ is the head.

In Colossians, the head-body metaphor was used to combat some heretical ideas that limited Christ's unique position of authority in the universe and in the church. Paul's concern there is to restore Christ to his rightful place of pre-eminence in all things—including his headship over the church (cf. disc. on Col. 1:18). In Ephesians, there is no direct polemic against false teachers. The idea of Christ's headship over the church is introduced to illustrate another dimension of Christ's exaltation.

In some ways, Christ's lordship over the church is similar to his lordship over all things. As Lord, he rules, guides, inspires. However, Christ's lordship over the church is of a different nature, because the church is his body and he is its head. As such, it is in vital union with Christ; it belongs to him and derives its meaning in union with him; it is **the completion of him who himself completes all things everywhere**. Thus, in some mysterious way, the church is necessary to Christ's completeness and he imparts to it his fullness.

This last phrase makes two important assertions: First, Christ **completes all things everywhere**. Up to this point in the text the author has indicated that God has put "all things under Christ's feet" and made him Lord over all things, including the church. Now he enlarges on this by indicating that Christ **completes all things everywhere**, literally, "all (things) in all (things)"! Perhaps these ideas are an expansion of 1:10, which states that it is God's plan "to bring all creation together, everything in heaven and on earth, with Christ as head." Does he envision that this is being done through the church (cf. 3:10)?

The concept of Christ's fullness or completion is brought out several times in Colossians, where it is stated that the full nature of God dwells in the Son (1:19; 2:9). The believer, in turn, comes to "fullness of life" through union with Christ in baptism. Ephesians presents the same thought on two different occasions: The apostle prays that his readers may "be completely filled with the very nature of God" (3:19) and exhorts them to reach "to the very height of Christ's full stature," literally, "to the stature of the fullness of Christ" (4:13).

The second assertion talks about **the completion of him** (Christ). Scholars have struggled over this very difficult theological concept (*plērōma*) and grammatical construction. Literally translated, the phrase reads, "the fullness of him who fills all in all." The GNB translation takes a position that in some way understands the church as "completing" or "filling up" Christ. Since "head" and "body" form an organic unity, it is possible to think of a relationship in which Christ not only completes the church but in which the church completes Christ as well. This completion should be seen in relation to Christ's function as the Lord over the church and not with respect to his divine nature. Christ is complete in himself as the divine Son of God, so the church has nothing more to add. But the church is Christ's body, and as such it is Christ's agent, the instrument through whom he works in the world. By fulfilling its function as the church it complements or completes the Christ to whom it is organically united. It functions as hands and feet for its exalted Lord. This thought is not unlike Colossians 1:24 where, by virtue of Paul's mystical union with Christ, he believes that his suffering for the church "fills up" or "completes" Christ's personal suffering.

Additional Notes

1:20 / A good discussion of Christ's post-Resurrection appearances in relation to the ascension can be found in F. F. Bruce, *The Book of Acts* (Grand Rapids: Eerdmans, 1979), pp. 30 ff.

1:21-22 / The many books and articles dealing with such concepts as principalities, powers, etc. in the NT is an indication of the difficulty there is in understanding them. Some helpful resources include G. B. Caird, *Principalities and Powers: A Study in Pauline Theology* (Oxford: Clarendon, 1956); W. Carr, *Angels and Principalities: The Background, Meaning and Development of the Pauline Phrase "hai archai kai hai exousiai"*, SNTSMS, vol. 42 (Cambridge: Cambridge University Press, 1981), esp. pp. 47–85 on Colossians and pp. 93–111 on Ephesians; G. H. C. MacGregor, "Principalities and Powers: The Cosmic Background of Paul's Thought," *NTS* 1 (1954), pp. 17–28; R. Yates, "The Powers of Evil in the New Testament," *EQ* 52–53 (1980–81), pp. 97–111; R. Yates, "Principalities and Powers in Ephesians," *New Blackfriar* 58 (1977), pp. 516–21; J. Y. Lee, "Interpreting the Demonic Powers in Pauline Thought," *NovT* 12 (1970), pp. 54–69.

P. T. O'Brien has written a very helpful article entitled "Principalities and Powers and Their Relationship to Structures," *RefThR* 40 (1981), pp. 1–10, in which he reviews a number of scholars (namely, Barth, Berkhof, Caird, Rupp, Sider, Yoder) who interpret principalities and powers as sociopolitical structures, tradition, law, authority, religion, etc. For additional disc. on this topic in Ephesians, see disc. and notes on 3:10 and 6:12.

1:23 / Cf. disc. and notes on Col. 1:18; also, G. Howard, "The Head/Body Metaphors of Ephesians," *NTS* 20 (1974), pp. 350–56. Some good information on *plērōma* and the technicalities of this verse can be found in the commentaries of Barth (*Eph. 1–3*), pp. 200–10; Mitton, pp. 76–79; Robinson, pp. 42–45, 87–89; Stott, *God's New Society*, pp. 62–65. More specialized studies include P. Benoit, "Body, Head and *Plērōma* in the Epistles of the Captivity," *RB* 63 (1956), pp. 5–44; A. R. McGlashan, "Ephesians 1:23," *ExpT* 76 (1965), pp. 132–33. This last article led to a reply from R. Fowler, "Ephesians 1:23," *ExpT* 76 (1965), p. 294. R. Yates provides a more thorough examination of the problem in his "A Re-examination of Ephesians 1:23," *ExpT* 83 (1972), pp. 146–51. Yates's conclusions produce the following translation (p. 154): "And he (God) has brought all things into subjection under his (Christ's) feet, and he (God) gave him (Christ) to be head over all things to the Church, which is his Body, the fulness (that which completes) of him (Christ) who all in all (completely) is being fulfilled (i.e., made complete as men and women are being reconciled to God through Christ's work and incorporated into him through his Body, the Church)."

5

Christ and the Salvation
of Believers

Chapter 1 of Ephesians is dominated by the theme of praise and thanksgiving. In verses 3–14 the apostle utilizes a redemptive eulogy to praise God for all the spiritual blessings that he has bestowed upon the believer. These blessings are mediated through the Son and are confirmed in the believer through the inner witness of the Holy Spirit. The use of baptismal themes suggests that the hymn may have been connected with the celebration of baptism in the early church.

From doxology, he turns to a prayer in which he expresses the wish that his readers personally understand and appropriate the blessings that he has just enumerated. Consequently, there are many verbal and doctrinal similarities between these two sections. In the prayer, the apostle asks that the believers be granted an increasing knowledge of the hope to which God has called them (1:18a) and the richness of God's blessing to them (1:18b) and that they will see God's power as manifested in Christ's resurrection, exaltation, and headship over all things, including the church (1:19–23).

The context makes it apparent that the mention of Christ's resurrection and exaltation provides the background for the thoughts that he develops in 2:1–10 and in 2:11–22. The apostle wants to demonstrate that the mighty power of God that was at work in Christ is also at work in the believer; what is true of Christ is also true for each believer in Christ. Unfortunately, this flow of thought is broken by the division of the text into chapters and verses. The Greek text permits one to appreciate the hymnic (liturgical) nature of this section because verses 1–7 form one sentence and the first main verb does not occur until verse 5 (**he brought us to life**).

In chapter 2, the apostle develops two specific themes that he has already mentioned: In 2:1–10, he picks up redemption and forgiveness

(1:7) and applies it to the reconciliation of sinful mankind by God; in 2:11–22, he applies the principle of unity from 1:10 to the specific case of Jews and Gentiles and shows how they have been brought together into one body.

Chapter 2:1–10 contains a number of contrasting features: First, there are the people who are mentioned. The author begins by referring to the Gentiles specifically (2:1), but then in 2:3 he expands his audience to include the Jews as well. By this, he shows that all of humanity was alienated from God and became recipients of his grace (2:3–7). And even though he returns to "you" (second person plural) in 2:8, one gets the impression that he still has both groups in mind until he addresses the Gentiles directly in 2:11.

Second, there is the contrast between their former pagan way of life (2:1–3) and their new life in Christ (2:4–10). At one time they were spiritually dead, and because of their sinful nature, they lived sinful lives, walked in the evil ways of the world, and disobeyed God; but now, as a result of God's grace and mercy upon their lives, they have been made spiritually alive and share in Christ's resurrection and exaltation. Their new creation is a manifestation of "good deeds" (2:10) rather than a life of disobedience and evil.

Third, these two ways of life reflect the contrasting forces that confront mankind: On the one side, there is the world ("the world's evil way"), Satan ("the ruler of the spiritual powers in space, the spirit who now controls the people who disobey God"), and the flesh ("our natural desires"); offsetting these are God's mercy, love, and grace, which make life, resurrection, and enthronement with Christ possible.

6

Salvation from Spiritual Death

In the past you were spiritually dead because of your disobedience and sins. ²At that time you followed the world's evil way; you obeyed the ruler of the spiritual powers in space, the spirit who now controls the people who disobey God.

³Actually all of us were like them and lived according to our natural desires, doing whatever suited the wishes of our own bodies and minds. In our natural condition we, like everyone else, were destined to suffer God's anger.

2:1 / The main contrast that the apostle makes in this section is between "death" and "life." He begins by reminding his readers of their past condition and then proceeds to describe the causes and effects of their spiritual death. One has to wait until verse 5 to pick up the contrasting idea of life ("**he brought us to life in Christ**") and the features that characterize existence in Christ.

Those who live without Christ are described as being **spiritually dead**. In such a condition there is no desire to relate one's life to God, because such a life is characterized by disobedience (lit., "trespasses," *paraptōma*, and "sins," *hamartia*). Many attempts have been made to distinguish these two terms and to define trespass as "false step," "deviation from a prescribed path," and so on and sin as "missing the mark" or "falling short of a standard." However, the usage of these terms in the NT varies and does not permit refined distinctions. In this context it is better to take them as all-encompassing phrases that describe the lives of those who are spiritually dead.

2:2 / In the past (**at that time**), that is, before they became Christians, these Gentiles **followed the world's evil way**. The word used in Greek is "walked" (*peripateō*) and as such expresses one's way of life or manner of moral conduct. The Gospels talk about an open gate and a "way" that leads to life or another that leads to death (Matt. 7:13, 14). Jesus is designated as "the way" (John 14:6), and those who are his disciples are described as followers of "the Way of the Lord" (Acts 9:2; 18:25, 26).

This "walk" or "way of life" is described by the following statements: First, it is **the world's evil way**. In other words, it is a pattern of life characterized by the world, which, in this context, means what is contrary to and apart from God. The First Letter of John 2:15–17 provides a good commentary on this concept by defining "world" as "what the sinful self desires," the things "people see and want," and "are so proud of." Paul admonishes believers not to "conform yourselves to the standards of this world, but let God transform you inwardly by a complete change of your mind" (Rom. 12:2).

Second, it is obedience to **the ruler of the spiritual powers in space**. The apostle already has spoken about Christ's exaltation over such spiritual powers (1:21), and he will go on to indicate that believers, likewise, are engaged in a vicious struggle against demonic forces (6:11, 12). Before one becomes a Christian, however, one virtually gives spiritual allegiance to these evil forces, particularly to the **ruler**, who is envisioned as Satan, or the Devil (6:11). That ruler is defined further as **the spirit who now controls the people who disobey God**. The apostle envisioned that people in their pre-Christian state obeyed Satan and were under the controlling power of evil spirits that led to their disobedience of God (cf. Luke 11:14–26; John 13:2; Acts 5:3; 2 Thess. 2:9).

2:3 / This dreadful condition of life also applied to Paul and his fellow believers before they became Christians. What was true of the Gentiles was true of all humanity, for "all men have sinned and are far away from God's saving presence" (Rom. 3:23): **All of us were like them**. To live as the Gentiles is to live according to one's **natural desires**. This does not appear to be a reference to the doctrine of original sin as taught elsewhere in Scripture (Rom. 1–3; 5:12–14). The phrase is more suggestive of a pattern of life that emerges when one is left to follow one's natural desires.

In such a condition, people do whatever suits the wishes of their **bodies and minds**. Literally, the phrase is "lusts of the flesh" (*sarx*). The word *sarx* does not imply that the body as such is evil but refers rather to the sinful principles, passions, or physical appetites that dominate one's life (Gal. 5:19–21). **Mind** includes one's intellectual and reasoning ability (cf. Col. 1:21). The consequence of such evil and ungodly action is **to suffer God's anger**. In other words, by following their natural desires, people became subject to the dreadful judgment of God ("we were by nature children of wrath," RSV).

Additional Note

2:1 / On spiritual death, see E. Best, "Dead in Trespasses and Sins (Eph. 2.1)," *JSNT* 13 (1981), pp. 9–25.

7

Salvation to Spiritual Life

EPHESIANS 2:4–10

But God's mercy is so abundant, and his love for us is so great, ⁵that while we were spiritually dead in our disobedience he brought us to life with Christ. It is by God's grace that you have been saved. ⁶In our union with Christ Jesus he raised us up with him to rule with him in the heavenly world. ⁷He did this to demonstrate for all time to come the extraordinary greatness of his grace in the love he showed us in Christ Jesus. ⁸⁻⁹For it is by God's grace that you have been saved through faith. It is not the result of your own efforts, but God's gift, so that no one can boast about it. ¹⁰God has made us what we are, and in our union with Christ Jesus he has created us for a life of good deeds, which he has already prepared for us to do.

2:4–5 / From the perversity of humanity as disobedient sinners deserving God's wrath, the apostle turns, in sharp contrast, to the mercy and love of God. God's mercy proceeds from his love and is his way of reaching out to those who are totally undeserving. **We were**, he claims, **spiritually dead in our disobedience**. However, the good news of the gospel is that God has acted decisively in Christ to correct that situation. And finally, in 2:5, one finds the verb that has kept the reader in suspense since the beginning of 2:1: Those who were spiritually dead (2:1) have become the recipients of God's mercy and love in that **he brought us to life with Christ**.

This action of God is the first of three experiences that the believer has in union with Christ. Literally, it reads that God's love and mercy has "made us alive together with Christ" (*synezōpoiēsen*), in order to stress the intimate union that the believer has with the Lord. All three verbs—"brought us to life," "raised us up," and "to rule with him"—are compound verbs prefixed with the Greek preposition *syn*, which means "together with." These terms are used to express the fact that the believer shares these experiences with Christ and thus with all those who are in the body of Christ. As believers die, are crucified or buried with Christ (Rom. 6:4, 6, 8; Gal. 2:20; Phil. 3:10; Col. 2:12), they also are made alive (Eph. 2:5), raised (Rom. 6:4; Eph. 2:6; Col. 2:12) and enthroned (Eph. 2:6; Col. 3:1).

There is no significant theological distinction between being "made alive" and "raised" with Christ. Both terms are a vivid contrast to the state of spiritual death that was mentioned earlier. In the Greek text (cf. RSV, NIV) the phrase **it is by God's grace that you have been saved** appears as a parenthesis and receives no further explanation until 2:8. Grace is God's unmerited favor to humanity, and reference to it here is a sharp reminder that the change from death to life is due entirely to God's initiative and not human action. "Saved," apparently, is equivalent to being brought to life with Christ. It appears in the perfect passive form as "you have been saved" (*sesōismenoi*)—the tense in Greek that describes a present state that has resulted from a past action. Salvation, therefore, is an accomplished fact (*fait accompli*), and its effects are continuous upon the believer.

2:6 / In addition to life and resurrection, the believer also is exalted (*synekathisen*) with Christ **to rule with him in the heavenly world**. Earlier, the apostle had talked about the believer's blessings "in the heavenly world" (1:3); then he mentioned Christ's exaltation in the "heavenly world" (1:20); and now the believer, by virtue of his union with Christ, is likewise enthroned in the invisible world of spiritual reality where Christ reigns supreme. The thought is similar to that expressed in Colossians 3:1, where believers are exhorted to set their mind on heavenly things because they have been raised to new life with Christ.

This teaching of the believer's participation in Christ is very similar to the thoughts that occur in the baptismal texts of Romans 6:1–11 and Colossians 2:11–13 and 3:1–4. Ephesians, however, makes no mention of the believer's death or burial with Christ in the way in which it is presented in Romans or Colossians. The death of which Ephesians speaks is not the mystical participation in Christ's death but the natural state of mankind as being dead in trespasses and sins. But even though the reference is to people who are "spiritually dead," it is through union with Christ that they have been made alive.

On the basis of the baptismal nature and teaching of Romans and Colossians, it is not unreasonable to assume that the author of Ephesians has the baptismal event in mind when he speaks of the Christian's participation in Christ. Although he does not explicitly mention the rite, his readers would recognize that the language of life, resurrection, and exaltation with Christ alluded to baptism. The new feature in Ephesians is that it places the believer in the heavenlies along with his exalted Lord. By doing this, the author shows that the fullness of life "in Christ" includes all that has occurred to Christ himself, including enthronement (1:20). As such, believers already share in Christ's heavenly **rule** (GNB).

The idea of enthronement or exaltation with Christ is difficult to grasp because there is a tendency among believers to think of this as something to be realized in the future—that is, at the end of this present age. Jesus, for example, tells his disciples this: "When the Son of Man sits on his glorious throne in the New Age, then you twelve followers of mine will also sit on thrones, to judge the twelve tribes of Israel" (Matt. 19:28; Luke 22:30). And some of the apocalyptic imagery in the NT speaks of a future time when the saints will be resurrected and reign with the Lord (1 Cor. 15:51–54; 1 Thess. 4:17; 2 Tim. 2:12; Rev. 3:21; 20:4; 22:5).

C. L. Mitton has noted in his commentary that some scholars go to great lengths to give a future meaning to the verbs in 2:5 and 6 even though they are in the past tense. They propose that the believer's resurrection can be referred to in the past tense because the future resurrection has already been guaranteed; or, the future state of believers with Christ is so secure that they already have a place in heaven assigned to them (pp. 89–90). These arguments have a certain kinship with the "prophetic future" wherein a coming event is so certain of being fulfilled that it is described as already having taken place.

Such interpretations, however, do not do justice to the thoughts in Ephesians, where the resurrection and exaltation of the believer are described as events that *have taken place* in union with Christ. In a number of cases, such views reflect attempts to make the eschatology of Ephesians—and Colossians—conform to the same pattern that is developed in the undisputed Pauline epistles.

One of the most significant aspects of Paul's understanding of eschatology is that he conceived of the eschatological process as having begun in the life, death, and resurrection of Christ. For him, these events represented God's breaking into the world and inaugurating his reign on earth. In Christ, therefore, the eschatological promises were already in the process of being fulfilled.

The fact that there is an "inauguration" of the eschatological process does not, however, eliminate the futuristic element. Paul retains the conviction that the eschatological process now begun is moving forward toward a final day of consummation. This has a significant bearing upon Paul's theology because it places the individual in tension between the two aeons—the one begun with the coming of Christ and the one yet to come at his Parousia. The Christian occupies a position between the times because the Kingdom has come and is yet to come. One could characterize this position as the "now" and the "not yet" of Christian existence—one of the great paradoxes of the Christian faith.

Various phases of this paradox are brought out in the Pauline letters. Christ has come (1 Cor. 15:3 ff.), yet he will come again (1 Thess. 4:16); the Christian has died to sin (Rom. 6:6), yet he or she is still in the flesh (1 Cor. 3:3); believers are citizens of heaven (Phil. 3:20a), yet eagerly await the Savior to come from heaven (Phil. 3:20b); Christians are new be-ings—a new creation (2 Cor. 5:17)—yet are to become new people at every moment of their lives (Rom. 12:1–2); believers have the first fruits of the Spirit (Rom. 8:23a), yet groan within themselves as they "wait for God to make us his sons and set our whole being free" (Rom. 8:23b); here believers receive all of Christ's abundant wealth (Phil. 4:19), yet there is a glory to be revealed (Rom. 8:18).

To a certain extent, Ephesians and Colossians retain a belief in the Parousia as the hope of God's people. In Colossians, the Christian has died with Christ (3:3a), but this new life is hidden with Christ in God, that is, its fullness will be revealed at the Parousia (3:3b); believers are resurrected with Christ (2:12; 3:1) but are, nevertheless, admonished to set their hearts on the things that are in heaven, where Christ "sits on the throne at the right side of God" (3:1). In Ephesians, the baptized who possess the Spirit do so as a first installment, a guarantee of a future inheritance (4:30). The church has been redeemed but still awaits its final glorification (5:27); the believer has been delivered from evil powers (2:1-3) but finds it necessary to be armed against principalities, powers, and so forth (6:12).

Even in Colossians and Ephesians mankind stands between the times—between promise and fulfillment. In one sense, the new "life" in Christ can be regarded as complete as "death" in Christ. Yet because it is in the world that human beings exist, Ephesians, as well as Romans and Colossians, lays great stress upon one's ethical life. Those baptized into Christ are "to walk in newness of life" (Rom. 6:4) or are admonished to "set" and to "keep" their minds on things that are in heaven (Col. 3:1–2). In Ephesians, the author is no less explicit about the Christian's walk. Those who are baptized into Christ are created for "a life of good deeds" (2:10) and are exhorted to "live a life that measures up to the standard God set when he called you" (4:1).

2:7 / When the apostle spoke about the resurrection and exaltation of Christ, he indicated that this was a demonstration of God's **power** (1:19, 20). But he speaks of the believer's resurrection and exaltation with

Christ as a demonstration of God's **grace** (**he did this to demonstrate . . . the extraordinary greatness of his grace in the love** (lit., "kindness") **he showed us in Christ Jesus**).

God already has demonstrated this grace in the present by blessing the believer so richly in Christ. To this, one naturally responds with comments such as "how wonderful," "how marvelous." This, however, is just a foretaste of the ongoing activity of God's grace **for all time to come**. The reference here is not to the "coming age." The word for "age" (*aiōn*) appears in the plural and should be translated as in the GNB or in a way that will convey the idea that all future generations beyond the present one will experience the extraordinary greatness of his grace as he manifests himself through the church (3:10).

2:8-9 / These verses often have been called the heart of Paul's gospel because they capture and summarize the essence of some of the great thoughts that he develops in such epistles as Romans and Galatians. In this context, grace and faith are mentioned as the key elements in the believer's union with Christ. The apostle dispels any idea that their change in status from spiritual death to life and exaltation with Christ is due to any human effort. Further, he concludes by stating that salvation is a call to a life of good works.

Grace can be defined as favor, graciousness, goodwill, and so on. When it is applied to God, it signifies that action of God by which he moved graciously upon undeserving humanity. The essence of grace is that it is God's (**for it is by God's grace**) and that it is free; otherwise, it would not be grace.

With respect to salvation, God always is the source of grace. When Scripture speaks about the "grace of our Lord Jesus Christ," it does so to indicate that Christ is the agent of God's grace—that is, he is the means by which God's grace is made known to humanity. Although the agency of Christ is not mentioned here, it definitely is affirmed in the preceding verses, where the parenthetical reference to God's grace (2:5) comes in the context of discussion about life in Christ.

Grace and faith are listed as the two essential elements in the salvation of mankind. Basically, faith is the means by which God's grace for salvation is appropriated. One popular way of discussing the nature of faith is to develop, in the form of an acrostic, the letters that spell out the word: *F*orsaking—*A*ll—*I*—*T*ake—*H*im! One side of faith is *passive*: it is "forsaking all." As such, it implies surrender before God, a willingness on the part of an individual to be open and receptive to God's grace. This, in a sense, also is a gift from God, because one's natural tendency is to be closed and unreceptive to God.

The other side of faith is *active*: "Forsaking all," *I take him*. Those who are willing to receive God's grace must respond personally in order to appropriate it. Faith is personal trust and confidence in God and the reception of the message of salvation that is offered in the Good News. In the NT, Christians are described as believers—that is, as those who have faith (*hoi pisteuontes*, Rom. 1:16; 3:22; 4:11; 1 Cor. 1:21) because they turned to God in faith (*pisteuein*, 1 Cor. 15:2, 11). Faith includes a willingness to surrender as well as a commitment to obey (cf. 2:10).

For it is by God's grace that you have been saved through faith. As in 2:5, the word for "salvation" occurs in the Greek perfect passive tense, thus reaffirming to the readers that their present and continuing state of salvation is the result of some action in the past when God's grace and their faith came together—undoubtedly when they were baptized into Christ as believers. In the framework of the NT, believers' baptism is a personal response to the proclamation of the gospel (Acts 2:38, 41, etc.).

Some commentators question this occurrence of "salvation" because Paul normally uses the word in the future tense as "you are being saved" (see Mitton, p. 94). Others wonder about the absence of such great Pauline themes as justification and reconciliation. However, believers need to recognize that the NT uses a number of different words and concepts when it talks about salvation or the process whereby one becomes a Christian. When, for example, one wants to know how to receive salvation, Scripture states that salvation is through *faith* (Mark 16:16; Acts 16:30, 31; Rom. 5:1; Eph. 2:8, 9), *repentance* (2 Cor. 7:10; 2 Pet. 3:9), *confession* (Acts 22:16; Rom. 10:9), *regeneration* (Titus 3:5), and *baptism* (Acts 22:16; 1 Cor. 6:11; 1 Pet. 3:21).

2:9 / Since grace, and to some extent faith, are gifts of God, the readers are reminded that their salvation is not due to human effort and cannot, therefore, lead to spiritual pride. The principle of grace prohibits boasting (Rom. 3:27). The GNB reading does a good job of clearing up the ambiguity in some translations with respect to the word "this" (*touto*). Because "this" (**it** in GNB) follows immediately after **faith** ("you have been saved through faith, and this is not your own doing, it is the gift of God," RSV, NIV), many have taken **it** to refer to **faith**, thus emphasizing faith as a gift. But even though the idea is true theologically, the Greek sentence does not permit such an identification, because the two words differ grammatically.

The apostle has more than the gift of faith in mind, for **it** refers to the entire process of salvation of which faith is but a part. And since salvation is all God's doing, mankind cannot work for it or boast about it. **Your own efforts**—literally, "not out of works"—is not the "works of the Law" to which Paul referred when he wrote to the Romans (3:20) and to the Galatians (3:10). To these Gentile readers, works would be any human efforts directed toward obtaining salvation. If successful, such efforts would lead only to boasting and self-aggrandizement.

2:10 / This verse continues to emphasize God's activity and neatly sums up some of the great thoughts that have been developed earlier in the epistle. First, **God has made us what we are** (lit., "we are his creation" or "workmanship," *poiēma*, as in RSV, NIV). This idea echoes the entire aspect of rebirth or re-creation that took place **in our union with Christ Jesus** (2:4–6; cf. 2 Cor. 5:17, where Paul writes that "when anyone is joined to Christ he is a new being"). All of this is God's doing and eliminates any sense of pride that would come if this were a "self-creation."

Second, God **has created us for a life of good deeds** (cf. 1:4, 6, 12, 14, 15). The whole context, which emphasizes God's gift of grace and faith, as well as the stress upon being God's creation in Christ, prohibits one from taking "good works" in any meritorious way, even though they are an essential ingredient of one's new life in Christ. The expression means that believers are created with a view *toward* good works; believers are saved *for* or *unto* good works, not *by* or *because of* them. Good works are the outcome, not the cause, of salvation.

The contrast here is between the spiritually dead who once walked (*peripateō*) in disobedience and sin (2:1, 2) and those newly created in Christ to a life (*peripateō*) of good works. Such a life belongs to one's calling as a believer because faith is a call to obedience. And all of this is part of God's will from the beginning. As he chose mankind "to be holy and without fault before him" (1:4), he also determined that faith would issue forth in deeds **which he has already prepared for us to do**.

This verse stands as a vivid reminder that there is more to salvation than just "getting saved." Though faith in Christ is important and is the beginning of the Christian life (the indicative), believers must remember that they are called to **a life** of faith, a life in which faith is demonstrated in **good deeds** (the imperative). James, for example, is one of the writers of the NT who places a strong emphasis upon the relation between faith and works (1:22; 2:14–26). On many occasions Christians are called upon to be examples of good deeds before the world (1 Tim. 6:18; Titus 2:7; 1

Pet. 2:12). Jesus put it very clearly when he said, "Not everyone who calls me 'Lord, Lord,' will enter into the Kingdom of heaven, but only those who do what my Father in heaven wants them to do" (Matt. 7:21). C. L. Mitton concludes his discussion on this verse with an appropriate comment: "This final phrase about our 'walking in them' reminds us that fine phrases or eloquent sermons about love are not what is required, but the actions, costly actions, which express in practical conduct the love which God's saving power has created in our hearts" (p. 99).

Additional Note

2:6 / For further direction on Paul's eschatology, see E. Lohse, *Colossians and Philemon*, pp. 177–83; C. K. Barrett, "Jewish and Pauline Eschatology," *SJT* 6 (1953), pp. 136–55; W. G. Kümmel, *Promise and Fulfillment* (London: SCM, 1957).

8

Christ and the Unity
of Believers

In 2:1–10, the apostle is addressing Jewish and Gentile believers. He begins by showing that both groups of people were living in disobedience and sin; both stood in need of God's mercy and love. The Good News in the passage is that a loving and gracious God acted to correct that through his Son. In union with Christ, believers become a new creation and are resurrected and exalted with their Lord. As such, they are lifted out of their former evil condition and made to share in Christ's victory over sin and live a life of good works.

Up to this point the emphasis is on the privileges that Jewish and Gentile believers enjoy in Christ. In 2:11–22, however, the author moves from their unity in Christ to discuss their unity in the church. In this passage he shows that the church no longer is to be perceived as a body of Jewish and Gentile believers; rather, it is a completely new creation ("one new people") in which all racial barriers and prejudices are obliterated. For the apostle, the church is a vivid example of how God is working out his plan to unite (1:10) and to complete (1:23) all things in Christ.

In some ways, this concept of a "new people" is a development of thoughts about the new creation in Christ that Paul has expressed in his epistles. In 2 Corinthians 5:16 ff., he refers to the process of reconciliation and how *all* humanity is reconciled to God as new beings; in Galatians 6:15 he indicates that racial distinctions are insignificant to the real issue of being a new creation ("it does not matter at all whether or not one is circumcised; what does matter is being a new creature"). The new thought in Ephesians is that these "new beings" in Christ now constitute a single new humanity as the body of Christ, the church.

In this section, the author describes the alienation in which the Gentiles found themselves before they became Christians (vv. 11, 12), indicates how Christ made a new people out of two distinct ethnic groups (vv.

13–18), and, by way of the imagery of the heavenly building, shows how the church grows together into a sacred temple in the Lord (vv. 19–22). The entire passage has many liturgical features, draws heavily upon the language of the OT, and is rich in baptismal theology.

Additional Note

Beyond the commentaries there are some helpful studies dealing with issues in this chapter: W. Barclay, "The One, New Man," in *Unity and Diversity in New Testament Theology*, ed. R. A. Guelich (Grand Rapids: Eerdmans, 1978), pp. 73–81. Barclay's main point is that "new" (*kainos*) means something new in quality and character; E. K. Lee, "Unity in Israel and Unity in Christ," in *Studies in Ephesians*, ed. F. L. Cross, pp. 36–50; R. P. Martin, "Reconciliation and Unity in Ephesians," in his *Reconciliation*, pp. 157–98. Martin offers a detailed literary and theological analysis of 2:19–21; W. A. Meeks, "In One Body: The Unity of Humankind in Colossians and Ephesians," in *God's Christ and His People*, ed. J. Jervell and W. Meeks (Oslo: Universitetsforlaget, 1977), pp. 209–21.

9

The Gentiles Apart from Christ

EPHESIANS 2:11–12

You Gentiles by birth—called "the uncircumcised" by the Jews, who call themselves the circumcised (which refers to what men do to their bodies)—remember what you were in the past. ¹²At that time you were apart from Christ. You were foreigners and	did not belong to God's chosen people. You had no part in the covenants, which were based on God's promises to his people, and you lived in this world without hope and without God.

I n this section the apostle begins by describing the condition of the Gentiles before they became Christians. Though he already has done this to some extent, the emphasis in 2:1–3 was upon their alienation from God as individuals. In that condition, they had many things in common with the Jews, and so the author speaks about all of humanity. In 2:4–10 he goes on to emphasize God's mercy, love, and grace and how God brought mankind into relationship with himself through Christ.

In 2:11–22 the concern is with the national and covenantal alienation between Jews and Gentiles rather than on the spiritual alienation between God and humanity in 2:1–10. Thus the emphasis here is upon those aspects of Christ's redemption that break down divisions and lead to a new people of God characterized by peace and unity. Their past life "apart from Christ" (2:12) and their present life "in union with Christ Jesus" (2:13) contains some vivid contrasts.

The Gentiles in the past:	The Gentiles in the present:
apart from Christ (v. 12)	in union with Christ Jesus (v. 15)
far away from God (vv. 13, 17)	brought near by the death of Christ (vv. 13, 17)
did not belong to God's chosen people (v. 12)	fellow citizens with God's people (v. 19)
foreigners . . . with no part in the covenant (v. 12)	not foreigners or strangers any longer (v. 19)
without hope (v. 12)	
without God (v. 12)	

2:11 / The Greek text begins with the emphatic "therefore remember." On the basis of all that these Gentiles have experienced from God through Christ (1:3–2:10), they are summoned to remember what they were **in the past**. They are addressed as **Gentiles by birth**. The inclusion of the article (lit., "you the Gentiles") indicates that the author is addressing a special class of people. It may be his way of giving special emphasis to the fact that the church is made up of two classes of people. Earlier (2:1, 2), he used only the second person plural ("you") in his reference to them.

Those who were Gentiles **by birth** ("in the flesh") were referred to by the Jews (**the circumcised**) as **the uncircumcised**. Circumcision is a physical rite performed on the Jewish male as a sign of the covenant (Gen. 17:11). Although circumcision is used in a spiritual sense in Scripture as something that God performs upon the human heart—thus not made with hands (Deut. 10:16; Rom. 2:28, 29; 4:11; 1 Cor.7:19; Phil. 3:3; Col. 2:11)—the emphasis here is upon the human rite because it is **what men do to their bodies**. In other words, the Gentiles were distinguished from the Jews both by birth and by the outward physical rite of circumcision. These two facts provide the basis for the conditions that the author lists in the next verse.

2:12 / In the past (**at that time**) the Gentiles were **apart from Christ**. In one sense, this was their major deprivation, for to be without Christ himself is to be deprived of any of the blessings that he gives. Hence the author mentions Christ for this very reason: As they have been blessed spiritually in Christ (2:1–10), he reminds them that it is through union with Christ that they are made one with the Jews and partake of the blessings that were theirs as God's covenant people. To be **apart** from Christ definitely stands in sharp contrast to being "in union with Christ Jesus" (2:13). Since the first reference is just "to Christ" (in contrast to Christ Jesus), it could be that a reference to "the Messiah" is intended.

You were foreigners: actually, this word belongs to the phrase "you had no part in the covenants" and, as such, means that as Gentiles they were strangers or foreigners to the covenants that God made with his people. These covenants include those made with Abraham (Gen. 15:8–21; 17:1–21) and Moses (Exod. 24:1–11) and the new and everlasting covenants about which the prophets spoke (cf. Isa. 55:3; Jer. 31:31–34; Ezek. 37:26).

The covenants that God made with Israel served both a present and future function in that they established Israel as God's special people and assured them of God's continued presence (they **were based on God's promises to his people**). The wording of the Greek text ("covenants of promise"), together with a possible reference to "the Messiah," suggest that the author may have those particular covenants in mind that promised the Messiah. But as Gentiles they were not entitled to any of the provisions that God had made for, or any of the promises he had made to, his chosen people.

Another aspect of their former estranged condition is that they **did not belong to God's chosen people**. The Greek uses the rather strong word *apallotrioō*, which conveys the ideas of estrangement or alienation (cf. RSV). Not belonging to Israel (lit., "commonwealth," "polity," *politeia*) meant that they had no rights of citizenship and no participation in the national or religious life of the Israelites. And since Israel was the only nation to whom God had revealed himself in a special way, the Gentiles had no access to the true God. Their life in **this world** was lived **without hope and without God**.

Given the context in which the word **hope** appears, it most naturally refers to the Gentiles' general state of hopelessness from not belonging to God's people and not, therefore, sharing in the hope of the coming Messiah. In Christianity, people **without hope** are those who have no certainty in the future events that pertain to the Lord's return and everlasting life (Acts 23:6; 1 Cor. 15:29, 32; Col. 1:5, 27; 1 Thess. 2:19; 4:13; 1 Pet. 1:3; 3:5).

J. A. Robinson makes an interesting observation about Jewish hope and Gentile hopelessness when he writes: "The Jew had a hope: the Gentile had none. The golden age of the Gentile was in the past: his poets told him of it, and how it was gone. The Jew's golden age was in the future; his prophets told him to look forward to its coming" (p. 57). For a short period of time the Greek mystery religions, with their doctrines of purification, immortality, brotherhood, and so forth, offered a ray of hope to the Greeks and Romans. This, however, never approximated the Jewish belief in the coming Kingdom of God or the certainty of Christianity, which based its hope on the verities of Christ's life and resurrection.

The Gentile's life in this world was also **without God**. This appears as a rather strange characterization of a people who were noted for their idolatry and polytheism (many gods). When Paul visited Athens, for example, "he was greatly upset when he noticed how full of idols the city was" (Acts 17:16). The irony is that, though there were many "gods and lords" (1 Cor. 8:5), they were, in effect, "no gods" (Acts 17:22–31; 19:26;

1 Cor. 8:4, 6; Gal. 4:8). By believing in such man-made idols or self-conceived deities, the Gentiles really had nothing—they were **without God**. The Greek word is *atheos*, from which the word "atheist" comes. This is the only occurrence of the word in the NT. In Greek literature, it was used to describe people who either were without God's help, lived in a godless manner, or did not believe in God at all (see Abbott, p. 59).

10

The Gentiles in Christ

But now, in union with Christ Jesus you, who used to be far away, have been brought near by the death of Christ. [14]For Christ himself has brought us peace by making Jews and Gentiles one people. With his own body he broke down the wall that separated them and kept them enemies. [15]He abolished the Jewish Law with its commandments and rules, in order to create out of the two races one new people in union with himself, in this way making peace.

[16]By his death on the cross Christ destroyed their enmity; by means of the cross he united both races into one body and brought them back to God. [17]So Christ came and preached the Good News of peace to all—to you Gentiles, who were far away from God, and to the Jews, who were near to him. [18]It is through Christ that all of us, Jews and Gentiles, are able to come in the one Spirit into the presence of the Father.

2:13 / The Good News of the gospel is that Christ came into such an alienated and hopeless world to reverse the misfortunes of the Gentiles: **But now, in union with Christ Jesus you, who used to be far away, have been brought near by the death of Christ**. There is nothing in the previous two verses that corresponds with the ideas of "afar" and **near** other than the obvious distance between the privileged Jew and the deprived Gentile. The imagery here comes from Isaiah 57:19, where the prophet says: "Peace, peace to the far and the near, says the Lord; and I will heal him" (RSV). These are the same words that Peter uses in his sermon on the day of Pentecost, when he is addressing a mixed audience (Acts 2:39; cf. also Rom. 10:15). In Ephesians, nearness to God has been made possible through the **death** (lit., "blood") **of Christ**.

2:14-15 / Since the author returns to the concepts of "far away" and "near" in 2:17, it appears that 2:14–16 is a rather long parenthesis on how Christ's death brought a divided humanity together. He already has given a number of reasons why the Jews and the Gentiles differed from each other (2:11, 12). These distinctions, which were racial, social, and religious, resulted in various expressions of hostility and enmity.

The apostle refers to the **Jewish Law with its commandments and**

rules as the cause of the divisions that existed between Jews and Gentiles. The effect of that "Law," he states, was like a wall that separated both races and kept them apart as enemies. However, through Christ's death the wall was broken down, a new humanity was created, Gentiles and Jews were reconciled to each other, and both were reconciled to God.

The phrase, **for Christ himself has brought us peace** is much more emphatic than it appears in English. Literally, it says, "Christ himself is our peace." Though it is true that he is the source of peace and brings peace through his life, he *is* peace—he gives peace because *he himself is peace*. This peace came about because Jews and Gentiles were made one people. The concept is reminiscent of Galatians 3:28, where Paul states that "there is no difference between Jews and Gentiles . . . you are all one in union with Christ Jesus."

Once again, the author turns to the role that Christ played in effecting this peace. Earlier, he used the death (blood) of Christ; here he states that **with his own body** (flesh) **he broke down the wall that separated them and kept them enemies**. Both of these phrases ("death," **body**) and the reference to the "cross" (2:16) are similar ways of describing the reconciling work of Christ. The author may consciously be using "flesh" in this context to refer to the Incarnation (cf. Rom. 8:3; Gal. 4:4; Heb. 2:14).

The image of **the wall** that Christ **broke down** must be understood in connection with the reference to the **Jewish Law** that follows in 2:15. Basically, **the wall** is a symbol of the divisions that the Mosaic Law ("the law of the commandments in ordinances") created and that kept the two races from having social and religious intercourse.

There has been considerable speculation with respect to the **wall** that is mentioned. Most scholars tend to believe that the author is referring to the wall that separated the Gentiles and the Jews in the temple area. Josephus, a Jewish historian in the first century, describes this wall as a stone barrier about five feet high (*Antiquities* 15.11). Gentiles may have wanted to approach the Temple out of curiosity or to offer gifts and sacrifices to the God of the Jews. Hence, warnings were posted at appropriate places to remind them of their limits and the severity of punishment that would follow if the barrier were crossed. One such warning, now in the Museum of Constantinople, was discovered by archaeologists in 1871. Translated from the Greek, it reads:

NO MAN OF ANOTHER NATION TO ENTER WITHIN THE FENCE AND ENCLOSURE ROUND THE TEMPLE. AND WHOEVER

IS CAUGHT WILL HAVE HIMSELF TO BLAME
THAT HIS DEATH ENSUES

(quoted in Robinson, p. 60)

The seriousness of this is vividly portrayed in Acts 21:27 ff., where Paul is accused of bringing Greeks ("Trophimus from Ephesus," no less) into the temple area and thus defiling "this holy place."

This wall, which so dramatically symbolized Jewish separatism, was broken down along with the Temple when Jerusalem was destroyed by the Roman general Titus in A.D. 70. But the destruction of that physical wall hardly eliminated the internal barriers that the Jewish Law had erected: That took place through the death of Christ when **he abolished the Jewish Law with its commandments and rules**. This meant the abolition of all distinctions that separated Jew and Gentile.

Other, but less common, views of the meaning of **wall** include *(a)* the curtain in the temple that separated the Holy Place from the Holy of Holies; *(b)* a rabbinic statement about building "a fence around the law"; *(c)* sin, which is a separation between God and man; or *(d)* a Gnostic concept of some kind of wall that divided the spheres of heaven and earth (see Barth, *Eph. 1–3*, pp. 283–87).

The **commandments and rules** are a reference to the ceremonial laws, such as dietary regulations, circumcision, rites of purification, sabbath and festival observances, sacrifices, and so forth. Colossians 2:8–23, which likewise mentions the abolition of rules and regulations, expands the list beyond Jewish ceremonial law because it is dealing with a number of man-made proscriptions that the false teachers had added ("Don't handle . . . taste . . . touch . . . "). There the emphasis is on the believers in Colossae not becoming enslaved to such legalism, because in Christ they have been freed from such powers. In Ephesians, the point is that the abolition of the Law serves to unite two previously alienated and hostile groups.

The breaking down of this ceremonial law, however, did not mean that all moral standards were abolished. The early Christians adopted many of the moral teachings of Judaism into their theology as long as they conformed to the standard that Christ taught or that he fulfilled in his life (cf. the Sermon on the Mount, esp., Matt. 5:17–48). J. Stott mentions that although Jesus did not abolish the moral law "as a standard of behavior," he did abolish it "as a way of salvation" (p. 101).

It took the early church considerable time to realize the implications of this truth and to effect what was true in principle. Theologically, it is a process begun by Stephen in Acts (chap. 7) and worked out by Paul in his Epistles to the Romans and to the Galatians. Practically, some of the divisions never were abolished completely, because the Jewish Christians in Jerusalem and Palestine remained more Jewish in theology and practice than their brethren outside Palestine (the Diaspora).

The largest percentage of early Christians were Jewish believers (Acts 1–12) who never fully separated themselves from certain forms of Judaism. When the Gentile mission was inaugurated, some of these Jewish Christians, represented by the Jerusalem and Palestinian churches, felt that the Gentiles should either become Jews before they became Christians—that is, submit to circumcision and the Law (the extreme view)—or at least be sensitive to Jewish food laws in cases of social fellowship. The account of Peter's vision at the home of Cornelius recounts how God declared that all foods are clean (Acts 10:1–43). The details of this and their implications for the Gentile mission are discussed at the Jerusalem council (Acts 15:1–35) as well as in Galatians 2.

The Good News in Ephesians is that Christ's death abolished the legal distinctions that separated Jews and Gentiles: The former divisive effect of the Law is annulled and has lost its power (cf. Col. 2:15). Instead of enmity between the two races there is **peace**; in place of two separate entities there is **one people**.

The effect of Christ's work in breaking down the barrier is twofold: First, it resulted in the creation of a new humanity (**in order to create out of the two races one new people in union with himself**). There is more here than simply the union or the mixture of two groups. This is not a case of the Greeks conquering the Jews or the Jews converting the Greeks to their faith and way of life. Rather, it is a completely new creation (lit., "one new man") that Christ has effected in union with himself (Gal. 3:28; Col. 3:11). To a certain extent, the church is the sum total of individuals who have become "new creatures" in Christ (2 Cor. 5:17; Gal. 6:15; Col. 3:10); but the author is thinking of something more profound—namely, the church as a corporate entity.

2:16 / Second, there is the aspect of reconciliation, which, for the apostle, has two foci: On the one side, the church effected a reconciliation between Jew and Gentile. The broken barrier—accomplished **by his death on the cross**—and the creation of the church (**one new people**) meant that the enmity between these two races was replaced by peace. Here the author uses the phrase "having slain (*apokteinas*) the enmity." The imagery of the cross suggests that he who himself was slain (Heb. 2:14) is now the one who slays (destroys) the enmity. Peace is illustrated by the metaphor of the body, the church. Jews and Gentiles are reconciled to each other because they are united into **one body** by means of the cross. Thus the church is presented as a living organism, composed of diverse parts, but existing peacefully as one body (cf. 4:4; 1 Cor. 10:17; 12:13; Col. 3:15).

The other side of Christ's work is that he brought about reconciliation between humanity and God (**and brought them**—i.e., the two who have been united in one body—**back to God**). Here there is no question of Jewish privilege or Greek ignorance, since both are equally represented as objects of reconciliation: Through Christ's work on the cross, God "changed us from enemies into his friends" (2 Cor. 5:18; cf. also Rom. 5:10).

2:17 / Before the author develops this concept of access he turns from Christ the reconciler to Christ the proclaimer: **So Christ came and preached the Good News of peace to all—to you Gentiles, who were far away from God, and to the Jews, who were near to him**. The idea of **peace** may be taken from Isaiah 57:19, which he used earlier (2:13), or he may be utilizing Isaiah 52:7, which announces: "How wonderful it is to see a messenger coming across the mountains, bringing good news, the news of peace."

Most scholars take Christ's preaching as an act related to his death-resurrection-exaltation and not to his earthly pre-resurrection ministry. The context appears to favor the idea that the peace that he effected on the cross is itself a proclamation and his way of announcing to the world that peace has been made. This verse could be in reference to Christ's post-resurrection appearances, in which his first followers are told not to fear (Matt. 28:5, 10), or to his benediction of peace in John 14:27 ("peace I leave with you; my own peace I give to you"). However, there is much to be said for the view that takes it as the preaching of the earthly Jesus himself or, at least, as the preaching of his disciples.

Jesus does adopt the words of Isaiah 61:1, 2, as his life's mission ("the Spirit of the Lord is upon me, because he has chosen me to preach the Good News to the poor, Luke 4:18, 19), and he does become involved with a segment of society that could be considered "afar off" (cf. Mitton, pp. 109–10). But regardless of what view one may take, the important point is that in the Christ event (life-death-resurrection-exaltation), peace was achieved and access to God was made possible. Thus the author reminds his readers that it is through Christ that Jews and Gentiles "are able to come in the one Spirit into the presence of the Father" (2:18).

2:18 / Perhaps there is an allusion here to the curtain in the inner temple that separated the people from God and through which only the high priest had access on the Day of Atonement (Heb. 9:1–14). The Good News of the gospel, however, is that Christ opened up a way of access to God by removing the curtain through his death (Heb. 10:19 ff.). The imagery suggested by the idea of "access" (*prosagōgē*) is that of an Oriental court where subjects were presented to their monarch by a *prosagōgos*.

In the church, it is Christ who has made the way into God's presence possible ("in union with him and through our faith in him, we have freedom to enter into God's presence with all confidence," Eph. 3:12). Access to God is through **the one Spirit** because all Christians are united by one Spirit in their baptism into Christ (1 Cor. 12:12, 13; Eph. 4:1–6). And as a church (the body of Christ), they now are a fellowship of the Holy Spirit. In addition to this verse, the role of the Spirit in worship is mentioned in 3:18–20 and in a similar passage in Colossians (3:16, 17).

There are a number of things that suggest that the author may have baptism in mind throughout this entire discussion (2:11–18). First, baptism provides the best answer as to where and when all this took place for the Jew and the Gentile—that is, when the "afar" were brought near and, together with the "near," united with Christ and made members of one another in the body of Christ. To be sure, Christ accomplished that at the time of his death on the cross, but the believer makes that his own through faith and baptism in Christ.

Second, there are many close parallels in this passage to the two baptismal passages in Colossians: Ephesians 2:11 is remarkably similar to Colossians 2:11–13; and 2:11–18 may be an adaptation of the Christ hymn in Colossians 1:15–20, which has considerable support as a baptismal hymn (see disc. on Col. 1:15–20).

Third, and perhaps most convincing, are those baptismal passages that specifically mention baptism into Christ as the means of breaking down all barriers, including racial distinctions. Thus Paul writes to the Galatians, "You were baptized into union with Christ . . . so there is no difference between Jews and Gentiles" (3:27, 28); and in Colossians the baptismal imagery of "putting off" and "putting on" is utilized, with the result that baptism eliminates the differences between Gentiles and Jews (3:9–11). It could be said that the author turns to baptismal language in Ephesians 2:11–18 to support his theological assertion of the unity between Jew and Gentile as one new people in Christ. And since baptism is mentioned in his great section on unity (4:1–6), one could infer that he understood baptism as the sacrament of unity (1 Cor. 12:13).

Additional Notes

2:14–15 / M. S. Moore presents a detailed analysis of these verses in his "Ephesians 2:15–16: A History of Recent Interpretation," *EQ* 54 (1982), pp. 163–69. For understanding the nature of Jewish and Gentile Christianity in the early church, see L. Goppelt, *Apostolic and Post-Apostolic History* (New York: Harper Torchbooks, 1970), esp. chap. 3, pp. 61–107.

2:17 / A thorough discussion of the expressions **near** and **far** is given by D. C. Smith, "The Ephesian Heresy and the Origin of the Epistle to the Ephesians," *Ohio Journal of Religious Studies* 5 (1977), pp. 78–103. Smith's investigation leads him to conclude that it is not that Gentile Christianity was threatening to lose its connection with Jewish Christianity, but "rather the issue is that certain Gentile—'Jewish'—Christians, on the basis of traditions derived in large part from hellenistic Judaism, are displaying contempt toward natural Jews who have become Christians. These opponents of the author of Ephesians, then, represent a fascinating synthesis of esoteric elements drawn from Judaism, Christianity, and Hellenistic religion in general" (p. 103).

11

The New Unity

EPHESIANS 2:19–22

So then, you Gentiles are not foreigners or strangers any longer; you are now fellow citizens with God's people and members of the family of God. ²⁰You, too, are built upon the foundation laid by the apostles and prophets,ᵈ the cornerstone being Christ Jesus himself. ²¹He is the one who holds the whole building together and makes it grow into a sacred temple dedicated to the Lord. ²²In union with him you too are being built together with all the others into a place where God lives through his Spirit.

d. the foundation laid by the apostles and prophets; *or* the foundation, that is, the apostles and prophets.

The thoughts in these verses on the incorporation of the Gentiles into a sacred temple in the Lord, conclude the section on Christian unity (2:11–22). The "**so then**" has the effect of pointing back to what was said in the previous verses and linking it to what follows. The main thought is that, because the Gentiles are now in Christ and have access in one Spirit to the Father, they are no longer "foreigners or strangers" but "fellow citizens with God's people and members of the family of God." By virtue of their faith in Jesus Christ, the "cornerstone," they are like an edifice that is built upon the foundation of "apostles and prophets" and that "grows into a sacred temple" in the Lord.

2:19 / Now that the apostle has discussed the effects that Christ's death had upon Jews and Gentiles (2:14–18), he returns to his discussion of the Gentiles to complete the contrasts that he began earlier. At one time they were foreigners who did not belong to God's people (2:12), but now they are no longer **foreigners** (*xenos*) or **strangers** (*paroikos*). **Foreigners** are people outside a country or community, with no special rights or privileges. The word for **strangers** (*paroikos*) often is translated as "sojourners," a term that accentuates the transient nature of the Gentiles. In that condition they were like aliens with an "immigrant visa," which granted them limited rights and privileges, but not full citizenship or permanent residency.

But the status of the Gentiles has changed remarkably: First, the author uses a political expression and affirms that they **are now fellow citizens** (*sympolitai*) **with God's people**, that is, they are on equal standing with the historic people of God. Second, he uses the imagery of a building (*oikos*) to affirm that they are members of the **family** (lit., "household") **of God**.

2:20 / From the concept of the **family** or "household" (*oikos*) of God, the author turns to discuss the building (*oikodomē*) of this family, utilizing an architectural metaphor. The language that he employs re-emphasizes that the Gentiles are part of an ongoing process: **You, too, are built upon the foundation laid by the apostles and prophets**.

If the Gentiles may have been guilty of forgetting or even scorning their relationship to God's redemptive work in history, these words would serve as a significant reminder that they are not the first or only people in God's eternal plan. Rather, they have been built (the Greek aorist tense refers to something that has happened) upon a foundation that already had been laid.

Apostles and prophets are named as forming the foundation of the church. Though some commentators take **prophets** to mean those in the OT, the word order—**apostles and prophets**—makes it more likely that the author has the NT prophets in mind (cf. Acts 11:27 ff.; 1 Cor. 12:28, 29; 14:1–5, 24 ff.). Both offices are used again in Ephesians (3:5; 4:11) with a clear reference to the NT period. They are considered the foundation of the church because of their importance as messengers and interpreters of the Good News.

The thoughts that the author is developing differ slightly from the picture that Paul gives in Corinthians. In Corinth, he is dealing with a divided church—a church that has polarized around such individuals as Paul, Peter, Christ, and Apollos. Paul seeks to dispel such party strife by showing that the ministry is the cooperative effort of a number of individuals, all of whom are servants of God and partners with each other (1 Cor. 1:10–13; 3:5–9). To anyone seeking to be the foundation of God's building, Paul warns that "God has already placed Jesus Christ as the one and only foundation, and no other foundation can be laid" (1 Cor. 3:11). In Ephesians, the **apostles and prophets** are **the foundation** and Jesus becomes the **cornerstone** (cf. 1 Pet. 2:4–8—quoting Isa. 28:16 and Ps. 118:22—where Christ is interpreted as the cornerstone).

The reasons for this apparent shift are not easy to discern. One author suggests that, by the time Ephesians was written, Christ's centrality in the church was guaranteed, but because of the heresies that threatened the church, it became necessary to establish an authentic line of tradition through the apostles and prophets (Houlden, p. 292). T. K. Abbott reasons that the cornerstone was more important to Orientals because of its function in connecting and bearing the weight of the building (p. 71). This view does have some appeal, because in the context of the passage the emphasis is upon the function of Christ in keeping this growing structure unified. The cornerstone would have provided the key around which the foundation and the superstructure were built (Stott, pp. 107–8).

Though it is natural to think of the cornerstone as being on the foundational level of a building, there is an attractive alternative to this concept that takes the phrase not as a foundation stone but as a "keystone" to be placed at the summit of a building to crown its completion. Some believe that this is a more fitting explanation of the thought in Ephesians, where Christ is the head of the body (1:22) and the church grows into him who is the head (4:15).

The variety of interpretations that attempt to make sense out of the difficult imagery and syntax should not distract the reader from the central message of this passage. The apostle is showing that the church consists of three significant elements: *(a)* the Gentiles, who are now part of God's people, the Jews; *(b)* the apostles and prophets; and *(c)* Jesus Christ. But this is more than just a random combination of parts: They are joined together by the principle of unity and growth.

2:21 / The construction of this verse in the Greek is very ambiguous and has led to a variety of translations and interpretations. Literally, it reads, "in whom every structure (*pasa oikodomē*) is joined together" (*synarmologeō*). The big question is whether *pasa oikodomē* should be translated as "every structure" or "the whole structure" and whether the thoughts should be taken literally or metaphorically.

Those opting for the former believe that this "sacred temple in the Lord" is like the Jewish temple, in which many buildings, rooms, and parts (see Moule, p. 85; Wescott, p. 41) made up the "whole Temple." C. L. Mitton accepts "every structure" as best grammatically but gives it a metaphorical rather than literal meaning. Hence, he follows a line of interpretation that takes the "parts" as the local congregations that make up the one universal or catholic church (p. 115).

From the context of the passage, however, one seriously wonders whether the apostle has local congregations in mind, because he has been so concerned about the unity of the entire body. Robinson, for one, admits that the words are ambiguous but, within the context of the passage, emphasizes the process of building and takes the phrase to mean "all that is builded," that is, whatever building is being done (pp. 70, 165). What is in the author's mind, therefore, is the entire operation of the building rather than single structures that make up the whole (cf. also Abbott, pp. 74,75; Barth, *Eph. 1–3*, p. 272; Foulkes, p. 87). The GNB follows this line of interpretation in its translation, **he is the one who holds the whole building together**.

The concept of a building process is continued in the following phrase: Christ is the one who **makes it grow into a sacred temple dedicated to the Lord**. Though the imagery is that of a building, the next verse (2:22) makes it clear that the author has a spiritual "house" in mind where God's presence is manifested. The **sacred temple** is the translation of *naon hagion*—*naos* being the inner part of the temple where God was believed to reside and meet his people. In early Christian theology, believers are referred to as God's sacred temple, not in a material sense, but as a "spiritual building" where God dwells and manifests himself. Christians are that holy (**sacred**) temple by virtue of being in the Lord.

2:22 / Once again, the apostle emphasizes that the Gentiles have a part in all of this: **In union with him you too are being** (present tense) **built together with all the others into a place where God lives through his Spirit**. This concept is reminiscent of Paul's ideas in his Corinthian letters, where he reminds the congregation that they are God's building—temple—in whom the Spirit of God dwells (1 Cor. 3:9, 16 ff.; 2 Cor. 6:16). To the Gentiles, all of this stands as a vivid contrast to the beginning of their lives, which was in "the flesh" (2:11).

This passage (2:19–22) contains a number of striking linguistic and conceptual parallels with the liturgical hymn in 1 Peter 2:4–10. Both epistles, for example, refer to Christ as the cornerstone and emphasize that Christians are part of a building process that is growing into a spiritual temple. The First Letter from Peter speaks of the "stone" rejected by the builders but that has become the elected cornerstone in Zion to the believing Gentiles.

In Ephesians, there is confirmation that the Gentiles, who were at one time far off, distant from the commonwealth of Israel, have been brought near and have become one with the people of God. In 1 Peter 2:9, 10, those who have been called out of darkness into light have now become the people of God; in Ephesians, this idea of the Gentiles becoming God's people is emphasized throughout 2:11–22, although the imagery of darkness and light is not used until 5:8–14 (cf. Col. 1:12, 13).

These similarities between 2:19–22 and 1 Peter 2:4–10 suggest that there was a tradition in the early church that described the role of Christ, the new status of Gentile believers (the indicative), and their ultimate goal (the imperative) by utilizing building imagery. Given the liturgical nature of both passages, it is not unreasonable to infer that these texts were used by the Gentile churches to celebrate their incorporation into the family of God. Although the imagery is different, there is a remarkable similarity in thought between the believers' union with Christ and their incorporation into Christ's body at the time of baptism.

Additional Note

2:20 / This idea of a "keystone" apparently was first initiated by J. Jeremias in his article *"akrogōnias," TDNT*, vol. 1, p. 792, and is championed by Barth in *Eph. 1–3*, pp. 317–19. C. L. Mitton lists a number of objections to this theory and sticks with the traditional view, which sees Jesus as the cornerstone of the building "from which the future building will be gauged" (p. 115). This view is also supported by R. J. McKelvey, "Christ the Cornerstone: Eph. 2:11–22," *NTS* 8 (1962), pp. 352–59. McKelvey concludes that "the interpretation which explains *akrogōniaios* of Eph. ii.20 as a topstone is to be abandoned in favor of the traditional understanding of *akrogōniaios* as a stone connected to the foundation of the building, which was located at one of the corners (probably the determinitive corner) and bound together the walls and the foundation" (p. 359). For further comments, see F. F. Bruce, "New Wine in Old Wine Skins: III. The Corner Stone," *ExpT* 84 (1973), pp. 231–35.

12

Paul and the Mission to the Gentiles

Whe apostle completed his section on the spiritual blessings in Christ (1:3–14), he proceeded to offer a prayer of
thanksgiving and petition (1:15–23). After this theological
discussion in 2:1–22, it appears that he is once again ready to turn to
prayer because the statement, "For this reason" (3:1), refers to what he
has just said; furthermore, the actual prayer in 3:14 ff. appears to relate to
this section and would be a fitting climax to the thoughts that he has
developed. But instead of a prayer, the apostle's thought is diverted to
another topic of discussion—one that is related to Paul's call and mission
as a proclaimer of God's secret. After a rather lengthy presentation of this
subject (3:2–13), he returns to his initial intention to pray and subsequently offers one of the most beautiful and comprehensive prayers in the
NT.

At first glance, Ephesians 3:2–13 appears to be a rather lengthy parenthesis on the vindication of Paul's apostleship to the Gentiles (it is one
long sentence in the Greek). The author has been discussing the unity of
Jews and Gentiles in Christ and how the Gentiles are legitimate heirs of
God's salvation (2:11–22); but for some reason he finds it necessary to
define God's secret more precisely and the human agent through whom it
was revealed. His definition of the secret (3:6) also extends some of the
imagery that he used before. In 2:19–22 the Gentiles were considered
fellow citizens who are joined and built together into a sacred temple. In
3:6, the theme of unity is re-emphasized by a number of similar expressions: "By means of the gospel the Gentiles have a part with the Jews in
God's blessings; they are members of the same body and share in the
promise that God made in Christ Jesus."

There are many close similarities between Ephesians 3:1–13 and Colossians 1:24–29:

Ephesians:

3:1—I, Paul, the prisoner of Christ Jesus

3:2—God in his grace has given me this work to do for your good

3:3—God revealed his secret plan and made it known to me

3:4—you can learn about my understanding of the secret of Christ

3:6—by means of the gospel the Gentiles have a part with the Jews in God's blessings; they are members of the same body and share in the promise that God made through Christ Jesus

3:8—I am . . . least . . . yet God gave me this privilege of taking to the Gentiles the . . . infinite riches of Christ

3:9—of making all people see how God's secret plan

3:10—by means of the church . . . might learn of his wisdom in all its different forms

3:13—[do not] be discouraged because I am suffering for you

Colossians:

1:23—I, Paul, became a servant

1:25—God . . . gave me this task to perform for your good

1:27—God's plan is to make known his secret to his people

2:2—And so . . . they will know God's secret, which is Christ himself

1:27—And the secret is that Christ is in you, which means that you will share in the glory of God

1:27—God's plan is to make known his secret to his people, this rich and glorious secret which he has for all peoples

1:26—the secret . . . but . . . now revealed to his people

1:26—the secret . . . hid through all past ages . . . but . . . now revealed

1:24—I am happy about my sufferings for you

In both epistles, the author is in prison and is suffering; he is considered the minister to the Gentiles; the "secret" has been hidden but is now revealed; this secret is identified as the inclusion of the Gentiles in God's plan of salvation; it is the message that Paul has been commissioned to preach.

There are, however, some notable differences between these two epistles as well. In Colossians, the call of Paul as a missionary to the Gentiles (1:25, 26) is not as specific as in Ephesians (3:8), where he definitely is identified as a prisoner of Christ Jesus for the sake of the *Gentiles*, to whom his preaching is directed (cf. Acts 21:17–34; 22:21–24; 26:12–23).

The goal of Paul's preaching varies slightly also: In Colossians, the proclamation is given "in order to bring each one into God's presence as a mature individual in union with Christ" (1:28); in Ephesians, it is oriented specifically toward the revelation of the "secret" ("to make all men see how God's secret plan is to be put into effect"). Ephesians does not touch upon the aspect of Christian maturity until 4:13.

But the main difference centers upon the nature of this "secret" that Paul has been called to preach. The brief mention of this in Colossians 1:27 almost goes unnoticed and hardly gives any indication of what the secret is all about. Ephesians, however, definitely is concerned about defining the "secret" (3:6) and presenting Paul as its chief exponent.

In 3:14–19, the author begins his prayer for spiritual growth and unity. The specific requests include strengthening of the readers' inner selves by God's Spirit (3:16), the indwelling of Christ in their hearts through faith (3:17a), a strong grounding in love (3:17b), comprehension of the love of Christ (3:18–19a), and filling with the perfect fullness of God (3:19b). In some ways, these requests are not unlike his earlier mention of wisdom (1:17), knowledge (1:17), and enlightenment for the readers (1:18).

There is no specific reference to the problem of the unity of the church. Mention of the Fatherhood of God (3:15) and the comprehension of Christ's love by all God's people (3:18) does, nevertheless, serve to remind the readers that their unity in Christ is to result in a unified Christian fellowship. The writer uses the expression "God's people" (*hoi hagioi*) on a number of occasions in the sense of belonging or togetherness (1:1, 15, 18; 2:19; 3:18; 6:18).

The concluding benediction (3:20, 21) points out that God is able to do far more than is requested, because the power of Christ is at work within the believer. The mention of the church is significant, for it is the sphere of the outworking of God's purpose on earth as well as in heaven (3:10). In stating this, Ephesians extends the mission of the church beyond that taught in Colossians.

The new features of this chapter center around the clarification of God's "secret," the prominence of Paul as an exponent of that secret, and the cosmic mission of the church. Beyond that, there is a definite repetition of the ideas that were used earlier in the epistle, for example:

the secret as made known by revelation	3:3	= 1:9
the role of apostles and prophets	3:5	= 2:20
the inheritance of the saints	3:6	= 1:14
the grace and power of God	3:7, 20	= 1:19
God's eternal plan	3:9	= 1:10; 2:7

the cosmic scope	3:10	= 1:3, 10
God's eternal purpose	3:11	= 1:4
access to God	3:12	= 2:12
God the Father	3:14, 15	= 1:17
the Son	3:11, 17	= 1:3, etc.
the Spirit	3:5, 16	= 1:13, 14; 2:22
the fullness of God	3:19	= 1:23

Presenting the Mystery of the Gospel

For this reason I, Paul, the prisoner of Christ Jesus for the sake of you Gentiles, pray to God. ²Surely you have heard that God in his grace has given me this work to do for your good. ³God revealed his secret plan and made it known to me. (I have written briefly about this, ⁴and if you will read what I have written, you can learn about my understanding of the secret of Christ.) ⁵In past times mankind was not told this secret, but God has revealed it now by the Spirit to his holy apostles and prophets. ⁶The secret is that by means of the gospel the Gentiles have a part with the Jews in God's blessings; they are members of the same body and share in the promise that God made through Christ Jesus.

⁷I was made a servant of the gospel by God's special gift, which he gave me through the working of his power. ⁸I am less than the least of all God's people; yet God gave me this privilege of taking to the Gentiles the Good News about the infinite riches of Christ, ⁹and of making all people see how God's secret plan is to be put into effect. God, who is the Creator of all things, kept his secret hidden through all the past ages, ¹⁰in order that at the present time, by means of the church, the angelic rulers and powers in the heavenly world might learn of his wisdom in all its different forms. ¹¹God did this according to his eternal purpose, which he achieved through Christ Jesus our Lord. ¹²In union with Christ and through our faith in him we have the boldness to go into God's presence with all confidence. ¹³I beg you, then, not to be discouraged because I am suffering for you; it is all for your benefit.

3:1 / As indicated in the introductory chapter, the phrase **for this reason** points back to the theological ideas that have been developed in the preceding section and that lead the apostle to prayer. **I, Paul**, is an emphatic expression to draw attention to the apostle and what he has to say (cf. 2 Cor. 10:1; Gal. 5:2; Col. 1:23; 1 Thess. 2:18). What is emphasized is that Paul is **the prisoner of Christ Jesus** for the sake of the Gentiles. The GNB rightly translates the article before prisoner as **the** rather than "a" prisoner (RSV). Thus Paul is represented, not as one prisoner among many, but as *the* prisoner of Christ Jesus, because of the significance of his ministry to the Gentiles (Acts 21:17–34; 22:21–24; 26:12–23). **Gentiles** is a very inclusive term and, as in 2:11, refers not to any one specific congregation but to all Gentiles (**Gentiles** also is preceded by an article and should read **you** *the* **Gentiles**). Other references to Paul's imprisonment are found in 6:20, Philippians 1:7, Colossians 4:10, and Philemon 1 and 9.

3:2 / The GNB (and NIV) **surely you have heard** is a better translation than the RSV "assuming that you have heard," which implies some kind of doubt rather than verification (cf. 4:21; Col. 1:23). The phrase does raise a question about the Ephesian destination of the epistle but fits the "circular letter theory," which would include a number of Gentile congregations.

In the process of developing Paul's role as the missionary to the Gentiles, the author mentions several important things: First, God gave Paul a commission (**God . . . has given me this work** (*oikonomia*) **to do for your good**); second, God gave him **grace**. The translation of this verse is a bit misleading, because the emphasis is upon God's grace—literally, "the stewardship of God's grace that was given to me for you" (RSV, NIV). Though Paul does connect God's grace with his mission (3:7, 8; 4:7; Rom. 1:5; 12:3; 15:15, 16), it is God's **grace** and not the work that is given in this context. This is slightly different from Colossians 1:25, where it is the office (*oikonomia*) that was given (cf. Mitton, pp. 125, 126).

3:3–4 / In the next ten verses the author concentrates upon the secret and how God used Paul to reveal that plan to the Gentiles. He begins by stating that **God revealed his secret plan and made it known to me**. This follows the connection between revelation and the "secret" that was alluded to in 1:9 and 10 but affirms that this revelation is from God and not something that Paul concluded from his studies or received from tradition (cf. Gal. 1:12, 16; 2:2).

Before the meaning of this secret is developed, the author reminds his readers that he already has **written briefly about this**. Though a few commentators see a suggestion in this phrase to an earlier epistle(s) to a Gentile audience, most take it as a reference to the brief mention of the "secret" in 1:9–10 and the outworking of it through the Jews and the Gentiles in 2:11 ff. With that as background material, they can go on and learn more about the apostle's **understanding of the secret of Christ**. The author is confident that as they read—probably in public during a worship service and then in private meditation—they will be able to appreciate the significance of Paul as a servant of Christ with respect to the **secret**. It is unlikely that it refers to a reading of the OT (see Foulkes, p. 92).

In the use of "secret," a number of things should be noted: In Colossians (1:27) the secret is the rather mystical concept of the indwelling Christ ("Christ is in you, which means that you will share the glory of God"); in Colossians 4:3, the "secret of Christ" alludes to the fact that the Gentiles are recipients of the Good News (cf. Rom. 16:25, 26); in Ephesians 1:9, the secret is God's plan to unite all creation through the agency of Christ; in Ephesians 3:4, along with 3:6, the secret is the unity between Jew and Gentile. This has partially been explained in 1:9–10 and 2:11–22, but now is made more explicit. Ephesians takes the concept of "the secret" from a revelation of a gospel that included the Gentiles (Colossians) and develops it into a doctrine on the unity between Jew and Gentile in the church (3:6).

3:5 / This verse is very similar to Colossians 1:26, which talks about the secret that was hidden through all past ages from all mankind but that God has now revealed to his people. There are, however, some notable differences: First, there is the nature of the secret itself. In Colossians, it is the message of the gospel to the Gentiles; in Ephesians, it is the unity between Jews and Gentiles. Second, the revelation is **by the Spirit to his holy apostles and prophets** rather than to "all mankind." This change is significant in Ephesians because it confirms the emphasis given in the epistle to church leaders and ecclesiastical authorities rather than to all the people. Initially (3:3) the author stated that Paul alone was the recipient of this revelation; now he broadens it to include other inspired leaders in the church (2:20; 4:11).

The opening phrase in this verse (**in past times mankind was not told this secret**) raises a question about how much of God's plan for the Gentiles was revealed before Paul came along. There are some glimpses of this in the OT where references to all the nations who come to the "light" or join the Lord surely includes the Gentiles (Gen. 12:1–3; Isa. 11:10; 42:6; 60:3; Jer. 16:19; Mic. 4:2; Zeph. 2:11). Paul himself uses Isaiah 49:6 to justify his call to the Gentiles when he disputes with the Jews (Acts 13:47). And in Romans 15:9–12, he uses a series of OT passages to demonstrate that the Gentiles always had a future in God's plan.

Thus, in a broad or general sense, one could say that God's purpose for the Gentiles was made known. But this is far short of the development in Ephesians, which envisions a universal community in which Jew and Gentile have equal share in what is to become known as the church, the body of Christ (cf. Stott, p. 118). The new revelation was made possible **by the Spirit**, that is, he is the agent who brought the secret to light.

3:6 / Up to this point the author has alluded to the secret a number of times: now, however, he becomes very specific and defines it in a way that will remove any doubt about its content. **The secret is this**: **By means of the gospel**, that is, by way of the proclamation of the word of truth that was believed and accepted (1:13), the Gentiles have been given a completely new status with all of the privileges pertaining thereto. The author describes this with a number of picturesque words prefixed with the preposition *syn*.

First, **the Gentiles have a part with the Jews in God's blessings**. The Greek word *sygklēronoma* is the same one Paul uses on occasions when he talks about believers becoming "heirs" of salvation and of the blessings of God (Rom. 8:17; Gal. 3:29; 4:7). Here the *syn* preposition gives it the force of "fellow heirs," indicating that the Gentiles share equally with the Jews all the privileges and blessings of sonship.

Second, they are **members of the same body**. Since there is no occurrence of this word (*syssoma*) anywhere in the NT, the Septuagint (the pre-Christian Greek translation of the OT), or classical literature, it becomes obvious that the author coined it in order to describe the intimate relation that Jews and Gentiles have to each other in the body of Christ, the church. A. T. Robinson notes that there is no English equivalent and, in order to capture its full meaning, offers this idea: "In relation to the Body the members are 'incorporate'; in relation to one another they are 'concorporate', that is, sharers in the one body" (p. 78).

Third, the Gentiles **share in the promise that God made through Christ Jesus**. Once again, the author uses a *syn* noun (*symmetochos*) to emphasize that the Gentiles participate equally with the Jews in the promises of God. Their entire relationship with the people of God is established by their incorporation in Christ as it came to them through the gospel. The gospel is the proclamation of all the privileges that Christ has made available to mankind, including the Gentiles. Earlier, the author indicated that God's ultimate plan was to bring all creation together (1:10). One gets the distinct impression that the unity between Jew and Gentile is but the first step in a broader cosmic unity that is going to include all of creation under the headship of Christ (cf. Rom. 8:19-21).

3:7 / Having stated the role of the gospel in bringing this unity about, the author reminds his readers once again that Paul **was made a servant of the gospel by God's special gift** (cf. 3:2). Paul's ministry was neither a self-chosen nor a self-appointed one but a gift of God's grace. The ability to carry out that mission came **through the working of his** (God's) **pow-**

er and not Paul's strength (Col. 1:29). In other words, everything that Paul received and achieved was the result of God's gift of grace and power.

3:8-9 / Readers of the Pauline epistles will recall similar statements to the one made here: **I am less than the least of all God's people**. When Paul's apostleship was being questioned by the Corinthians he remarked that "even if I am nothing, I am in no way inferior to those very special apostles of yours" (2 Cor. 12:11). And on occasions when Paul is haunted by his former persecution of the church, he reminds himself of his unworthiness and inadequacy (cf. 1 Cor. 15:9; Gal. 1:13–15; 1 Tim. 1:12–14). In this context, it appears that Paul's feeling of inferiority comes from reflecting upon the grace of God and how it has worked in his life and among the Gentiles. He is overcome, not by a guilty conscience or questions about his authority, but by a heart that is overflowing with the marvels of God's grace.

The next phrase indicates that there is a double function to Paul's apostleship: First, there is his ministry of the proclamation of the gospel to the Gentiles (**God gave me this privilege of taking to the Gentiles the Good News about the infinite riches of Christ**). Though Paul has commented on his mission to the Gentiles, he appears to be amazed—and thankful—that God's grace was rich enough to include them and that he was God's instrument in bringing the message of reconciliation to them. F. Beare draws attention to the article before **Christ**, thus indicating that "the Christ," or "the Messiah" who was promised to the Jews, is now proclaimed to the Gentiles as well (p. 669). This could be a conscious thought in the author's mind, given the context of a passage in which incorporation between Jews and Gentiles is stressed.

The translation **infinite riches** (*anexichniastos*) captures beautifully the idea behind this Greek word (RSV and NIV, "unsearchable"; NEB, "unfathomable"). J. Stott lists ten different English equivalents that he has discovered in various translations and commentaries—all attempting to define the word without confining its meaning (p. 120). Basically, it means "not to be tracked out," "beyond comprehension," or "inscrutable." Paul expresses this idea when he writes to the Romans: "How great are God's riches! How deep are his wisdom and knowledge! Who can explain his decisions? Who can understand his ways?" (11:33). The same thoughts occur in Job 5:9 and 9:10 with respect to God's creation and providence—they lie beyond human comprehension and defy description.

A current analogy may be found in the modern attempt to conquer the cosmos. The present universe, as it is known, is accessible and "trackable." But as one reaches farther and farther into space, one discovers that there are many more universes and galaxies to explore—literally, an infinity in space. And so it is with the riches of Christ! They are **infinite** to the extent that the moment one discovers some of them a new door is opened to God's treasury, which in turn leads to a supply of riches that is endless and even beyond comprehension. These **infinite riches** are none other than Christ himself.

3:9 / The second aspect of Paul's mission is **making all people see how God's secret plan is to be put into effect**. Literally, the phrase reads "to enlighten" (*phōtisai*), or "to bring to light what is the stewardship (*oikonomia*) of the mystery." The Greek word for "all people" (*pantes*) is omitted in some manuscripts, so the emphasis is on bringing God's secret plan to light. Although not stated, the intention appears to be that the revelation is to **all people** (as the GNB).

The idea of "illuminating," or making all of humanity see how God's secret plan is to be put into effect, suggests something more than proclamation; it conveys the idea that Paul was used specifically to show the world how God publicly disclosed what had been kept secret. This Paul accomplished by explaining the incorporation of the Jews and Gentiles into the body of Christ. Everything that has taken place is part of God's master plan (*oikonomia*). The reference to God as the **Creator of all things** is somewhat enigmatic. Does it mean that this secret plan of God is part of his creative activity, or does it emphasize that his secret was hidden from the time of creation and **hidden through all the past ages**?

The parallel in Colossians 1:26, for example, mentions the secret hidden "through all past ages from all mankind" but without reference to God as the Creator. F. Beare concludes that the mention of God's creative activity is "in keeping with the writer's consistent association of creation and redemption, and his emphasis on the cosmic aspect of the saving work of Christ" (p. 670). It does confirm that God is the **Creator of all things**, including that which is momentarily concealed but which, in his plan, is **put into effect**.

3:10 / What had remained hidden "through all the past ages" (3:9) is now (*nun*), **at the present time**, made manifest. This verse makes one of the most inclusive statements about the church in the entire NT. Simply put, it announces that the church has a cosmic function in the plan of God.

With this verse, the author reaches the climax of his development on the "secret plan of God." C. L. Mitton calls this "God's master plan" and outlines the sequence by which this revelation took place: "It was made known first to Paul (3:3), then to the apostles and prophets (3:5), then to *all men* (3:9). Only then, as God's reconciling power in Christ became effective in his Church and produced a united fellowship out of elements which in the world had seemed irreconcilable, did the powers of evil realize what God was achieving" (p. 127). This unfolding of God's plan as presented in Ephesians may be diagrammed in the following way:

Paul (3:3)	Apostles and prophets (3:5)	All mankind (3:9)	Angelic powers and rulers in the heavenly world (3:10)

In this last stage God's plan comes full circle: What was alluded to in the opening hymn of praise (1:10) is now complete. The grand purpose of the church is that through its agency, **the angelic rulers and powers in the heavenly world might learn of God's wisdom in all its different forms**. These angelic rulers and powers are those beings that the author mentioned in 1:21 and to which he will return in 6:12. Colossians used similar expressions when it taught Christ's—and consequently the believer's—victory over these evil forces (Col. 1:16; 2:15, 20; cf. also Rom. 8:38; 1 Pet. 3:22).

In order to understand this verse it is necessary to realize that the author is utilizing an ancient cosmological system. In pre-Copernican times, astronomers believed that the earth was the center of the universe and that it had no motion. The earth was surrounded by a series of spheres that contained celestial bodies, such as the sun, moon, stars, and planets, which revolved around the earth. Beyond these spheres (usually seven) was the highest heaven, where God made his abode. In time, it was believed that these spheres were inhabited by some kind of "heavenly beings," which acted as sovereign rulers within these spheres. These heavenly powers could be either good and friendly or evil and hostile.

With respect to salvation, some religious systems, such as that of the Gnostics, believed that the human soul had to pass through these spheres as it ascended to its permanent abode with God in the highest heaven. But as it moved upward, it was confronted by the rulers and authorities of these spheres, who, in most cases, were hostile and needed to be placated or appeased in some way so that safe passage through the spheres could be guaranteed. This developed into elaborate systems of magic, sorcery, and astrology, many of which were current during Paul's time.

The Good News in the book of Colossians is that Christ has defeated these evil powers through his death on the cross. Consequently, they no longer have any control or authority over mankind; believers share in that victory by virtue of their faith in Christ and their union with his death and resurrection in baptism (Col. 2:20).

Ephesians retains a similar cosmology: Christ is exalted and rules "above all heavenly rulers, authorities, powers, and lords (1:21); the Christian is engaged in a battle against "the wicked spiritual forces in the heavenly world, the rulers, authorities, and cosmic powers of this dark age" (6:12); and in 3:10, these forces exist as witnesses to what God has done and is doing through the church. Thus, all forms of life—whether on earth or in the far regions of the cosmos—know about God's eternal plan and purpose.

Scholarly interpretations vary greatly in their approach to the cosmology presented in such epistles as Ephesians and Colossians. Some believe that the concepts are obsolete and need to be demythologized, that is, reinterpreted in terms that have meaning for the modern era. A good example is M. Barth, who understands these concepts as politicoeconomic structures of society rather than as cosmic intelligences (cf. notes on 1:21, 22). At the other extreme there is the position represented by such spokesmen as J. Stott, who takes exception to the kind of interpretation given by Barth and others. Stott does not accept the view that Paul was referring to earthly social structures that are included in the redemptive activity of God. In his book *God's New Society*, he provides a short history of the study of the principalities and powers (pp. 267–75) and makes a passionate appeal that readers of the NT understand them as supernatural beings rather than as "structures, institutions and traditions" (p. 273).

It is unclear what effect this revelation of God's secret through the church is to have upon these heavenly beings. All the text says is that **by means of the church** they might know God's **wisdom in all its different forms**. Are they objects of God's redemptive activity, or are they merely cosmic spectators to a drama that is being worked out on earth through the church? The rest of the NT is silent on this subject, and there are only a few verses that allude to some kind of intelligent activity among the angels (cf. 1 Cor. 4:9; 1 Pet. 1:2).

The author describes the unity of the church as the manifestation of

God's wisdom—wisdom to the extent that God's divine purposes were being accomplished throughout all the "past ages" down to the **present time**. Only an all-wise God could bring hostile nations and powers together into a unified whole.

God's wisdom, the author continues, exists **in all its different forms**. This is a translation of the Greek *polypoikilos*, which basically means "many-sided" and which other versions render as "manifold" (RSV, NIV) or "varied forms" (NEB). God's manifold wisdom is like looking through a kaleidoscope that reveals an amazing array of shapes and colors as one turns it gently; it is like beholding a marvelous tapestry that a designer has woven from a variety of different strands (Stott, p. 123). In this verse, the author has a magnificent vision of a triumphant and unified church that demonstrates the entire creative and redemptive purposes of God to all humanity (3:9) as well as to all cosmic powers (3:10).

3:11 / The recent disclosure of God's secret was something that God had planned to do from eternity. In a way, the apostle is sharing a philosophy of history in which he sees each successive age as a further revelation of the eternal plan that God is working out for humanity. Many Christian writers have suggested that history be spelled HIS-STORY (cf. Stott, p. 127). The One who "chose us in him before the foundation of the world" (1:6, RSV) has now made that election possible **through Jesus Christ our Lord**.

As in the opening hymn, the author indicates that Christ is the agent through whom God accomplishes his purposes. Here he uses three specific titles for Christ: He is "the Christ," that is, the Messiah for whom the Jews hoped; he is **Jesus**, the one whom the early Christians believed was historically present with them in the Incarnation; he is the **Lord**, who through death and resurrection has been exalted to the Father's right hand.

When this verse states that God's eternal purpose was **achieved through Christ Jesus our Lord**, it implies that everything Christ did and said was important. The apostle is drawing attention to the entire Christ-event (incarnation-life-death-resurrection-exaltation), for in this, God accomplished his redemptive purpose for mankind. Ephesians 2:1–10 serves as a good commentary on how the apostle views the work of Christ as applied to the believer; 2:11–22 performs a similar function in showing how Jews and Gentiles are united in Christ to form his body. The church is a living testimony to the redemptive and unifying power of God on earth (3:9) as well as to all heavenly beings (3:10).

3:12 / Lest the readers conclude that the God who worked out this eternal plan is somehow removed from the everyday affairs of mankind, the apostle turns to a practical concern and reminds them that their **union** with Christ grants them the privilege of communicating with God (**in union with Christ and through our faith in him we have the boldness to go into God's presence with all confidence**). The words in Greek are "boldness" (*parrēsia*), "access" (*prosagogē*), and "confidence" (*pepoithēsis*). *Parrēsia* is used in the NT in the context of speaking, such as boldness in proclaiming the gospel (Acts 4:31; Eph. 6:20; Phil. 1:20) and confidence in approaching God (Heb. 4:16; 10:19).

Christians have that boldness in approaching God because their faith and union with Christ has given them **confidence**. In Christ, all barriers have been removed that would keep the believer from approaching God openly and confidently. Christ has revealed the Father as one who has forgiven his children and who loves them. B. F. Wescott aptly comments that "the right of address and the right of access are coupled together as parts of the right of personal communion with God" (p. 49).

3:13 / In this verse there appears to be an abrupt shift in the author's thought, and he returns to his previous mention of being a prisoner (3:1). By reading between the lines one could get the impression that the Gentile congregations had become discouraged (*egkakeō*, "become weary," "despair," "lose heart," "be afraid") because their great spokesman had been imprisoned. Undoubtedly, much prayer went up to God on Paul's behalf (Col. 4:18). It could be that his discussion on the revelation of God's secret and the reminder of the believer's freedom in approaching God led him to encourage his readers not to become **discouraged** over the circumstances surrounding his imprisonment.

Most commentators draw attention to the fact that the Greek phrase is capable of a number of translations and meanings because the verb "do not be discouraged" (*mē egkakein*) does not have a subject. Consequently, it could read *(a)* "I ask that 'I' may not be discouraged," or *(b)* "I ask that 'you' not be discouraged." The context of the passage, together with Paul's positive attitude toward his sufferings (Rom. 5:3; 2 Cor. 12:10; Col. 1:24), suggests that the author's concern is with the members of the Gentile congregations who may have become disheartened over Paul's imprisonment. Consequently, they are once again reminded (cf. 3:1) that Paul is suffering on their behalf; but this time the author adds that it is for **your benefit**, literally, "for your glory" (*doxa*). The immediate **benefit**, or "glory," is that through Paul's ministry and subsequent imprisonment, the Gentiles have become members of Christ's body. This, in turn, should prevent them from losing heart. It is doubtful that Ephesians is teaching that the sufferings of the martyrs are the glory of the church—a concept that developed in later centuries.

Additional Notes

3:3 / For an extended discussion of the "secret," see R. E. Brown, *The Semitic Background of the Term "Mystery" in the New Testament* (Philadelphia: Fortress, 1968); A. E. Harvey, "The Use of Mystery Language in the Bible," *JTS* n.s. 31 (1980), pp. 320–36.

3:10 / There is additional disc. of these concepts in the commentary on Col. 1:16; 2:15, 20, and Eph. 1:21, 22 and 6:12. See the bibliographies listed in notes on Eph. 1:20 and 6:12; cf. also Caragounis, *The Ephesians Mysterion*, pp. 139–42; Beare, pp. 671–2; Stott, pp. 267–75.

14

Praying for Enlightenment

For this reason I fall on my knees before the Father, ¹⁵from whom every family in heaven and on earth receives its true name. ¹⁶I ask God from the wealth of his glory to give you power through his Spirit to be strong in your inner selves, ¹⁷and I pray that Christ will make his home in your hearts through faith. I pray that you may have your roots and foundation in love, ¹⁸so that you, together with all God's people, may have the power to understand how broad and long, how high and deep, is Christ's love. ¹⁹Yes, may you come to know his love—although it can never be fully known—and so be completely filled with the very nature of God.

This section follows the same structural pattern that the author established earlier in the epistle. He began with a great hymn of thanksgiving for all of the spiritual blessings that God provided in Christ (1:3–14) and followed this by a prayer for his readers to understand their hope and inheritance in the Lord (1:15–20). In 2:1–3:13, the author provides a lengthy exposition on the believer's position in Christ (2:1–10), the incorporation of Jews and Gentiles into one body, the church (2:11–22), and Paul's personal role in revealing God's eternal and secret plan (3:1–13); this, too, is followed by a prayer that the readers will understand the magnitude of God's plan and be filled with the perfect fullness of God (3:14–19). An appropriate benediction closes the main doctrinal section of the epistle (3:20–21).

These similarities, however, should not prevent one from seeing some of the significant differences in the prayer. One devotional writer put the distinction in the following way: In the first prayer, "the apostle petitions God for knowledge; and in the second, he prays for love. The first is a prayer for revelation; the second is for enablement. It is not enough merely to *know*; we must *be*. The fruit of divine knowledge is the expression of divine life" (Strauss, p. 160).

There are two significant features of this prayer that should be noted. First, it has many parallels to the praise and prayer in chapter 1. In a sense, 3:14–21 could be considered a further application of the ideas developed earlier: prayer is offered to the Father (1:17=3:14 f.); prayer is for the

Spirit (1:17=3:16); the sphere of God's action is in the mind (1:18) or the inner self (3:16); there is an aim for knowledge and fullness (1:18 f.=3:18 f.); there is a linking of knowledge and power (1:19=3:19); and finally, praise and glory is offered to God (1:6, 12, 14=3:21).

Second, this prayer has a wonderful and ever-expanding progression to it. The author begins by listing three specific requests: He prays that his readers may (a) receive inner strength from the Holy Spirit (3:16), (b) experience the abiding presence of Christ in their hearts (3:17a), and (c) root and ground their lives in love (3:17b). The author envisions two significant developments from this: first, a deeper understanding and appreciation of the extent of God's love (3:18); second—the ultimate goal—being "completely filled with the very nature of God" (3:19).

3:14 / C. L. Mitton begins his exposition of this prayer by rightfully noting that "this short paragraph is one of the gems of the NT" (p. 129). The section opens with the same phrase (**for this reason**) as 3:1, where it appears that the author initially wanted to offer this prayer but was momentarily diverted. To **fall on** one's **knees** is an expression of deep emotion and humility—prostration in the spirit of submission (Rom. 11:4; 14:11; Phil. 2:10). Another posture of prayer was to stand with one's face and hands lifted up to God (Matt. 6:5; Mark 11:25). Either way, it is the motive and inner attitude that is important, not the method. Once again, God is the **Father** to whom the prayer is directed.

3:15 / In Greek, there is a play on words between "Father" (*patros*) and **family** (*patria*) that is not obvious in the English. The author indicates that God, as Father, is the one **from whom every family in heaven and on earth receives its true name**. The meaning of the text is ambiguous and raises a number of problems: First, *patria* means a family, clan, or tribe that descends from a common ancestor. It cannot be translated as "fatherhood," although the idea of fatherhood is there and has led some commentators to think of God as the prototype or archetype of all fatherhood. This is different from saying that God is the father of all, which the passage is not teaching.

Second, the phrase **every family** (*pasa patria*) presents a problem analogous to "every building" in 2:21. Some translations use "the whole family," but to do so requires an article (*pasa hē partia*). The GNB **every family** is the correct translation. But this does not clarify the meaning.

Given the context of the passage, which includes the unity of all people and reference to "angels, rulers, and powers," it appears that the apostle understands that **every family**, that is, every human and divine father-hood, derives its pattern and meaning from God, the divine prototype. The family on earth could be the Jews and the Gentiles that make up the church as the family of God. By **every family in heaven**, either the apostle envisions some kind of heavenly community in which family structures are meaningful, or he is using it as an inclusive way of saying that all conceivable family patterns, whether on earth or in heaven, receive their **true name** from the Father. Mitton's suggestion that the verse could mean "local congregations" (on the earth) and "a company of departed Christians" (in heaven) is intriguing though not entirely convincing (pp. 131–32).

3:16 / In this prayer, the apostle draws upon the vast reservoir of God's resources—**I ask God from the wealth of his glory**. The glory of God is the essence of all that God is, and so there is no limit to his ability to give. Normally, one's prayers are limited by the inability to comprehend God's riches and ask accordingly (3:20; James 4:3, 4). Ephesians reminds believers that God gives according to the **wealth of his glory**!

The first request is for inner strength from the Holy Spirit. **Inner selves** is an inclusive term that can mean the heart, mind, spirit, and so on—anything that stands in contrast to the outer man (cf. Rom. 7:22; 2 Cor. 4:16). This inner strengthening is to take place by means of the **power** (*dynamis*) imparted by the Holy **Spirit**. It is the means by which God works within the believer's life.

3:17 / Second, there is the abiding presence of Christ in one's heart (**that Christ will make his home in your hearts through faith**). Here is another way that God prepares the believer to fulfill his ultimate purpose. This statement reverses Paul's usual terminology on the believer's union with Christ by emphasizing that Christ dwells within the believer. This indwelling is to be perceived as Christ taking up residency in the believer's heart, that is, in his or her inmost being. Furthermore, it is a relationship granted **through faith**, a thought reminiscent of 2:1–10 and the baptismal passages that connect faith with the indwelling Christ (Rom. 6:1–11; Gal. 3:26, 27; Col. 2:11–13; cf. also Gal. 2:20). Faith is one's inner response to the action of God through his Spirit.

Although the requests for strength from the Holy Spirit and for the indwelling of Christ are two separate expressions, they conform to Paul's theology that equates the Spirit as the Spirit of Christ: To have Christ is to have the Spirit; to be in the Spirit is to be in Christ (Rom. 8:9 ff.).

The third request is that the readers may have their **roots and founda-**

tion in love. The tense of these verbs in Greek (perfect passive, *errizōmenoi, tethemeliōmenoi*), indicates this is an action that already has taken place but is to continue as a reality in the believer's life (cf. Col. 1:23; 2:7, for similar exhortations toward stability). To illustrate the depth of life that he is after, the author uses a botanical and architectural metaphor: One sends its roots deep into the soil, whereas the other is grounded on a firm foundation. The GNB indicates that the soil or foundation is **love**.

This translation does not indicate a rather serious textual question at this point. In the Greek, it is permissible to take the phrase **in love** with rooted and grounded (as GNB) or to take it with the preceding phrase to read "that Christ may make his home in your hearts, through faith in love." A. T. Robinson, for one, takes it in this latter sense; by faith the Gentiles are partakers of Christ, but they are bound together in love (p. 175).

Most scholars, however, take love as the soil into which the roots grow or the foundation upon which a structure is built. Love is seen more as the result of Christ dwelling within the believer than the sphere in which he dwells. The ultimate truth is that those who are strengthened by the Spirit and in whom Christ dwells will have their lives rooted and grounded in love. Since love is the possession of Jews and Gentiles, both can grow together in their understanding of Christ's love.

3:18 / After making these three specific requests, the apostle concludes by mentioning the *effect* that his prayer will have upon their understanding of God. He is still addressing the Gentiles and indicates that their reception of God's gifts is not something that they experience in isolation but **together with all God's people** ("all the saints").

These words are especially appropriate to people of a Greek background, with their tendency toward rationalism and love for knowledge (cf. 1 Cor. 1:22; 8:1-3; Col. 2:18, 23; 1 Tim. 1:4; 6:4). But even though the author has been developing a Christian philosophy of history with respect to God, humanity, and the world, the emphasis is upon love rather than knowledge. He would not condone a Gnostic system that elevates knowledge as the highest gift. The real test of one's spiritual maturity is whether or not one is rooted and grounded in love; love, not knowledge, leads to a deeper understanding of God.

With the emphasis upon love rather than knowledge, one cannot help but feel that the author is attacking some form of Gnosticism (cf. Introduction). Besides stressing knowledge (*gnōsis*) in itself, the attainment and possession of knowledge often led to a kind of spiritual elitism in the church. In Corinth, for example, this developed into a division between the "spiritual," that is, those who possessed a higher knowledge, and the "fleshly," those who were less enlightened (cf. 1 Corinthians). The Apostle John confronts a similar problem in his first epistle, where a manifestation of Gnosticism threatened to divide the church. This made it necessary for him to emphasize the close relationship between knowledge and love: "Whoever does not love does not know God, because God is love" (1 John 4:8; cf. also 2:9; 3:11–19; 4:13–21).

Knowledge, when grounded in love, will unify, not divide, God's people. Thus the apostle prays that the Gentiles will realize that their spiritual insight and maturity are not unique to them; they do not exist in isolation from the way that God has worked out his purposes historically, particularly among the Jews. And as they are members of the same body, fellow heirs, and so forth (3:6), they share a knowledge of Christ's love and the fullness of God **together with all God's people**.

This knowledge of God's truth is not the possession of a few privileged individuals; it is not a matter of secret doctrines for a small inner circle. Knowledge of God's mystery is given to individuals in and for the community of believers in the same way that all spiritual gifts are given for the welfare of the entire body (4:11–16; 1 Cor. 12:4–13; 14:12, 26). This is a timely message to Christians of any age when individualism tends to destroy the unity of the body of Christ.

The prayer includes the **power to understand**—in other words, strength to comprehend or the complete ability to realize **how broad and long, how high and deep, is Christ's love**. This spatial imagery should be seen as the author's attempt to show the magnitude of Christ's love and should not leave the reader searching for objects that the author may have in mind. There are a number of interpretations of this passage that refer to the shape of the cross, the church, the temple, the visible universe, and so forth. At best, however, such suggestions are "curiosities" (Stott, p. 137), or fanciful and ingenious interpretations (Mitton, p. 134).

When the author begins to reflect upon Christ's love, he quickly discovers that there is no tangible way to describe it, and so l.. esorts to these rhetorical expressions. Christ's love can only be described in spatial images. Paul had a similar experience when he dwelled upon God's love in Christ and exclaimed that absolutely nothing can separate the believer from the "love of God which is ours through Christ Jesus our Lord" (Rom. 8:31–9). Ephesians uses spatial imagery in a way analogous to the psalmist when he describes God's love (Ps. 103) or the omnipresence of God (Ps. 139). Every part of the universe is suffused with the love of Christ.

3:19 / But even as the apostle summons his readers to understand Christ's love, he realizes that any effort to do so falls short of its intended goal. No matter how much power of comprehension one has, Christ's love **can never be fully known**; it "surpasses knowledge" (RSV); it exceeds one's "capacity of comprehension" (Beare, p. 679). What an indictment of those people who claimed such knowledge for themselves! Though it is legitimate and necessary to seek such comprehension, it is folly to claim full attainment of it. (For another discussion of love and its superiority to knowledge cf. 1 Cor. 8:1–3; 13:1–3).

Although believers never fully understand Christ's love, it is a step toward being **completely filled with the very nature of God**. This is the second result of his prayer that the apostle envisions. He began by praying that the power of the Holy Spirit, the indwelling of Christ, and grounding in love would lead to an understanding of Christ's love. But the ultimate goal is that the believers attain the fullness that belongs to God, that is, all the riches and glory that belongs to him. "God's fullness or perfection becomes the standard or level up to which we pray to be filled" (Stott, p. 138).

The concept of "fullness" (*plērōma*) in Colossians (1:19; 2:9, 10) and Ephesians (1:23; 3:19; 4:13) is another way by which the author describes the indicative and imperative or the "already" and the "not yet" of the Christian life. In union with Christ, believers have been granted this fullness; but their possession is a goal that remains to be fulfilled as they appropriate God's gifts and grow in their capacity to receive them (1:14; 4:30). The apostle seems to be emphasizing the reality of this within the context of the church and not alluding to some kind of heavenly perfection that awaits God's people when this earthly pilgrimage is over.

Additional Notes

On 3:14–21, see W. E. Hull, *Love in Four Dimensions* (Nashville: Broadmans, 1982).

3:14 / For further discussion on **every family** in 3:14, see Abbott, pp. 93–94; Mitton, pp. 130–32.

3:18 / See N. A. Dahl, "Cosmic Dimensions and Religious Knowledge (Eph 3:18)," in *Jesus and Paulus*, ed. E. E. Ellis and E. Grässer (Göttingen: Vandenhoeck & Ruprecht, 1975), pp. 57–75. Also, Barth, *Eph. 1–3*, pp. 395–97; Moule, p. 100; Robinson, p. 176.

Praising Through Doxology

EPHESIANS 3:20–21

To him who by means of his power working in us is able to do so much more than we can ever ask for, or even think of: ²¹to God be the glory in the church and in Christ Jesus for all time, forever and ever! Amen.

3:20 / The apostle has prayed earnestly for certain things, but he realizes that even his requests fall far short of what God is able to do. Thus he concludes this doctrinal section with an appeal to the infinite wealth and understanding of God: **To him who . . . is able to do so much more than we can ever ask for, or even think of**. He has opened to his readers the marvels of God's secret and how they have been incorporated into the body of Christ. But in spite of this vast and eternal plan of God, he reminds them that God has the resources to do much more **by means of his power working in us**. "Our experience of his power, as it is brought to bear within us, is a limited but true index to the nature of the power that governs the universe and brings all things to their appointed end" (Beare, p. 680).

3:21 / Most of the doxologies in the NT connect the glory of God to Christ in some way (Rom. 11:36; 16:27; Gal. 1:5; 1 Tim. 1:17; 1 Pet. 4:11; Jude 24, 25); this is the only passage that refers to glory **in the church and in Christ Jesus**. Some commentators take this as part of the author's liturgical language, which should not be pressed for any kind of theological precision (see Houlden, p. 305). However, given the teaching about the church in Ephesians, the relationship of the church as the body to its head, Christ, and the occurrence of so much liturgical language in the epistle, it seems more likely that the author's statement is chosen deliberately. Christ (head) and his church (body) form the entire sphere of God's glory as well as provide the means by which that glory is proclaimed to all humanity. This praising of God's glory is to go on **for all time, forever and ever! Amen**. This **amen** is a final liturgical declaration that may everything the apostle has written indeed be so.

The Appeal and Pattern
for Unity

EPHESIANS 4:1-6

I urge you, then—I who am a prisoner because I serve the Lord: live a life that measures up to the standard God set when he called you. ²Be always humble, gentle, and patient. Show your love by being tolerant with one another. ³Do your best to preserve the unity which the Spirit gives by means of the peace that binds you together. ⁴There is one body and one Spirit, just as there is one hope to which God has called you. ⁵There is one Lord, one faith, one baptism; ⁶there is one God and Father of all mankind, who is Lord of all, works through all, and is in all.

Chapter 4 begins what often is referred to as the ethical or practical section of the epistle. If one could say that chapters 1–3 provide the *theological basis* for Christian unity, then chapters 4–6 contain the *practical instruction* for its maintenance. In other words, unity has been established (the indicative); now it becomes the duty of the believers to strengthen and maintain unity in their fellowship (the imperative).

This generalization does not mean that chapters 4–6 are devoid of theological content. The division of the epistle into such broad categories is somewhat misleading, because, as in the case of Colossians, the apostle throughout his epistles frequently combines theological and ethical statements (cf. disc. on Col. 3:1 ff.). In Ephesians, the moral teaching is based upon what has been said in the earlier chapters (1–3) but also grows out of new theological concerns of the author, particularly with respect to the unity of the church. The liturgical style that characterized much of the first half of the epistle is maintained throughout the second half as well.

It has been suggested that the main theme in Ephesians is unity—a unity that has been effected by the reconciling work of Christ who has united all things in heaven and earth (1:10) and who has brought Jews and Gentiles together into the church. The apostle now exhorts his readers to maintain that unity in their personal, domestic, social, and ecclesiastical lives.

In the opening exhortation (4:1–3), he immediately draws attention to his main concern: The readers need to manifest those virtues characterizing their new life in Christ that "preserve the unity which the Spirit gives" (4:3). This admonition is followed by a list of all the unifying elements of the church (4:4–6), which, in turn, are given further application throughout the remaining chapters.

4:1 / **I urge you, then** ("therefore," RSV), refers to what has been said in chapters 1–3. As in 3:1, the apostle reminds his readers that his vocation is the ground of his captivity (**I who am a prisoner because I serve the Lord**). The Greek preposition *en* also points to the sphere of his captivity: He is a prisoner "in the Lord."

The exhortation begins by calling the readers to **live a life that measures up to the standard God set when he called you**. The concept of *calling* is an important one in Biblical thought. On a number of occasions the prophets remind the people of Israel that they have been "called" by God to fulfill a specific function (see Isa. 41:9; 42:6; 43:1; 44:2; 45:3, 4; Hos. 11:1). Christians, likewise, have a calling from God, as is evident in the Lord's disciples (Mark 1:20), the Apostle Paul (1 Cor. 1:1), and the Gentiles (Eph. 3:8).

In Ephesians, the Gentiles have been told that God has chosen them to be his children (1:4, 5), appointed them to praise God's glory (1:12), called them to a wonderful hope (1:18), and incorporated them into the body of Christ for a life of good works (2:10); now they are admonished to demonstrate their calling and position in Christ by a worthy ethical life.

To **live a life** is a translation of the Greek *peripateō*, which means "to walk." At one time their "walk" conformed to "the world's evil way" (2:2); now they are exhorted to "walk" (**live a life**), that is, bear witness to, their new life in Christ and the unity that is theirs in the church. They are a part of God's grand design for the world, which includes the uniting of all things in heaven and on earth (1:10).

4:2 / In this verse the apostle presents a list of personal attitudes that are essential for unity in the body of Christ. There is a striking similarity to the list in Colossians 3:12–15, but here the application is developed around the theme of unity. J. Stott refers to these virtues as the "five foundation stones of Christian unity" (p. 149). As was noted in Colossians, many of these virtues are related, and it is sometimes difficult to draw distinctions between them.

Humility (*tapeinophrosunē*) is that attitude of mind that enables one to see people other than oneself. The Greeks disdained the idea of a submissive or subservient attitude, but Christianity, by virtue of Christ's example in the Incarnation (Phil. 2:5–11), gave it new meaning. When Paul met with the Ephesian elders, he reminded them that his ministry among them was carried out "with all humility" (Acts 20:19). Humility is especially important in the body of Christ, where interpersonal relationships are so important. The Philippian church is a good example of how pride, selfishness, and conceit produce a fractured fellowship (Phil. 2:1–4).

Gentleness (*prautēs*) is consideration toward others. A gentle person will not insist upon his or her personal rights or be assertive at the expense of others. J. Stott notes how humility and gentleness go together by drawing upon an insight from R. W. Dale: "For 'the meek man thinks as little of his personal claims, as the humble man of his personal merits' " (p. 149).

Patience (*makrothumia*) and **being tolerant to one another** (*anechō*, lit., "endure someone or something") form another single thought. Patience would be the willingness and the ability to deal with people in a deliberate but courteous way—in the manner that God deals patiently with his people (Rom. 2:4; 9:22; 1 Tim. 1:16; 1 Pet. 3:20; 2 Pet. 3:15); Christians are called upon to demonstrate this virtue in dealing with one another (1 Cor. 13:4; Gal. 5:22; 2 Tim. 4:2). Such mutual tolerance within the body will go a long way in maintaining a spirit of unity.

The fifth virtue is **love**. Though it could be argued that love is not a separate quality from patience but "an amplification of what patience means" (Mitton, p. 138), love could be taken as the crowning virtue that embraces all the rest. Love is emphasized a number of times throughout the epistle (1:4; 3:17; 4:15, 16). And although love may include being helpful to one another, the author realizes that all virtues need to be practiced if there is to be unity within the church.

4:3 / **Do your best** is a very emphatic expression coming from the word *spoudazō*, which means "to exert zealous effort," "to take pains," **to preserve the unity**. The entire expression—**do your best to preserve the unity**—underscores the apostle's concern that his readers make an effort to guard carefully the unity that has been given to them. In principle, this unity already exists as something **which the Spirit gives**; now God's people are admonished to preserve and manifest that unity.

Ephesians is the only epistle in the NT that uses the word **unity** (*enotēs*, 4:3, 13). Elsewhere, unity is described by such concepts as "fellowship," "communion," "one man," "one body," and so on. The unity here is a gift of **the Spirit** and should thus manifest itself in the human spirit.

Peace is introduced as the quality or means that **binds** believers together (lit., "in the bond of peace"). This is different from Colossians 3:14, where love binds all things together in perfect unity. In Ephesians, **peace** was obtained when the hostilities that separated Jews and Gentiles were broken down and both races were united in one new man in Christ (2:14–16); now it is presented as the bond by which that unity is kept.

Now that the author has exhorted his readers to maintain their unity through proper conduct, he presents the theological base from which all unity arises. Verses 4–6 contain a list of seven "ones" that relate the unity of the church to the unity of Christ and God.

There are a number of theories about the origin of this passage. Some scholars have found striking parallels in certain forms of Hellenistic Judaism and Stoic philosophy. F. Beare, for example, lists a number of non-Christian sources that bear witness to the concern that existed in the ancient world about the unity of the cosmos, God, Law, Truth, and all areas of life (pp. 685–86). The assumption is that the author of Ephesians adopted such formulas, gave them a specific Christian content, and incorporated them into his epistle.

Most commentators, however, take verses 4–6 to be a compilation of verses and ideas that Paul has used throughout his writings. The main difference between Paul's undisputed writings and the epistle to the Ephesians is not so much the content as it is the structure in which these formulations occur. Only Ephesians collects and arranges the thoughts into a pattern that resembles a liturgical hymn or a creedal confession.

Though the author may be indebted to such Pauline texts as 1 Corinthians 8:6 and 12:4–13, the application that he gives to the ideas found there conforms to his specific concern for unity within the body of Christ. In Corinthians, for example (1 Cor. 12:4–13), a local concern is dealt with regarding a misunderstanding of spiritual gifts and their application in the church's worship and corporate life. It is emphasized that all spiritual pride and disunity should disappear because such gifts come from the same Spirit. In Ephesians, Christ is the dispenser of spiritual gifts, and the unity that embraces all of society is based upon the "oneness" of God himself as the ultimate source of unity (see Houlden, p. 309).

Structurally, there are several features of this passage that are worth noting: First, the author moves from the church ("body") to the Godhead. One may have expected him to proceed from the unity of God to the unity of the church, but his order appears to be determined by his concern for unity within the body. Verse 4 flows quite naturally from his exhortation in verse 3 calling for the church to preserve the unity that the Spirit gives; thus, "there is one body and one Spirit."

Second, there is an obvious emphasis on all the members of the trinity and the believer's relationship to the Spirit, Son, and Father. Though there have been a number of ingenious attempts at outlining the apostle's thoughts, there does not appear to be any conscious symmetry or parallelism in his mind. J. Stott, for example, applies four of the expressions to different members of the trinity: "First, the one Father creates the one family. Secondly, the one Lord Jesus creates the one faith, hope and baptism. Thirdly, the one Spirit creates the one body (p. 151). Basically, however, the passage teaches that the unity of the Godhead is the foundation of the church's unity. "Its unity is of the same order as the unity of Christ and of God; as there cannot be other gods or other lords, so there cannot be other churches" (Beare, p. 686).

4:4 / **There is one body and one Spirit**: The union of body and spirit is especially noticeable in such passages as 1 Corinthians 8:6; 12:4–6, 13. The emphasis in Ephesians undoubtedly is related to the concept that believers are members of the body by virtue of the work of the Holy Spirit (Rom. 8:9; 1 Cor. 12:13). There is only one body because there is one Spirit.

Besides being one in body and Spirit, **there is one hope to which God has called you**. **Hope** is the goal or inheritance toward which the body strives in the Spirit (1:14, 18; Col. 1:4, 5). All who have been called by God share in the hope that is common to all believers.

4:5 / From "the body," the apostle moves to "the Head" (Christ) and what unites the believer to him. **Lord** is the Greek *kyrios*, which is attributed to Christ on a number of occasions (1 Cor. 8:6; 12:3; Phil. 2:11). The church is established by its acknowledgment of Jesus as "the sovereign Lord."

Faith may be taken in two ways: First, it could signify "the faith," that is, that body of teaching that contains all the truths about Christ's life, work, and so forth. In the early church this became a common expression for the Christian message (Gal. 1:23; Phil. 1:27; 1 Tim. 3:9; 4:1, 6; Titus 1:4; Jude 3). But the absence of the article "the" in this passage makes it more likely that the author is thinking of one's belief in Jesus as

Lord and thus the acceptance and acknowledgment of him as Lord.

Baptism refers to the rite of water baptism, because it is the visible expression of one's faith in the Lord and is the means by which one becomes a member of Christ's body, the church (Rom. 6:1–11; Gal. 3:26, 27; Col. 2:11–13). It is doubtful that **one** baptism carries the idea that baptism is unrepeatable or that it is a polemic against other baptismal practices current at the time. All that is implied is that the one proper, or correct, baptism is the baptism of faith into Christ. Baptism is a sacrament of unity because it expresses a common faith in the one Lord.

The idea of baptism as a sacrament of unity is not unique to Ephesians. Behind Paul's rather sarcastic remark to the Corinthians—"Were

you baptized as Paul's disciples?" (1 Cor. 1:13)—lies the implication that their baptism into Christ should unify rather than divide. This is even more forcefully expressed in 1 Corinthians 12:13, where there is a specific reference to "baptism into the one body by the same Spirit." The direct mention of Jews and Greeks in this Corinthians passage, as well as in Galatians 3:27, 28, and Colossians 3:10, 11, fits well into the theme of unity in Ephesians.

Though faith, Lord, body, and Spirit all belong to the baptismal event, there is no way of knowing whether these phrases contain a baptismal formula or confession. If one subscribes to the liturgical setting of Ephesians, then it would be possible to envision these verses as a confession that a baptismal candidate recited or the witnessing congregation sang as a hymn. The opening admonition to live a life that coincides with God's call could be taken to refer to the new life that is received in baptism. However, the appearance of this formula in Ephesians does not necessarily mean that the epistle is a baptismal treatise or liturgy. Its application of baptismal imagery and theology simply conforms to the author's purpose in describing the unity of the church. But behind the formula lies the idea of baptism as the "sacrament of unity," the rite by which Jew and Gentile have been made members of the body of Christ. Both their faith and their baptism is in Jesus Christ as **Lord**.

4:6 / The writer's thoughts reach their climax in the unity of God (**there is one God and Father of all mankind**). The Christian community shared the Jewish concept of monotheism (one God) and through their relationship with Christ, appreciated God as Father (Rom. 8:15; 1 Cor. 8:6; Gal. 4:6; Eph. 3:14). Although there is no personal pronoun in Greek, and God's fatherhood is not limited to humanity (3:15), the GNB inserts **mankind** to indicate that it is God's relationship to redeemed humanity that is in the author's mind (so RSV, but not NIV). **Mankind**, however, is omitted in the next phrase, **who is Lord of all, works through all, and is in all**; it is not clear whether the translators intended the first **mankind** to carry through the remaining expressions without being mentioned again, or whether they are taking the expression **all** (*pantōn*) to mean everything, all things, the universe, and so on. The KJV "in you all" reflects a reading that does not have good manuscript evidence and that has been abandoned in subsequent translations.

Given the context of the passage, it would appear that the author has the community of God's people in mind (Stott, p. 151) even though such thoughts can embrace the entire universe. The concepts express God's transcendance ("**Lord of all**"), his omnipresence (**through all**) and his immanence (**in all**). One wonders if there is a veiled reference to the triune God, for in Christian thought, God's omnipresence and immanence are manifestations of the Son and the Spirit. The verse is similar to Paul's benediction in Romans 11:36, where he states: "For all things were created by him, and all things exist through him and for him."

17

The Giving of Spiritual Gifts to the Body

EPHESIANS 4:7–11

Each one of us has received a special gift in proportion to what Christ has given. ⁸As the scripture says:

"When he went up to the very heights,

he took many captives with him;

he gave gifts to mankind."

⁹Now, what does "he went up" mean? It means that first he came down to the lowest depths of the earth.ᵉ ¹⁰So the one who came down is the same one who went up, above and beyond the heavens, to fill the whole universe with his presence. ¹¹It was he who "gave gifts to mankind"; he appointed some to be apostles, others to be prophets, others to be evangelists, others to be pastors and teachers.

e. the lowest depths of the earth; *or* the lower depths, the earth itself.

4:7 / The apostle has been discussing the unity of the whole (4:1–6); now he turns to the individual parts and shows how diversity within the body contributes to its unity. The body is unified but it is not uniform; every person has a special gift that makes a contribution to the whole.

In the verses following, the apostle lists the various gifts that are necessary for the body to function properly and ultimately to attain its goal of maturity—"reaching to the very height of Christ's full stature" (4:13). **Each one of us has received a special gift** (lit., "but grace was given to each one of us"). Christ's giving is always a matter of his grace, and just as the apostle has emphasized how he personally was the recipient of grace (3:2, 7, 8), he reminds the readers that each one of them has received the same privilege. Later, he will show how that privilege leads to responsibility (3:12–16).

The gift is **in proportion to what Christ has given**. Though grace suggests the unlimited favor of God, this phrase shows that, as it was given to **each** individual, it does have certain limitations. No one person has all the gifts that are necessary for the body; rather, the gifts of each member are supplemented by the gifts of all members. It is the working together of each part that produces the unity and growth that the apostle envisions.

Here it is the gift that **Christ has given**, not the gift of the Spirit, as in Corinthians (1 Cor. 12:7-13).

The unity of this passage is broken by a parenthesis that the apostle inserts at 4:9-10. He has introduced Christ as the giver of spiritual gifts, but before he goes on to enumerate them (4:11), he pauses to reflect upon the "giver" and how Christ's dispensing of these gifts relates to the humiliation and exaltation of Christ. This "so-called" parenthesis (4:9-10) is one of the most difficult and controversial passages in the entire epistle: First, there is the translation of an OT quotation; second, there is the application of the quotation to Christ; and third, there is the meaning of these verses within the context of Ephesians.

4:8 / **As the scripture says** clearly indicates that the author is quoting from the OT. The problem, however, is that the quotation in Ephesians differs considerably from Psalm 68:18, which is the only likely source of the quotation.

Psalm 68:18	Ephesians 4:8
He goes up to the heights,	**When he went up to the very**
taking many captives with him;	**heights he took many captives with**
he receives gifts from rebellious men.	**him; he gave gifts to mankind.**

The GNB translation does not indicate that there is a change from the second person (you) to the third person (he), but it does show that the author has changed the phrase "he receives gifts from" to "he gave gifts to." Scholarly reaction to this has varied from accusations of deliberate alteration (see Houlden, p. 310), an "unintentional misquotation" (Mitton, p.146), or a piece of rabbinical exegesis (Beare, p. 688), to J. Stott's explanation "that the two renderings are only formally but not substantially contradictory" (p. 157).

Initially, the psalm celebrated an earthly triumph of the Israelites over their enemies and the return of the defeated foes with the spoils of war to the capital city. This serves also as a picture of God's victory over all his enemies during the Exodus and his enthronement in the holy city. At a later period, the rabbis interpreted this passage as referring to Moses' ascension of Mount Sinai to receive the Law (Exod. 19). It became associated with the festival of Pentecost as the celebration of the giving of the Torah (Law). In this usage of the psalm, the rabbis understood that Moses ascended the mountain to receive gifts, that is, the Law, *for* mankind so that he, in turn, might *give* it to mankind (see Barth, *Eph. 4-6*, p.

472; Beare, p. 688). An ancient Targum (an Aramaic translation of the Hebrew) actually changes the wording of the original psalm to "he gave gifts to men."

When the author of Ephesians comes to discuss the spiritual gifts that Christ bestowed upon the church, he draws upon that psalm because he sees Christ's ascendency to the Father as a prophetic fulfillment of it (**when he went up to the very heights**). As Moses was given the Law for the people of Israel, Christ, as a second but greater Moses, gave the Spirit to the church, which, in turn, included the gifts mentioned in 4:11 (**he gave gifts to mankind**). The **many captives** refers to the principalities and powers that he led captive (1:20–22; Col. 2:15).

Commentators either are troubled by the author's cavalier use of the OT (Houlden, p. 310) and disregard for the original meaning of the OT text or they accept this as "a true testimony of the Spirit of Prophecy" (Moule, p. 107). J. Stott reconciles the problem by stressing that "receiving" was for the purpose of "giving" and finds this principle illustrated in Peter's sermon on the day of Pentecost (Acts 2:33), when he states: "He has been raised to the right side of God and received from him the Holy Spirit, as his Father had promised; and what you now see and hear is his gift that he has poured out on us" (pp. 158 f.).

4:9 / The author leaves the quotation and expands upon the meaning of ascend and descend: **Now, what does "he went up" mean? It means that first he came down**. In other words, Christ's ascension implies a previous descension. The best Greek manuscripts do not contain the word **first**, even though it does help to clarify the meaning. The phrase **down to the lower depths of the earth** raises the second major interpretative problem in this passage. Commentators are full of suggestions, which include *(a)* the earth, *(b)* the region below the earth, such as Hell or Hades, *(c)* Christ's descent at the Incarnation, *(d)* Christ's humiliation on the cross and his subsequent death and burial, and *(e)* Christ's return at Pentecost to give his spirit to the church.

Since the apostle does not clarify what he meant, one assumes that his readers must have known to what he was referring. Some may have thought of a tradition in the early church that spoke of Christ visiting the underground between the time of his death and resurrection (1 Pet. 3:19; 4:6). However, it could be just an expressive way of being as inclusive as possible. It thus serves to balance the phrase **above and beyond the heavens** in 4:10.

4:10 / From descent the apostle turns to ascent and stresses that the same person is meant in both cases: **So the one who came down is the same one who went up**. This must be a reference to an early heresy known as Docetism, which denied the reality and integrity of the Incarnation (cf. 1 John). What the author would be saying is that the same Jesus who became incarnate, who suffered and died, who descended to Hades (?), is the same person who was exalted to the right hand of the Father and who is the dispenser of spiritual gifts.

The ascension is **above and beyond the heavens**. Ancient cosmology depicted at least seven heavens above the earth (see disc. on 3:10). Here again the apostle is saying that Christ has been exalted to "the highest honor and glory possible" (Foulkes, p. 116); his presence permeates everything between the deepest deep and the highest high ("everything in heaven and on earth," 1:10). Early Christian theology described Christ's ascension as an exaltation in, through, or beyond the heavens (1:20, 21; Heb. 4:14; 7:26).

The purpose of the ascension is that Christ will **fill the whole universe with his presence** (cf. 1:23). This could mean that Christ simply pervades everything with his presence or that, by doing so, he brings all things into subjection under his sovereignty. At any rate, the central truth about the ascension is that it makes Christ accessible "to all men everywhere at all time" (Mitton, p. 149). In the context of the gifts, this passage shows that the ascended Lord is the same person who descended to the earth in order to give these spiritual gifts to the church.

4:11 / After this brief commentary on Psalm 68:18, the apostle returns to his thoughts on the special gifts that Christ has given to the church (4:7). From his rendering of the psalm, he repeats—as if to re-emphasize—that Christ is the giver: **It was he who "gave gifts to mankind"; he appointed** (lit., "gave") **some to be apostles, others to be prophets, others to be evangelists, others to be pastors and teachers**.

Although a verse like this may look relatively simple on the surface, there are a number of issues that make its meaning difficult and even ambiguous: First, within the canon of the NT there is often an overlapping of functions attributed to an office. Deacons and elders, for example, perform a similar ministry, and few scholars agree on how presbyters, bishops, and elders are to be distinguished from each other.

Second, churches may have varied in their organizational structure from place to place. Thus, what was true for one specific congregation may not have applied to all the other churches. It is a fairly well accepted theory that the "charismatic" leadership of the early church gradually was replaced by regulated offices such as elders, bishops, deacons, and so on. The Pastoral Epistles (1 and 2 Timothy, Titus), for example, stress the various offices of the church rather than the variety of gifts mentioned in 1 Corinthians 12.

Third, there also is the question of authority in the early church. Initially, spiritual and ecclesiastical authority belonged to the early leaders—the apostles, prophets, elders, and so on. Gradually, however, this authority was replaced, or rather superseded, by the canon of Scripture. As the early church leaders died out, the church was forced to look at the inspired writings that they had left behind as their source of authority. Thus Paul's apostolic authority could be maintained for succeeding generations through his letters to the churches.

A fourth problem about Ephesians is the intention of the author. What were his reasons for presenting the list that he does? Why does he omit the others that are mentioned in 1 Corinthians? Does his selection conform to his presentation of a universal rather than local church? Unfortunately, the answers to these questions are not always easy to determine.

Finally, any interpretation of these "gifts" runs the risk of imposing contemporary ideas upon ancient categories. Since the church today does not generally use the office of apostle, for example, the temptation is to find a modern counterpart in such church leaders as area superintendents, overseers, and so on (see Stott, p. 160). There may be a certain legitimacy to this, but it does not help to clarify the original meaning of an office and/or gift and to understand it in the context in which it is used. Here, it is not a case of putting new wine into old skins; the church has new skins into which it is trying to pour old wine.

There are several things that can be noted about Ephesians: First, **apostles**, **prophets**, and **teachers**, are the only three categories that are taken over directly from 1 Corinthians 12:28: "In the church, then, God has put all in place: in the first place, apostles, in the second place, prophets, and in the third place, teachers." The **apostles** and **prophets** have already been mentioned in the founding of the church (2:20; 3:5); the other offices (**evangelists, pastors/teachers**) occur for the first time.

Second, the office of evangelist occurs only two other times in the NT. Philip is an "evangelist" (Acts 21:8), and Timothy is exhorted by Paul to "do the work of a preacher of the Good News" (evangelist). There is no way of knowing whether the author thought of **evangelists** as foundational to the church in the same way as **apostles** and **prophets**. Certainly their function as proclaimers of the Good News could be considered in this way.

Third, it appears that attempts to separate these offices into foundational and continuing ministries, or those intended for the universal (**apostles, prophets, evangelists**) and local church (**pastors/teachers**) are arbitrary. Had the apostle intended to make such distinctions, one would have expected him to mention presbyters, bishops, and deacons as well. What is certain, however, is that Christ gave (**appointed**) these offices to the church for the specific function of having the church attain its full maturity in him (4:12–16).

Apostles: This term comes from the verb *apostellō*, which means "to send out." An apostle is one who has been sent. In the NT it is used of the Twelve, of those who are associated with specific churches (2 Cor. 8:23; Phil. 2:25), and of Christians generally (John 13:16). In the early church, the qualifications of an apostle of Christ were to have seen Jesus (1 Cor. 9:1, 2) and been a witness to the Resurrection (Acts 1:21–23). Apostles were individuals who were sent out as messengers, probably upon the commission of a church (after the Lord's death), to exercise some kind of leadership in spiritual and organizational matters.

Prophets: In Biblical literature, a prophet is a proclaimer (forth-teller) as well as a predictor (fore-teller). These individuals received a specific message from God, either directly or through his Word, and by way of divine utterances made the will of God known in specific situations. In most cases, it was the communication of a specific and immediate message of God to his people or to the church (see Stott, pp. 161–62).

Evangelists: The most obvious definition of an evangelist is "a preacher of the Good News" (2 Tim. 4:5). These would be itinerant individuals who would move about into unevangelized areas in order to proclaim the gospel. An evangelist may also have the gift of making the gospel understandable or of leading individuals to accept it as God's word for them.

Pastors and teachers: A common debate at this point is whether the author intended to express two distinct offices or whether pastors and teachers are two functions of the same office. The absence of the article before teachers (*tous de poimenas kai didaskalous*) leads one to suspect that these words express two aspects of the same office—an office that has a pedagogical and pastoral (shepherding) ministry.

This is the only occasion in the NT where the noun *poimēn* is used as a title for a church leader. Undoubtedly, it comes from the application of the shepherd imagery that characterized the Lord's relationship with his disciples. Jesus is the good shepherd (*ho poimēn ho kalos*, John 10:11–18; cf. also Matt. 18:12–14; Luke 15:3–7; Heb. 13:20; 1 Pet. 2:25; 5:4); on several occasions, leaders in the church are exhorted to "be shepherds of the flock that God gave you" (1 Pet. 5:2; Acts 20:28); church leaders are to pattern their "pastoral" (shepherding) ministry after the example of Christ.

If the primary function of a pastor is to *care* for the flock in a loving and pastoral way, then the main function of the teacher would be the *feeding* of the flock through the verbal instruction that is given. It is very difficult to separate the two, because pastoring and teaching are so closely related. To quote John Stott: "Perhaps one should say that, although every pastor must be a teacher, gifted in the ministry of God's Word to people (whether a congregation or groups of individuals), yet not every Christian teacher is also a pastor since he may be teaching only in a school or college rather than in a local church" (pp. 163–64). Pastoring, which includes an element of teaching, implies a long-term responsibility for the spiritual needs of people.

Additional Notes

4:8 / R. Rubinkeiwicz examines the targumic version of the psalm in his article, "Ps LXVII 19 (= EPH IV 8): Another Textual Tradition or Targum?" *NovT* 17 (1975), pp. 219–24. See also G. V. Smith, "Paul's Use of Psalm 68:18 in Ephesians 4:8," *JETS* 18 (1975), pp. 181–89.

4:9 / For further explanation of these theories, see Abbott, pp. 114–16; Barth, *Eph. 4–6*, pp. 433–34; Beare, pp. 688–89; Mitton, pp. 146–49; Stott, *God's New Society*, pp. 156–59. On the theory of Christ's descent at Pentecost, cf. G. B. Caird, "The Descent of Christ in Ephesians 4, 7–11," in *Studia Evangelica*, vol. 2, ed., F. L. Cross (Berlin: Akademie Verlag, 1964), pp. 535–45.

4:11 / An old but valuable discussion can be found in J. B. Lightfoot, "The Christian Ministry," in *Philippians* (London: Macmillan, 1898), pp. 181–269. On the offices, cf. K. H. Rengstorf, "*apostolos*," *TDNT*, vol. 1, pp. 407–47; G. Friedrich, "*prophētes*," *TDNT*, vol. 6, pp. 781–861; G. Friedrich, "*euaggelistēs*," *TDNT*, vol. 2, pp. 736–37; J. Jeremias, "*poimēn*," *TDNT*, vol. 6, pp. 485–502; K. J. Rengstorf, "*didaskalos*," *TDNT*, vol. 6, pp. 781–861.

18

The Attainment of Unity

He did this to prepare all God's people for the work of Christian service, in order to build up the body of Christ. ¹³And so we shall all come together to that oneness in our faith and in our knowledge of the Son of God; we shall become mature people, reaching to the very height of Christ's full stature. ¹⁴Then we shall no longer be children, carried by the waves and blown about by every shifting wind of the teaching of deceitful men, who lead others into error by the tricks they invent. ¹⁵Instead, by speaking the truth in a spirit of love, we must grow up in every way to Christ, who is the head. ¹⁶Under his control all the different parts of the body fit together, and the whole body is held together by every joint with which it is provided. So when each separate part works as it should, the whole body grows and builds itself up through love.

4:12 / After listing the offices, the apostle now clarifies their function or purpose. In conformity with Corinthians, the gifts are given to the church for the good of the entire body (1 Cor. 12:7; 14:26, 31). The work and the results that the author of Ephesians goes on to describe fit the ministry entrusted to the pastors and the teachers.

The first and immediate function of church leaders is **to prepare all God's people for the work of Christian service**. The GNB correctly combines preparation and ministry, thus avoiding the error of some earlier translations that made two coordinate clauses out of the sentence (cf. KJV; RSV, 1947 ed.). In the body, every member and not only the ministers must be taught to serve. The word *katartismos* ("training," "preparing," "equipping"), conveys the idea of an harmonious development in which all parts are brought to a condition of being able to perform according to their created purpose (2 Tim. 3:17).

The second phrase, **to build up the body of Christ**, expresses the ultimate goal of the gifts that are given to the church. Here the author uses building imagery to indicate that the body is being built as God's people are prepared for doing the work of the ministry (*diakonia*). Every member must contribute to this process, or the body will be deficient in certain areas of its growth.

4:13 / From these two general statements, the author goes on to define more specifically the various aspects of Christian growth in the body of Christ. The building up of the body of Christ includes several important features: First, there is an intellectual component (**and so we shall all come together to that oneness in our faith and in our knowledge of the Son of God**). Here is a call for the Christian community to collectively work toward attaining the unity of the faith (*eis tēn enotēta tēs pisteōs*). Since Ephesians already has spoken about the unity that is inherent in the "faith" (4:5), one sees this as another reminder that the readers are to progressively appropriate what is theirs by possession. The emphasis here is upon the corporate attainment of this unity (**we shall all come together**) rather than upon individuals striving for spiritual growth apart from the body.

In addition to faith, the apostle mentions **knowledge of the Son of God** as a second condition of unity. **Son of God** is another designation for Jesus (Rom. 1:4; Gal. 2:20), and there does not appear to be any specific reason why this term is used here. What is important is that the **Son of God** is essential to unity because he is the object of Christian faith and knowledge. The realization of unity, in other words, is only to be found in a personal relationship of faith and knowledge to the person of Jesus Christ.

A second feature of bodily growth includes personal maturity—**we shall become mature people** (*eis andra teleion*). Although there are some scholars who take this as a reference to individual or personal maturity (Mitton, p. 154) or to Christ as the "Perfect Man" (Barth, *Eph. 4–6*, pp. 484–96), the context shows that the author is still thinking about the corporate nature and unity of the church. As a body it is to grow up as **mature people**, a goal that, of course, can only be attained as each individual member grows in the unity of the faith and in the knowledge of the Son of God.

The third feature that the apostle mentions is something equivalent to Christ-likeness (Mitton, p. 154)—**reaching to the very height of Christ's full stature**. This is the final prepositional phrase that is used (*eis . . . eis . . . eis . . .*) and represents the final stage of the Church's maturity. Christian maturity, whether individually or corporately, is that quality of life that belongs to Christ. As the church attains Christ's full stature there is a reciprocal benefit in that Christ also finds his fullness in the church (1:23).

So far, the apostle has been describing Christian unity as a goal that is to be attained. True, there is diversity within the body with respect to the spiritual gifts that Christ has given to the church, but that diversity is to promote the unity of the faith and to assist the body in reaching its ultimate goal. Believers are to grow out of their individualism into the corporate oneness of the person of Christ. In the following verses he describes some circumstances that hinder the attainment of unity, and then he provides some insights on bodily growth.

4:14 / Although unity is an ideal to be realized, the writer is aware that the church's pilgrimage toward that goal is characterized by immaturity and instability. Currently, the body of Christ acts very much like **children**, a designation that implies immaturity, erratic temperament, individualism, self-assertion, and so on. When the church attains its goal, then it will no longer act in a childish way.

Children also are unstable, that is, they can be like a little boat, **carried by the waves and blown about by every shifting wind of the teaching of deceitful men**. The church acts in an immature and unstable way when it permits various false teachings and doctrines to distract it from attaining its maturity in Christ. There is no way of knowing whether the author has any specific heresy in mind (such as Gnosticism or Docetism, cf. Acts 19:26–35), or whether it is a general exhortation toward sound doctrine. Either way, the teaching of false doctrine promotes sectarianism and individualism rather than corporate unity within the body of Christ.

The apostle expands upon the deceitfulness of mankind by employing a metaphor that comes from a game of dice—**who lead others into error by the tricks they invent**. The Greek *kubia* basically means "dice playing" but ultimately developed into such concepts as craftiness, trickery, and deceit.

It appears from the text that false teachers deliberately try to mislead the church through crafty and deceitful teachings. "The people are being swept along by the prevailing crazes and new fashions of thought; but also they are being manipulated by unscrupulous and clever men who by every trick they know are trying to divert them from the main life of the Church into divisive and sectarian movements" (Mitton, p. 155). All these negative qualities will disappear (**then we shall no longer be** . . .) when the body of Christ has attained its goal of unity and maturity in Christ.

4:15 / From the negative, the apostle returns to the positive direction that the church is to take. A divided church is characterized by rivalry, suspicion, hatred, pride, selfishness, lack of direction, and so forth (cf. Phil. 2:2–4). **Instead**, he pleads that the church should be characterized by the qualities of truth and love (**by speaking the truth in a spirit of love**). Literally, the phrase should be translated "truthing in love" because there is no verb in the Greek text for **speaking**, and the essential meaning is that truth needs to be conveyed in love and not by deceit and craftiness.

Truth and love form two essential components of the church's life. The significant teaching in this phrase is how these two virtues belong together. Christian truth has a moral as well as an intellectual side; it affects the entire person, not just the brain. And though the possession of truth is crucial to the life of the church, it also is important how that truth is obtained and maintained. It is clear that Christian teachers cannot resort to the kind of trickery that characterizes the false teachers (4:14).

"Truthing in love" suggests the idea of living out the truth in a spirit of love. Some congregations may have all "the truth," but no love; others may have considerable love, but no truth. What is needed is a combination and balance between the two. J. Stott makes a very fitting and astute statement on this point when he writes: "Truth becomes hard if it is not softened by love; love becomes soft if it is not strengthened by truth. The apostle calls us to hold the two together. . . . There is no other route than this to a fully mature Christian unity" (p. 172).

As with the apostle's other exhortation, this one is directed toward the corporate life of the church as well. The individual must learn to live as a part of a greater whole—**we**, that is, the entire body, **must grow up in every way to Christ, who is the head**. The church is a living body, capable of manifesting such growth because of its relationship to Christ, the Head.

4:16 / As the head of the body, Christ directs and controls the growth that is to take place. Thus he is the source as well as the goal of the church's growth. To illustrate, the author employs a physiological metaphor similar to the one in Colossians 2:19. In Colossians, the emphasis is upon the nourishment and cohesion that the Head gives the body; in Ephesians, the head-body relationship remains, but emphasis is given to the interdependence of individuals within the body in much the same way that muscles, nerves, limbs, and so on are joined together in the human organism. The *syn* verbs (*synarmologoumenon*, "to fit or join together," and *symbibazomenon*, "to bring, unite, knit together"), underscore this concern, and that they are in the present tense indicates that this is an ongoing process within the body of Christ.

Again, the author draws attention to the importance of parts in relation to the whole: **The whole body grows and builds . . . when each**

separate part works as it should. It is one thing for individual members to be related to the Head (4:15); but it is equally significant that the growth of the body depends upon the way these members relate to one another and perform their appropriate function as members of the body. This building and growing process takes place **through love**. As the readers have been exhorted to demonstrate love to each other (4:2, 15), they are reminded again that **love** is the soil out of which such growth in unity takes place (cf. 3:17).

The Old and the New Life

In the Lord's name, then, I warn you: do not continue to live like the heathen, whose thoughts are worthless [18]and whose minds are in the dark. They have no part in the life that God gives, for they are completely ignorant and stubborn. [19]They have lost all feeling of shame; they give themselves over to vice and do all sorts of indecent things without restraint.

[20]That was not what you learned about Christ! [21]You certainly heard about him, and as his followers you were taught the truth that is in Jesus. [22]So get rid of your old self, which made you live as you used to—the old self that was being destroyed by its deceitful desires. [23]Your hearts and minds must be made completely new, [24]and you must put on the new self, which is created in God's likeness and reveals itself in the true life that is upright and holy.

U p to this point in the epistle there have been only occasional references to the ethical life of the Christian (2:10; 4:1–3, 15). In 4:1 it appeared that the apostle was preparing to begin a lengthy description of the new life in Christ, but this led, instead, into a further exposition of the unifying elements of the church (4:4–16).

At 4:17, however, there is a clear break from the theological aspects of unity to an emphasis upon the ethics of unity and how that unity can be maintained within the church. This large section begins by admonishing the readers not to walk—that is, to live—ethically like the heathen and continues with a description of the new standards that are to govern their life. In contrast to Colossians, there does not appear to be any moral crisis that necessitated these exhortations; rather, they form an important part of the author's overall theme of unity.

The large ethical section of 4:17–5:21 may be broken up into several smaller parts: First, 4:17–24 forms a general appeal for the readers to abandon their former way of life, on the principle that their new life in Christ has meant a radical change in their behavior; second, 4:25–5:2 includes a selected list of vices and virtues that are essential for maintaining unity within the body; third, the ethical life of the old and new life is contrasted by the imagery of light and darkness (5:3–14); and fourth, there is another appeal to the Christian's "walk" in 5:15–21, including some exhortations within the context of Christian worship.

4:17 / That the apostle feels his ethical exhortations are urgent, significant, and authoritative is implied by his reference to **the Lord** (lit., "this, therefore, I say and bear witness in the Lord"). His basic concern is that they break away from their former pagan (**heathen**) way of life. The description that is given resembles closely the one in Romans 1:18–24.

The heathen way of life includes **worthless . . . thoughts**; the Greek word behind this (*mataiotēs*) expresses the idea of futility and even vanity. In other words, their life apart from God has no meaning or value.

4:18 / The heathen also have darkened minds; deprived of the true source of light and the illumination that God gives to his children (1:18), they live in a state of intellectual darkness.

They live in alienation; being **ignorant** (*agnoia*) and **stubborn** (lit., "hardness of heart," *dia tēn pōrōsin tēs kardias autou*), they are separated from all life with God. In Ephesians, the author does not explain how this came about. In Romans, Paul indicates that God made himself known through natural revelation but that mankind rejected this revelation and turned to self- and idol worship instead (cf. Rom. 1:18–23). Stubbornness, or "hardness of heart" (RSV, NIV, NEB), is a good translation of *pōrōsis* and is preferable to "blindness" (see note on 4:18).

4:19 / All this has had two further degrading effects upon their lives. Callousness (**they have lost all feeling of shame**): Vice, or "licentiousness" (RSV), is another way of describing all sorts of sexual license and perversion (*aselgeia*, "licentiousness," "debauchery," "indecent conduct"). And this indecent conduct was practiced **without restraint**. *Pleonexia* describes greedy individuals continually seeking to gratify their desires. In this context, the author's thought is that the pagan way of life is characterized by an increasing desire to participate in more and more forms of sexual immorality.

In this description one can see how the apostle envisions the futility of paganism. By rejecting God's revelation the non-Christian becomes hardened in heart and conscience. This sad state of affairs leads to participation in various kinds of immoral behavior. Ultimately, it becomes a vicious circle because new perversions must be sought to replace the old (Mitton, pp. 161–62).

4:20 / In contrast to their former pagan way of life, the apostle reminds them that they learned something quite different when they became Christians—**that was not what you learned about Christ!** The Christian walk is the exact opposite of the way of life that he has just described. The references to learning, hearing, and being taught undoubtedly refer to the time when these Gentiles became Christians through the proclamation of the Good News about Jesus and their subsequent instruction in the Christian faith. The phraseology suggests the existence of a "school" or at least catechetical instruction being passed on to new converts.

4:21 / Although the GNB mentions that the believers "learned about Christ," the Greek has no preposition and literally states that *they learned Christ (emathete ton Christon)*! The implication appears to be that the voice of Christ is actually heard through the apostles who proclaimed the gospel (Mitton, p. 163; Stott, p. 179). In addition to proclamation (*kerygma*) there is teaching (*didachē*), of which Christ is the object (**and as his followers you were taught the truth that is in Jesus**).

There does not appear to be any reason why the author switches from "Christ" (4:20) to **Jesus** (4:21). A number of commentators feel that this may be a deliberate reference to the historic personality of the Lord because some false teachings at that time made a distinction between Christ and Jesus. This, however, is speculative, and it could be that the apostle simply wishes to remind his readers that truth is embodied in Jesus—who, of course, is the Christ.

4:22–24 / In 4:22–24 the author refers to the kind of instruction that new believers would have received at the time of their baptism (cf. Col. 3:8–12). In the Greek text there is no new sentence at the beginning of 4:22, so the exhortation to **get rid of your old self** and **put on the new self** must be seen in the context of baptismal instruction. This passage shows that there is a close relationship between baptism and ethics. Christian morality cannot be considered apart from Christian revelation. The point is quite clear that what was begun at baptism must be continued in the experience of the Christian. Baptism, in other words, is the beginning of a new ethical way of life.

There are three important verbs that govern the thought of 4:22–24. To "put off" (**get rid of**) and "put on" are both aorist infinitives and as such express a single act that is based on a past experience. The readers have "put off" (*apothesthai*) the old self and "put on" the new self at the time of their baptism. This is the indicative of their Christian life and forms the basis for the imperative to live out that life ethically.

The GNB captures this idea beautifully by showing that the apostle is admonishing the readers to **get rid of** the **old self which made** them **live as** they **used to** before they put it off in their baptism. That former way of life **was being destroyed by its deceitful desires**. The **new self**, on the other hand, which the believers put on in baptism, **is created in God's likeness**.

In Colossians 3:10, Paul talks about this new life as being renewed in God's image. Undoubtedly, both Ephesians and Colossians allude to the restoration of the image of God in humanity that was lost after the Fall (Gen. 1:27) but that is restored through incorporation into Christ. This new creation **reveals itself in the true life that is upright and holy**.

But coming between the reminder that the readers have put off the old self and put on the new is the exhortation for continual renewal of their hearts and minds (lit., "in the spirit of your mind"). *Ananeousthai* is a present infinitive, thus indicating that creation in God's likeness is a continuing process even though it is an established fact. Here is another reminder to believers that they must *become* what they *are*!

Additional Notes

4:17 / A helpful table of comparisons between Romans and Ephesians is provided by Mitton, p. 159, and by Stott, *God's New Society*, pp. 177–78.

4:18 / J. A. Robinson supports the translation "blindness." See his lengthy discussion on the word *pōrōsis* in his commentary, pp. 264–74.

4:20 / Barth, *Eph. 4–6*, has many helpful comments in his discussion "The School of the Messiah," pp. 529–33.

20

Specific Ethical Directions

No more lying, then! Everyone must tell the truth to his fellow believer, because we are all members together in the body of Christ. ²⁶If you become angry, do not let your anger lead you into sin, and do not stay angry all day. ²⁷Don't give the Devil a chance. ²⁸The man who used to rob must stop robbing and start working, in order to earn an honest living for himself and to be able to help the poor. ²⁹Do not use harmful words, but only helpful words, the kind that build up and provide what is needed, so that what you say will do good to those who hear you. ³⁰And do not make God's Holy Spirit sad; for the Spirit is God's mark of ownership on you, a guarantee that the Day will come when God will set you free. ³¹Get rid of all bitterness, passion, and anger. No more shouting or insults, no more hateful feelings of any sort. ³²Instead, be kind and tender-hearted to one another, and forgive one another, as God has forgiven you through Christ.

¹Since you are God's dear children, you must try to be like him. ²Your life must be controlled by love, just as Christ loved us and gave his life for us as a sweet-smelling offering and sacrifice that pleases God.

The moral exhortations that are given in this section are especially appropriate for maintaining unity within the body of Christ. The vices that are mentioned are destructive to Christian fellowship; the virtues promote the corporate unity of believers. But though the apostle may consciously have selected these qualities to strengthen his central thesis, it should be noted that his teaching has a wider application and is appropriate for people outside the church as well.

Basically, this section includes the vices and virtues that belong to the old and the new life. Consequently, whenever the author lists a vice that is to be "put off," he substitutes a virtue that promotes human relationships: Lying is replaced by truth (4:25); anger is removed by reconciliation (4:26); a person who once robbed goes to work (4:27); harmful words give way to helpful ones (4:29); bitterness, passion, anger, and insults give way to tender-heartedness, forgiveness, and love (4:31–5:2).

4:25 / In the exhortation that there be **no more lying**, the apostle uses the same word (*apotithēmi*) that he used in 4:22. Lying is to be put away because it does not belong in one's new life. Colossians 3:9, 10 is even more explicit when it states: "Do not lie to one another, because you have put off the old self with its habits, and have put on the new self." The Ephesians passage appears to be a quotation from Zechariah 8:16 ("speak the truth to one another"). The GNB translates *plēsion* ("neighbor") as **fellow believer**, thus accentuating that **we are all members together in the body of Christ**. Although lying is wrong under any circumstances, the apostle shows that it is detrimental to the Christian community. "Without openness and truth, there can only be disunity, disorder and trouble" (Foulkes, p. 132).

4:26–27 / The second exhortation is directed toward controlling anger. The Greek imperative, "be angry" (*orgizesthe*), is probably a "concessive" or "permissive imperative" and is translated properly **if you become angry** (cf. Ps. 4:4). The important point is that anger is restricted by a series of negative admonitions:

Do not let your anger lead you into sin. Believers must learn to keep their anger in check. If one is legitimately angry (righteous indignation?), caution must be taken that it does not become the cause for such sins as pride, hatred, or self-righteousness.

All anger is to be dealt with before the day is out. The translation "do not let the sun go down upon your anger" (RSV), suggests that there is no justification for carrying anger over into the next day; that surely would lead to sin.

No opportunity should be given to **the Devil**. The apostle understands that anger that is unjustified, that promotes other sinful actions, and that is permitted to remain in one's life ultimately gives God's adversary access to the believer's heart, thus destroying the harmony of the church.

4:28 / The third exhortation seeks to terminate stealing (*kleptō*). Those who became Christians and continued their former practice of stealing (**robbing**) are told to end this practice and **earn an honest living**. Stealing is an attempt to get something for nothing. Thieves seek to enrich themselves at the expense of someone else's labors. Individuals practicing this sin are to **start working in order to earn an honest living**.

Manual labor, however, is more than a cure for theft or a method of personal gain. The apostle raises the motive of work to a higher level and indicates that those who labor honestly will be able to fulfill their corporate duty to **help the poor**, that is, anyone having a need. The biblical motive for possessions is not personal or selfish gain but the opportunity to assist others (for biblical injunctions on giving, see Matt. 19:21; Luke 14:13; John 13:29; Acts 2:44; 4:32–6; 6:1–4; Rom. 15:25–29; 2 Cor. 8 and 9). The ultimate goal for work is to have something to give away. The readers of Ephesians are to share in that concern for humanity.

4:29 / The fourth injunction deals with **harmful** speech—do not let any evil or rotten (*sapros*) word come out of your mouth. According to Mitton, this would include "words of a complaining, sneering, cynical, sarcastic type, all of which spread demoralisation in a community" (p. 171). In their place, use **only helpful words**. Both individuals and the body of believers need words that **build up**, that will edify and **do good to those who hear**. The Greek word translated **good** is *charis*, meaning grace. Proper speech, in other words, communicates something about God's grace. Although silence may be considered a virtue at times, the believer is encouraged to make a positive contribution to the life of the body by graceful speech. "Evil speech grieves the Holy Spirit, who works through good words" (Wescott, p. 80).

4:30 / It appears that the author refers to the **Holy Spirit** because of his connection with a person's speech. "The Spirit," states J. A. Robinson, "claims to find expression in the utterances of Christians . . . (cf. 5:18). The misuse of the organ of speech is accordingly a wrong done to, and felt by, the Spirit who claims to control it" (p. 113). Improper speech makes **God's Holy Spirit sad** (*lupeō*, "grieve," "pain"). "The sins against the brotherhood are also an offense against the divine Spirit which inhabits the body of believers" (Beare, p. 701).

Once again, the readers are reminded that they have been sealed with the Holy Spirit—**for the Spirit is God's mark of ownership on you** (cf. 1:13). Since he is a **guarantee** of the believer's destiny (**that the Day will come**), they are asked to revere him in their speech and thus be worthy of their inheritance.

4:31 / The presence of the Holy Spirit within the believer is sufficient reason to clean up one's speech by abolishing the following vices: **Bitterness** (*pikria*) comes from harboring resentful feelings; **passion** (*thumos*) is a bitter outburst of anger, **anger** (*orgē*) may be understood as resentment that lingers on in one's life; **shouting**, or clamor (*kraugē*), is boisterous face-to-face confrontation, whereas **insults** (*blasphēmia*) can be abusive and slanderous words spoken about someone.

Lastly, there is malice, or **hateful feelings of any sort**. This term may be considered a separate category or, as some commentators suggest, it may be a category that embodies all the previous vices that have been previously mentioned (Mitton, p. 173). Thus the GNB **hateful feelings of any sort** and the NEB "bad feelings of every kind." Any one or all of these vices grieve the Holy Spirit when they manifest themselves in the life of the believer.

4:32 / This verse provides a striking contrast to the previous one by emphasizing the virtues that should characterize believers in their interpersonal relationships. **Instead of** those negative and destructive qualities, believers are admonished to **be kind and tender-hearted to one another**. Both of these virtues promote a spirit of acceptance, tolerance, and patience within the congregation.

Beyond that, the readers are to **forgive one another**. The word used for forgiveness (*charizomai*) is also the word from which grace (*charis*) is derived. Within this context, the author's meaning is that believers are to respond to each other with the same grace, forgiveness, and generosity that they have experienced from God: hence **forgive one another, as God has forgiven you through Christ**. Christians have been forgiven by Christ (*echarisato*, past/aorist tense) but they are to go on forgiving (*charizomenoi*, present tense) one another on the strength of the example that Christ has provided.

5:1 / The thought of God's gracious activity in Christ leads the apostle to summon his readers, whom he addresses as **God's dear** (beloved) **children**, to imitate God (lit., "be imitators of God as beloved children"). The GNB **try to be like him** tends to weaken what in Greek is an emphatic imperative expression (*ginesthe*).

This is the only place in the NT where believers are called upon to imitate God. Elsewhere, Paul asks his converts to imitate him because they are his children (1 Cor. 4:14–16; 11:1; 1 Thess. 1:6; 2 Thess. 3:7,9) and because he, himself, is an imitator of Christ. Here, the imitation of God is introduced within the context of forgiveness, and the apostle wants to use God's example in Christ as a pattern for one's personal relationships. It is doubtful that he would make a distinction between imitating Jesus and imitating God since one can only know God through Jesus.

5:2 / Since forgiveness and love are bound together, believers are admonished to have their life **controlled by love**. That love finds its example in Christ who **gave his life for us**. By implication, the Christian's love is to be expressed as a self-giving sacrifice (cf. 5:25). Love is the essence of God and is to be the main feature of the believer's walk (*peripateō*). By mentioning Christ's death, the apostle thinks of some words that were applicable to Jewish sacrifices—namely, **a sweet-smelling offering and sacrifice that pleases God**. The sacrifice of Jesus and the sacrificial life of love that believers live are pleasing to God.

21

Living in the Light

EPHESIANS 5:3–21

Since you are God's people, it is not right that any matters of sexual immorality or indecency or greed should even be mentioned among you. ⁴Nor is it fitting for you to use language which is obscene, profane, or vulgar. Rather you should give thanks to God. ⁵You may be sure that no one who is immoral, indecent, or greedy (for greed is a form of idolatry) will ever receive a share in the Kingdom of Christ and of God.

⁶Do not let anyone deceive you with foolish words; it is because of these very things that God's anger will come upon those who do not obey him. ⁷So have nothing at all to do with such people. ⁸You yourselves used to be in the darkness, but since you have become the Lord's people, you are in the light. So you must live like people who belong to the light, ⁹for it is the lightᶠ that brings a rich harvest of every kind of goodness, righteousness, and truth. ¹⁰Try to learn what pleases the Lord. ¹¹Have nothing to do with the worthless things that people do, things that belong to the darkness. Instead, bring them out to the light. (¹²It is really too shameful even to talk about the things they do in secret.) ¹³And when all things are brought out to the light, then their true nature is clearly revealed; ¹⁴for anything that is clearly revealed becomes light.ᵍ That is why it is said,

"Wake up, sleeper, and rise from death,
and Christ will shine on you."

¹⁵So be careful how you live. Don't live like ignorant people, but like wise people. ¹⁶Make good use of every opportunity you have, because these are evil days. ¹⁷Don't be fools, then, but try to find out what the Lord wants you to do.

¹⁸Do not get drunk with wine, which will only ruin you; instead, be filled with the Spirit. ¹⁹Speak to one another with the words of psalms, hymns, and sacred songs; sing hymns and psalms to the Lord with praise in your hearts. ²⁰In the name of our Lord Jesus Christ, always give thanks for everything to God the Father.

²¹Submit yourselves to one another because of your reverence for Christ.

f. the light; *some manuscripts have* the Spirit. g. anything that is clearly revealed becomes light; *or it is light that clearly reveals everything.*

In the previous section (4:25–5:2), the apostle concentrated upon those vices that were disruptive to the unity of the Christian community. From there, he moved to the sins of immorality. In a sense, sexual sins also destroy the trust, unity, and respect that Christians have for each other and should, therefore, be banished. But in this case, the main point is that sexual sins are an offense to God, and they incur God's wrath because they are considered idolatrous. The new walk is explained further by the imagery of darkness and light. As the readers have been admonished to walk in "love" (5:1, 2), they are to walk in "the light" that they have received.

Given the general application of this epistle, it seems unlikely that these exhortations address anything specific that the readers faced. In a sense, they are similar to the denunciations that one finds elsewhere in the NT (Romans, 1 Corinthians, Gal. 5:19–21; Col. 3:5–8). But at the same time, it is possible that some form of Gnostic teaching had gained access to the Christian community. In some cases, for example, the heresy at Colossae (2:8–23), the teaching emphasized a rigid asceticism; but a variation of it tended toward libertinism, taking the attitude that those who had received spiritual knowledge (*gnōsis*) were free to participate in sexual indulgences. Those who separated body and spirit argued that it did not matter what one did with the body; they thus sinned with impunity. Perhaps these exhortations are addressing a situation in which such teachings were taking hold.

5:3 / The writer is emphatic in stating that, since his readers are **God's people**, the question is not only one of nonparticipation; rather, such sins should not **even be mentioned** among them. When believers approach such sins with an attitude of indifference (as in Gnostic libertinism), then it is not uncommon to discuss and to make light of one's personal sins or the sins of others. This is to be avoided in their fellowship.

Immorality (*porneia*) covers a wide variety of unlawful sexual activity, such as prostitution, adultery, fornication, and promiscuity. **Indecency**, or impurity (*akatharsia*), is tied to immorality and probably means sexual perversions of various kinds. **Greed**, or covetousness (*pleonexia*), in the context of immoral behavior would be the desire to engage in sexual activity solely for selfish reasons. Christians are to remove such evil from their lives as well as from their conversation. Such perversions are a contradiction to one who is called to imitate God and to walk in Christ's love (5:1, 2).

5:4 / The list of prohibitions goes on (in the Greek there is no new sentence) to include words that are **obscene, profane, or vulgar**. **Obscene** words are ugly, base, shameful (*aischrotēs*); **profane** or foolish words (*mōrologia*) are those uttered by a fool (*mōros*), words void of any decency or honor; *eutrapelia* (**vulgar**) has a positive side meaning "wit" or "pleasantry." Here, however, it is used negatively in the sense of coarse jesting, dirty insinuations, and so forth. All of these have no place in the life of a believer.

In place of foolish and shameful talk, believers **should give thanks to God** (the Greek does not include the words **to God**). The basic meaning appears to be that thankfulness, rather than indecency, should dominate one's speech. Though **thanks** should be expressed to God for all things, the context may imply that **thanks** be expressed to God for sexual activity and speech when it is proper to do so (cf. Mitton, p. 179).

5:5 / The emphatic **you may be sure** and the "do not let anyone deceive you with with foolish words" (5:6), suggest that there was a serious moral threat at the time. Immorality, indecency, and greed exclude people from the inheritance that God has prepared for them. **Greed**, or covetousness (*pleonexia*), is equated with idolatry because sexual passions can become objects that dominate one's life and destroy one's relationship to God. A similar statement occurs in Colossians 3:5 in the context of "putting off" immoral practices.

Even though much is said about the "Kingdom of God" in the NT, Galatians 5:21 is the only passage that specifically mentions this concept within the context of immoral behavior: Those who indulge in the "sins of the flesh" will not receive "the Kingdom of God" (Gal. 5:19–21). But the phrase **Kingdom of Christ and of God** is unique in the NT (unless "Lord" in Rev. 11:15 means God). The author of Ephesians makes no distinction between the two, because he understands the rule of Christ and God somehow to be synonymous (cf. 1 Cor. 15:24–28). The main point, however, is that God's rule (**Kingdom**) is denied to people who practice immoral behavior.

5:6–7 / There is no way of knowing specifically who was attempting to deceive these believers with **foolish** (lit., "empty") **words**. Since Ephesians does not appear to have a local situation in mind, the **anyone** could mean "everyone" who engages in using empty or foolish words. Mitton refers to this as "arguments that sound plausible and attractive but which run counter to true reasoning and intuitive insights" (p. 181). This could be an amplification of the reference to "the deceitful men" who teach by error and trickery (4:14).

The false teachers would want the Christians to believe that there is nothing wrong about participating in illicit sexual behavior and dirty talk. Such teaching, however, is deceptive; it leads people to believe something that is not true. The hard fact is that **God's anger will come upon those who do not obey him**; eventually, wrongdoers will be punished for their sins.

5:7 / Believers are admonished to **have nothing at all to do with such people**. Actually, the language is much stronger than this translation suggests. The Greek uses the term "partner" (*symmetochos*), meaning do not join in with these people and participate in the evil things that they are doing. This verse does not mean that believers should avoid all contact with immoral people; otherwise the exhortations that follow about light penetrating the darkness would have no purpose (cf. Col. 4:5, 6: "Be wise in the way you act toward those who are not believers"). Rather, they are a warning against participating in the vices of others.

5:8 / In 5:8–14, the apostle talks about the Christian life in the familiar imagery of darkness and light. Since they are **the Lord's people**, they are no longer in darkness; nor do they participate in the unfruitful works of darkness. They are now "light in the Lord" (RSV), and the life that they are to live as children of light is characterized by goodness, righteousness, truth, and whatever is pleasing to the Lord. The section ends with the quotation of a saying that calls upon the spiritually dead to arise from their slumber and experience the light of the Lord (5:14).

The language, imagery, and theology of this section (5:8–14) strongly suggest that the author has baptism in mind. First of all, there is convincing evidence that the early church was in possession of a catechetical form that employed the motifs of darkness and light. These motifs play an important part in the passage, and it is quite likely that the author is borrowing thoughts from such an existing tradition.

Second, there is the contrast between the "then" and the "now." This, as has been noted on other occasions, relates to the concept of baptism as a change of status for the individual. The same readers who had been strangers, alienated from God (2:12–22) and subject to the powers of the world (2:1, 2), had also lived in darkness (5:8, 11). Now, however, in addition to having been brought near to God (2:13 ff.), being victorious, and experiencing salvation in Christ (2:5–9), they are characterized as **in the light** and are admonished to **live like people who belong to the light** (5:8). This imagery reaches a climax in 5:14 with the affirmation that Christ is the instrument of light.

Earlier, the author contrasted the status of these believers in terms of being "dead" and "alive" (2:1–5) and "far away" and "near" (2:11–13); here, as a continuation of darkened minds (4:18) and renewed hearts (4:23), he uses the imagery of darkness and light to describe their moral condition. Darkness symbolizes their life of sin and participation in the evils that he has just denounced; light is life in obedience to God.

The English translation **you yourselves used to be in the darkness** does not quite do justice to the original meaning of the text, which states that "you were darkness" (*ēte gar pote skotos*), that is, they were identified as darkness, not just surrounded by it in their environment. Moule states it very succinctly when he writes: "So had the night of spiritual ignorance and sin penetrated them that they were, as it were, night itself, night embodied" (Moule, p. 131). The same language applies to their new status as believers: **Since you have become the Lord's people, you are in the light**, literally, you "are" light (*nun de phōs*). Since they have become light (the indicative) the ethical charge that follows (the imperative) exhorts them to be what they are, that is, **live like people who belong to the light**. This change from darkness to light was, of course, due to their new relationship in the **Lord** through faith and baptism.

5:9 / Just as a seed, plant, or tree fulfills its true nature by producing fruit (**a rich harvest**), a believer, who is light in the Lord, will produce **a rich harvest** of the virtues of goodness, righteousness, and truth—quite the opposite of the fruit of darkness in 5:3, 5. By insisting on the moral implications of light, the author would be opposing any false theories, such as those in the Gnostic system, that made enlightenment a mystical experience and viewed the ethical life with indifference and even disdain. To *be* light is to walk in the light (John 3:19, 20; 1 John 1:5–7; 2:8–11).

The fruit of light is similar to the fruit of the Spirit mentioned in Galatians 5:22, although **goodness** is the only concept that occurs there. The items on the list here in Ephesians are probably selected for their relevance to the concern about unity within the body of Christ that the author has been describing. The virtues of goodness, righteousness, and truth are essential to healthy personal and social relationships.

5:10 / Although part of the process of becoming a Christian is the acceptance of the truth as it is found in the Good News, the other part is learning by careful thought and experience what it means to be a Christian. Earlier, when the author was running through a list of pagan vices, he reminded the believers that this was "not what you learned about Christ" (4:20). In other words, through instruction and guidance, probably in the form of a baptismal catechism, new converts were taught what to believe and how to act. Here they are exhorted **to learn what pleases the Lord**.

The word *dokimazō* has the meaning of "putting to the test," "proving," "examining." The Christian life, in other words, is not just a simple acceptance of doctrines and rules; believers are called upon to exercise intelligent judgment as they relate their theology to specific moral situations in society. The things that **please** (*euaristos*) **the Lord** include the rich harvest of "every kind of fruit" (5:9).

Both *dokimazō* and *euaristos* occur in Romans 12:2, where Paul writes that because of the inner transformation of their minds, believers "will be able to know [*dokimazō*] the will of God—what is good and pleasing [*euaristos*] to him and is perfect." Beare notes that *euaristos* ("well-pleasing," "acceptable") is nearly always used of a sacrificial offering (Rom. 12:2; Phil. 4:18): "So here it suggests the thought that the life of the Christian is ever laid upon the altar. All of our actions are to be an offering to God . . . and we must therefore take care that they are *acceptable* to him" (p. 709).

5:11 / In contrast to the fruitful works of light (**a rich harvest**, 5:9), the works of darkness are unfruitful, or **worthless**. Believers are admonished not to have anything to do with people who belong to the darkness. Again, as in 5:7, the apostle uses a *syn* noun (*sygkoinōnos*), by which he means do not become a participant, a partner, in the unfruitful works of darkness. **Instead**, believers are to correct, convict, or reprove (*elegchō*) such evil by exposing it **to the light**. The Christian life is not only the avoidance of evil; it is active participation in the things that expose evil.

5:12 / What the GNB puts in a parenthesis (**it is really too shameful even to talk about the things they do in secret**) is really a strong admonition against discussing the works of darkness in secrecy. This could be a veiled reference to the secret rites of the mystery religions or just a more general reminder that much of the evil that goes on is done in secret, under the cloak of darkness. Since the evil deeds are so shameful, it is wrong even to talk about them (cf. similar thoughts in John 3:19–21).

5:13 / Here the author returns to his thoughts in 5:10 (hence the parenthesis in the GNB) by affirming that **when all things are brought out to the light, then their true nature is clearly revealed**. The repetition of *elegchō* (5:11) reaffirms the positive nature of light in exposing and reproving the works of darkness. In that process, people will come to see the true nature of evil and, it is hoped, turn to the light. As stated by Beare, "The power of light not only reveals, but penetrates and transforms into its own likeness whatever it illumines" (p. 711).

5:14 / The continuing emphasis in the first part of this verse is that darkness cannot exist in the presence of light. It appears that the most reasonable way to understand the imagery of darkness and light and the quotation that follows is in the context of baptism. Darkness, sleep, and death are striking figures that symbolize the condition of an individual apart from Christ. Baptism could be seen as the act by which a person awakens from sleep, rises from the dead, and responds to the light of Christ. Thus: **"Wake up, sleeper, and rise from death, and Christ will shine on you."**

There has been considerable speculation about the origin of this saying. Some scholars see it as a rather free synopsis from ideas in such OT passages as Isaiah 26:19 and 60:1, 2; others speculate that it may come from an Apocryphal text or from some Hellenistic literature with a Gnostic or mystery religion's background; and others have found parallels and allusions to it in the Dead Sea Scrolls.

The introductory phrase, *dio legei* (cf. 4:18, where an OT citation is introduced), suggests that some written source is being quoted. But the failure to find such a literary formula opens the possibility that this was a well-known expression in the Christian community. The GNB **that is why it is said** leaves room for such a possibility.

Although the reconstruction of the setting of this quotation remains highly speculative, it is possible to envision when it may have been used by the church. Here, the first thing that comes to mind is the actual baptismal service, where the saying may have been part of a hymn that was recited or sung. The early church created and used many songs in worship services (Eph. 5:19, 20; Phil. 2:6–11; Col. 3:16; 1 Tim. 3:16), and there is no reason to doubt that such hymns could have been used on the occasion of baptism as a "call" to the candidate. It may have been sung when the candidate came out of the water after immersion. In the unbelieving state he or she has been regarded as asleep and dead; consequently, the believer is summoned to rise to a new life.

Another possibility is that the saying, together with the preceding discussion on darkness and light (5:8–13) and the following exhortations on Christian living (5:15 ff.), belongs to the context of instruction (catechesis) just prior to baptism. Those being baptized would be reminded of their former life of darkness and then invited to **wake up** from their sleep and **rise from death**.

Although some of this is speculative, it does appear that the author is consciously alluding to baptism and that his readers would catch this allusion in the material he is using. His purpose, however, is neither to create nor to provide a baptismal liturgy to be used on the occasion of baptism, even though the material he utilizes is so oriented.

The exhortations of 5:8–14 fall within the context of a larger section (4:17–5:20) and illustrate the apostle's use of traditional catechetical material. His quotation from an existing baptismal hymn emphasizes that Christ is the source of all spiritual light. Now that Christians are light in the Lord, they are to walk (*peripateō*) as children of light. This, he goes on to say, includes wisdom (5:15), an understanding of God's will (5:17), fullness of the Spirit (5:18), as well as joyfulness and thanksgiving (5:19, 20).

5:15 / Within the context of Christian teaching, theology and ethics belong together: Behavior must be based upon correct doctrine; knowledge should not be regarded as a substitute for proper behavior. Basically, it is another way of reminding believers to be what they are. Consequently, they are to walk carefully and to live as **wise** rather than **ignorant** people. Wisdom, here, has a practical dimension, that is, the ability to discern between right and wrong. For Mitton, "This means that the recognition that we live in a world where evil actions are followed by evil consequences is the first step toward wise conduct" (p. 187).

5:16 / The next exhortation advises the readers to **make good use of every opportunity**. Literally, the term *agorazō* comes from the language of the marketplace and means "to buy up" or "redeem." *Kairos* ("time") is the God-given opportunity that the believer has to walk in wisdom and to demonstrate the qualities of life that project light into darkness. Time is a precious commodity entrusted to believers for the purpose of doing good in an evil world (**evil days**). Far too often Christians are so heavenly minded that they are no earthly good!

5:17 / In this brief exposition on Christian wisdom (5:15–17), the apostle has reminded his readers that wisdom has a practical dimension and that they are wise when they make good use of every opportunity. His final exhortation is that they not be foolish (**don't be fools**) but discern God's will with respect to the course of their moral action.

5:18 / Ephesians 5:18–21 is an exhortation directed toward the worshiping community and stands in sharp contrast to the attitudes and actions of those who live in darkness (5:8–12). Instead of prohibiting certain conduct and conversation, the believers are encouraged to express their spiritual joy with song and thanksgiving. In 5:16, 17, they are reminded to be wise and learn God's will; in 5:18–21 they are shown how that is accomplished.

240

These verses are adapted from Colossians 3:16, but here the main emphasis is upon the Spirit rather than on Christ's message (the word of Christ). The admonition—**do not get drunk with wine**—leads one to suspect that the author was thinking about religious cults, such as the worship of Dionysus, in which intoxication manifested itself in wild frenzies and ecstatic behavior that were interpreted in religious terms. Christians have a better way of experiencing spiritual elation—it is by being **filled with the Spirit**.

It should be noted that this is not a prohibition against the use of wine but against the excessive use of any alcoholic beverage leading to drunkenness (1 Tim. 3:3, 8; Titus 1:7; 2:3; *asotia*, "debauchery," "profligacy," "waste"). The contrast is not between wine and the Spirit but between the two states that they produce: Intoxication with wine has a degrading effect; intoxication with the Spirit (cf. Acts 2:13) can have an uplifting effect upon the Christian community.

5:19 / This uplifting effect manifests itself in several ways. One is in worship: This verse suggests that early Christian worship had a certain spontaneity about it and had not become fixed by liturgical order. **Psalms** (*psalmos*), **hymns** (*hymnos*), **and sacred songs** (*hōidais pneumatikais*) are listed as ways believers can praise the Lord. Though it is impossible to make any real distinctions between these categories (cf. disc. on Col. 3:16), some authors think that **psalms** are OT musical pieces accompanied by the plucking of strings, as on a harp, **hymns** are songs of praise to God, and **sacred songs** are more spontaneous pieces of inspired music or words of exhortation. The important thing is that such worship is a corporate, not an individual, experience. Believers are to **speak to one another** as they praise the Lord.

5:20 / A second manifestation is in thanksgiving: Though thanksgiving undoubtedly is a component of worship, it is another sign of being filled with the Spirit. Spirit-filled Christians, in other words, live in a continual attitude of gratitude for everything. This, as J. Stott wisely notes, should not be pressed too literally: "For we cannot thank God for absolutely 'everything' including blatant evil. . . . the 'everything' for which we are to give thanks to God must be qualified by its context, namely *in the name of our Lord Jesus Christ to God the Father*" (p. 207).

5:21 / The final manifestation noted is in submission: Scholars, and consequently Bible translators, are divided on how this verse fits into the context. Grammatically, it belongs to the section on worship (5:18–21) and should be seen as another manifestation of the spirit-filled believer. As singing and thanksgiving are to be expressed corporately, members also must willingly submit to one another. Fullness of the Spirit leads to mutual subordination and unity, not to individual pride and disunity (cf. 1 Cor. 14:26–33; Phil. 2:1–5). At the same time, 5:21 is a transitional verse from which the author goes on to give illustrations of how that submission is to be observed in specific domestic relationships (5:22–6:9).

If 5:21 is taken as an independent sentence, then it serves as a heading for the specific relationships that follow. Some translations, namely, GNB and RSV, use it this way. The NIV, however, lets it stand with the previous section. In either case, the position of the verse is not as important as its teaching—a teaching in which believers are exhorted to **submit** themselves **to one another** out of **reverence for Christ**. "We are not asked to yield to the wishes of others, no matter what they wish, but only when what they ask of us is in line with *reverence for Christ*" (Mitton, p. 196).

Additional Notes

5:4 / P. W. Van der Horst goes through a lengthy examination of the word *eutrapelia* and concludes that "the warning in Eph. v. 4 need not be read as a denouncement of humor and wittiness in the church" ("Is Wittiness Unchristian? A Note on *eutrapelia* in Eph. v. 4," in *Miscellanea Neotestamentica, Supplements to NovT*, vol. 48, ed. T. Baarda, A. F. J. Klijn, and W. C. Van Unnik [Leiden: Brill, 1978], 163–77).

5:8 / Cf. disc. on Colossians, pp. 108–10. Extensive studies on the catechetical teaching in the early church can be found in P. Carrington, *The Primitive Christian Catechism*, and E. G. Selwyn, *I Peter*. Especially helpful is Selwyn's Table II, pp. 376–78, which he calls "Further Catechetical Material: The Children of Light (Filii Lucis)." Much of the language used in Ephesians reminds one of the symbolism in the Fourth Gospel, where following Christ as the light of the world means to have the light of life and not to walk in darkness (8:12; cf. also, 3:19 ff.; 9:5; 12:35, 36, 46).

5:14 / On the history of interpretation of this passage, see Barth, *Eph. 4–6*, pp. 573–77; R. Orlett, "Awake, Sleeper," *Worship* 35 (1961), pp. 102–5. Houlden, p. 185, list parallels between this passage and Acts 12:7. Most scholars support some kind of association of this saying with a baptismal hymn, believing that it could have been used as an "awakening call" for the unbeliever to step out of his or her darkness into the light of Christ.

5:18 / C. L. Rogers believes that the wild, drunken practices connected with the worship of Dionysus form the general background for this command. See his

"The Dionysian Background of Ephesians 5:18," *BibSac* 136 (1979), pp. 249–57; also, Beare, p. 714; Mitton, pp. 188–89.

In addition to the commentaries on the hymnody of the early church, cf. H. Schlier, "*ōidē*," *TDNT*, vol. 1, pp. 164–65; G. Delling, "*hymnos . . . psalmos*," *TDNT*, vol. 8, pp. 498–501.

22

Wives and Husbands

Wives, submit yourselves to your husbands as to the Lord. [23]For a husband has authority over his wife just as Christ has authority over the church; and Christ is himself the Savior of the church, his body. [24]And so wives must submit themselves completely to their husbands just as the church submits itself to Christ.

[25]Husbands, love your wives just as Christ loved the church and gave his life for it. [26]He did this to dedicate the church to God by his word, after making it clean by washing it in water, [27]in order to present the church to himself in all its beauty—pure and faultless, without spot or wrinkle or any other imperfection.

[28]Men ought to love their wives just as they love their own bodies. A man who loves his wife loves himself. ([29]No one ever hates his own body. Instead, he feeds it and takes care of it, just as Christ does the church; [30]for we are members of his body.) [31]As the scripture says, "For this reason a man will leave his father and mother and unite with his wife, and the two will become one." [32]There is a deep secret truth revealed in this scripture, which I understand as applying to Christ and the church. [33]But it also applies to you: every husband must love his wife as himself, and every wife must respect her husband.

What motivates the author to move from general admonitions on moral life and corporate worship to specific instructions regarding household relationships? Beare suggests that his arrangement of material follows the conventional pattern of Hellenistic philosophical literature, which concluded its doctrinal exposition with a brief presentation of the social code (p. 716). Another author places the code, particularly this section on husbands and wives, within the context of the ethical instructions that preceded it: "What," he asks, "was more necessary than to counter immorality with a true doctrine of man and wife?" (Houlden, p. 331).

A third suggestion comes from J. A. Robinson, who sees the code related structurally to the preceding instructions on worship (5:18–20). The church is not a fanatical and disorganized Spirit-filled community; rather, it is regulated by order and the principle of subjection of one member to another (p. 123).

A fourth theory explains the arrangement in Ephesians on the basis of Colossians, which, according to a number of commentators, the author was using as a model. Colossians, likewise, has a section on instruction and worship (3:16–17) before it moves on to discuss "Personal Relations in the New Life." The differences between the Colossian and Ephesian codes can be accounted for by the specific purpose they have in each epistle.

Finally, there is the principle of submission in 5:21. This statement relates to mutuality within the church but also forms a transition to the section on the household code. In other words, the author states a general principle; now he provides specific examples of how it is to be applied in relationships between husband and wife, parents and children, and masters and slaves.

Beyond these observations, one must rightfully question the purpose for such a lengthy exposition on the relationship between husband and wife in this epistle (Ephesians has eleven verses, whereas Colossians has two). Is it the writer's primary intention to (a) offer domestic guidance regarding the husband-wife relationship (as is the case in 6:1–9 with child-parent and master-slave)? Or (b) is he using the example of husband and wife for an ecclesiological purpose, that is, to portray the nature of the relationship between Christ and the church? Or (c) is he using Christ's relationship to the church as a prototype for an ideal Christian marriage?

It appears that the author's primary intention is to emphasize the quality of relationship that should exist between husband and wife. In order to do this properly, and thus bring out the deepest implications of marriage, he resorts to the analogy of Christ and the church. And what could be a more fitting analogy! As Christ is head over the church, the husband is the head of his wife (5:23); as the church submits itself to Christ, wives submit themselves to their husbands (5:24); husbands are to love their wives with the same sacrificial love as Christ, who feeds and takes care of the church, his body (5:25, 29). The Lordship of Christ and his relation to the church epitomize the ideal union between husband and wife.

But though this appears to be the author's main purpose, the analogy works in the opposite direction as well. Throughout the epistle he has been expounding on the nature of the church and how Christ, the Head, is related to his body, the church. Marriage gives him an illustration—albeit imperfect—of how his readers can understand his ecclesiology. Thus, the church is under Christ's authority just as the wife is under the authority of her husband (5:23); Christ loves and cares for the church in the same way that a husband ought to love his wife (5:28). The analogy, in other words, has both a domestic and an ecclesiological function.

M. Barth, although he agrees with these two foci of this section, does not think that either of them are foremost in the author's mind. Marriage, along with the other problems raised in Ephesians, such as sin, death, ethnic divisions, institutions, and so forth, all come under the power and riches of God's grace. "The intention of Paul is to show that 'the grace of our Lord Jesus Christ' gives husband and wife the basis, the strength, and the example which they need in order to live in that 'peace to [or by] which God has called' them (1 Cor. 7:15). The 'peace' between God and man, Jews and Gentiles, of which Paul spoke in Eph. 2:14–16 shall be extended into every house and praised by the conduct of husband and wife" *(Eph. 4–6,* p. 655).

The subjects of husband-wife relationships, the equality of women, and the role of women in the church continue to be debated and controversial issues today. With respect to Ephesians, several things must be noted: First, the author is talking about husband-wife relationships, *not* male-female differences and the equality, rights, roles, and so on of women. Some of those issues are dealt with in other epistles, such as 1 Corinthians and 1 Timothy. Second, the relationship between husband and wife is not modified *or* qualified by arguments that are used elsewhere in Scripture, such as the order and glory of creation (1 Cor. 11:3–16) or the sin of Eve (1 Tim. 2:9–15); nor is submission demonstrated by such outward things as women covering their heads in public worship (1 Cor. 11:3–16) or remaining silent in the presence of men during worship (1 Cor. 14:33–38). The submission taught in Ephesians is a *mutual subordination* between husband and wife that is *based on the prototype of Christ and his church*; Christ is the example who determines the qualities of headship and submission. Third, the teaching with respect to husband and wife—as well as the other categories in the code—must be seen within the larger context of the position of women and marriage in the first century (cf. disc. in Chap. 18 on Colossians; Barth, *Eph. 4–6,* pp. 655–62).

In a sense, the need for order lies behind all the instruction that encompasses the domestic code. The authors of the NT did not want Christianity to be misunderstood by society or to have new Christians feel that their freedom in Christ meant the abolition of current standards regulating domestic life. But in Ephesians the motive goes beyond "good order." The household rules illustrate the principle of subordination that is essential to the unity and harmony within the body of Christ. The church, in other words, becomes a pattern for all social order.

5:22-24 / In Colossians, wives are exhorted to be obedient (*hypotassō*) to their husbands because it is the proper thing for Christians to do (3:18). Obedience is required on the basis of the socially acceptable norms of the day. In Ephesians, wives are called to submission for a different reason, namely, the divine order to creation that appears to be at the heart of the entire passage. This principle of "creationism" is assumed rather than explicitly stated, as it is, for example, in 1 Corinthians 11:3 ("Christ is supreme [*kephalē*] over every man, the husband is supreme over his wife, and God is supreme over Christ").

The husband has **authority over his wife**—literally, the husband is "head" of his wife. What is significant in Ephesians is that the so-called hierarchical order of creation is qualified profoundly by a number of important factors: First, the submission of the wife to her husband is exercised within the wider principle of mutual subordination. Members within the body of Christ are to "submit . . . to one another because of your reverence for Christ" (5:21). This, however, does not abolish the concept of authority: "The principle of mutual subordination is not applied so as to destroy the complementary principle of authority, without which there can be no ordered social life among men" (Beare, p. 717). Second, the *motive* for submission is placed within the context of the wife's relationship to the Lord— **wives, submit yourselves to your husbands as to the Lord**. Those who submit must do so as if they were submitting to Christ.

Third, submission is regulated by the divine pattern of Christ's relationship to the church. Those to whom submission is given likewise must find the pattern of their obedience and conduct in Christ. Hence the reciprocal exhortations: wives, submit **as to the Lord** . . . "just as Christ loved the church" (5:25).

From these principles it becomes obvious that a husband's authority is regulated by Christ's example and the principle of love. Authoritarianism, self-assertion, self-centeredness, and so on have no place in a marriage that is based on these principles. Submission is not "obedience," for the word "obey" (*hypakouō*) is used only for children and slaves (6:1, 5). When a husband relates to his wife out of love (*agapē*), there will be no problems with respect to submission or obedience.

The author is aware of the limits of his analogy, because there is no way that a human, fallible husband can even approximate the extent and quality of love that Christ has for the church. This seems to be the case when he states that Christ is the **Savior of the church, his body** (5:23). Only Christ can be considered the savior of the body because of his work for and relationship to it. Nevertheless, "The sacrificial concern of the Lord for the salvation of the Church should have a parallel, even if at a much lower level, in the loving and sacrificial concern of the husband for the welfare of his wife" (Foulkes, p. 156).

5:25 / Lest husbands come to believe that Ephesians 5:21–33 is a document legitimizing their authority to restrict the freedom of their wives, it should be noted that the admonitions for husbands to love their wives puts a greater responsibility on them. *Agapē* means to subordinate one's own interests, pleasures, and personality for the benefit of someone else. In fact, Christ's love, which the husband is to model, was completely sacrificial—**Christ loved the church and gave his life for it**. The **church** is considered as the sum total of persons for whom Christ died (Rom. 4:25; 8:32; Gal. 1:4; 2:20). **Loved** (past tense) refers to some definite action in the past, such as the cross.

5:26–27 / The sense of the corporate nature of the church is carried over into these two verses that describe the **washing** of the church and its subsequent results. At first glance, 5:26, 27 appears as an interpolation, because the thoughts of 5:25 and 5:28 join so nicely together. Yet, there is no textual evidence that these verses are of questionable origin; nor is there any suggestion that they do not fit into the context of the writer's discussion on Christ and the church. It appears that the mention of Christ's death for the church (5:25) triggered certain thoughts the author had about baptism. Perhaps he was thinking of Jesus' death as a baptism in which his followers are to share (Mark 10:38, 39). Christian baptism is a baptism into Christ's death (Rom. 6:3; Gal. 3:27; Col. 2:11, 12, 20).

Beyond the relationship between Christ's death and baptism, there appears to be another analogy at work, namely, the nuptial or ceremonial bath that a bride took before marriage. In the cultures of that day it was customary for a bride to take such a bath before the marriage day. Following the bath, the bride, clad in her lovely garments, would present herself before the bridegroom. Does the author conceive of baptism as a bridal bath that sanctifies the church? Does Paul have this imagery in mind when he writes to the Corinthians, "You are like a pure virgin whom I have promised in marriage to one man only, Christ himself," (2 Cor. 11:20)? On the basis of context, it seems more probable that when the author speaks of Christ giving himself up for the church (5:25) he thinks of baptism as the rite that symbolizes this death and by which the church is made clean by the washing in water.

There are a number of reasons why the thoughts in verse 26 are associated with baptism: First, there is the imagery of washing and cleansing **(after making it clean by washing it in water)**. The cleansing of the church, which here is viewed collectively or corporately, took place when its individual members were baptized. The readers would have been aware of the baptismal teaching in the early church that conceived of baptism as a moral washing (John 13:10; Acts 2:38; 22:16; 1 Cor. 6:11; Titus 3:5; 1 Pet. 3:20, 21; Heb. 10:22).

Second, the relationship between baptism and the **word** (lit., "the washing of water by/in the word"). Baptism, in the context of the NT, was accompanied by a *spoken word*. Here it could mean either *(a)* some kind of gospel utterance; *(b)* a confession from the candidate in which he or she expresses faith in the Lord; *(c)* some prebaptismal words of instruction, or *(d)* a baptismal formula, such as baptism into the name of Christ (Acts 2:38; 8:16; 19:5; 22:16; 1 Cor. 6:11) or into the names of the trinity (Matt. 28:19). In spite of all these possibilities, it would be safe to conclude that **word** refers to some form of confession or formula that accompanied baptism.

The new, or perhaps unusual, idea of Ephesians at this point is that the entire church receives this bath. This idea of a corporate baptism may have its origin in the preceding discussion on the unifying elements of the Christian church (4:4–6) in which, among other things, the writer mentions the one body (4:4) and the one baptism (4:5). Although baptism ordinarily is received by the believer, its application to the church as a whole is justified on the basis of the church's corporate and unified nature.

5:27 / The reason or the ultimate purpose behind the baptism of the church is now stated: **in order to present the church to himself, in all its beauty—pure and faultless, without spot or wrinkle or any other imperfection**. This is where the analogy of the bride and the bridal bath—if it is implied—breaks down. In a marriage the bride presents herself to the bridegroom; it would be inappropriate for the bridegroom to present the bride to himself (Mitton, p. 201). Here Christ takes the initiative by cleansing the bride (church) through baptism and presenting it to himself "free from all disfigurements or deformities" (Mitton, p. 204; Mitton also draws attention to the parallel between individual and corporate holiness in 1:4 and 5:27). The husband is to love his wife, "not just because of the beauty he finds in her, but to make her more beautiful. Christ sees the Church in all her weaknesses and failures, and yet loves her as His body and seeks her true sanctification" (Foulkes, p. 160).

Baptism has a three-dimensional focus: It is a past event that is grounded in the redemptive work of Christ ("he gave his life for it," i.e., the church); it continues to be a present reality by which individuals are baptized into the body of Christ and by which they are cleansed; and it has an ethical and eschatological function (**in order to present**). Sanctification and cleansing lead to the church's ultimate glorification and splendor.

5:28 / Even though husbands cannot love their wives in the same way that Christ demonstrated his love for the church, the divine model is still in the author's mind: **Husbands ought to love their wives just as they love their own bodies**. It appears that the husband, based on the principle that in marriage the two will become one (5:31), should regard his wife as his own body. He will, therefore, love his wife just as he loves his own body. Such union and intimacy seems to agree with the phrase, **a man who loves his wife loves himself**. This is true in the sense that husband and wife are "complementary parts of one personality" (Beare, p. 725).

This interpretation fits the drift of the author's thought better than one that sees these statements as encountering some kind of "prudential" or "pragmatic self-interest," as Mitton, for example, suggests: "It is easier to do what is right and good if one can see at the same time that it will produce something beneficial to ourselves" (p. 205). What we have, instead, is a fusion of the bride image into the body image (Houlden, p. 334). Thus, "As the Church is Christ's body, so in a true sense the wife is the husband's body. Through her he extends his life" (Wescott, p. 85).

5:29 / By placing 5:29 and 30 in a parenthesis, the GNB understands these verses as a commentary on 5:28. The love that a husband has for his own body and, consequently, for his wife is illustrated in some very practical ways: First, **he feeds it and takes care of it**. In other words, once a husband has come to think of his wife as his own flesh he will **feed** (lit., "nourish," *ektrephō*) and **take care** (lit., "cherish," *thalpō*) of her as Christ does with respect to his body, the church. On the human level this is true because **no one ever hates his own body**. (The Greek uses the term "flesh" rather than **body**, probably because it anticipates the quotation in 5:31 from Gen. 2:24, which states that the two shall become one "flesh." Unfortunately, the GNB leaves "flesh" out of Eph. 5:31 and leaves it in Gen. 2:24.)

5:30 / The second illustration is through being **members of his body** (cf. 1 Cor. 6:15—"You know that your bodies are parts of the body of Christ"). The meaning of this phrase must be seen in relation to the previous statement on Christ's love and care for the church: **We are members of his body**; therefore, Christ "feeds" and "takes care of" us. Although there does not appear to be any conscious application of this truth to the readers, it would remind them of Christ's concern for each one of them. Foulkes finds a helpful analogy from the vine and the branches in John 15: "As in the divine purpose the wife becomes part of the very life of her husband, and he nourishes and cherishes her, even so the Lord does to us as members of Himself, part of His own life that he has joined to Himself" (Foulkes, p. 161).

5:31 / The OT verse (Gen. 2:24) from which the author has been drawing his imagery is finally quoted and confirms the thoughts that he has been expounding on the relationship between husband and wife in marriage. Prior to marriage, a man and a woman are bound in an intimate relationship with their parents; but the marriage bond transcends that former bond by uniting the two as one flesh. For the author, this verse appropriately expresses the intimacy, unity, and, according to his thoughts, the identity of the husband and wife within marriage—a condition undoubtedly created by their sexual union (cf. 1 Cor. 6:16, 17, where Gen. 2:24 is used with reference to an immoral relationship with a prostitute).

Some of the older commentaries suggest that this verse has a secondary reference to Christ and how he left his heavenly home in order to be joined with his bride, the church. Moule, for example, writes: "We may reverently infer that the Apostle was guided to see in that verse a Divine parable of the Coming Forth of the Lord, the *Man* of Men, from the *Father*, and His present and eternal mystical Union with the true Church, His Bride" (p. 143; cf. other examples in Abbott, pp. 173, 174). Such an interpretation, however, is highly speculative and presses the analogy beyond its intended purpose as an illustration of unity.

The significance of the meaning of this quotation and the context from which it is taken cannot be overstated. In Scripture, it is used as the main argument against such problems as polygamy, sexual immorality, and divorce. No one verse speaks more strongly for the sacredness and permanency of the marriage bond and for fidelity within marriage.

5:32 / As appropriate as Genesis 2:24 is in describing the essence of marriage, and as overcome as the author is by the beauty of such a relationship, he still is preoccupied with thoughts about Christ and the church. Consequently, he sees in the oneness of husband and wife a great revelation that, for him, applies to **Christ and the church**. "The husband's position as head, and his duty of sacrificial love and devoted care for his wife are but pictures, imperfect, but the best that this life can offer, of Christ as Head, and of His love, self-sacrifice and concern for His church. The dependence of the wife on her husband and her duty of submission are a picture of how the Church should live and act towards her divine Lord" (Foulkes, p. 162).

The phrase **there is a deep secret truth revealed in this scripture** is a translation of the Greek *to mystērion touto mega estin* ("this mystery is great!"). "Mystery," as used earlier in this epistle, referred to God's plan for mankind, which had been hidden but now has been revealed (1:9; 3:3–6, 9; cf. also 6:19). Here it refers to a deep insight or **a deep secret truth** that is revealed. A mystery, in this context, is not a secret but a revelation—the union between Christ and the church.

One cannot help but notice that the references to "mystery" in Ephesians have unity as a theme. The mystery that is revealed in 3:3–6 has the effect of *uniting* Jew and Gentile into the body of Christ; in 5:32, one application of the mystery is the *union* between Christ and the church. In the former case there is the creation of *one new people in union with himself* (Christ); in the latter, the *two become one*. Stott notes that in Ephesians the metaphors of the church—"the body, the building and the bride—all emphasize the reality of its unity on account of its union with Christ" (p. 231). The Latin rendering of *sacramentum* for mystery (**secret**) does not legitimize viewing marriage as a sacrament (cf. Barth, *Eph. 4–6*, pp.744–49).

The precise meaning of the author's thoughts is by no means easy to determine—as is obvious from the variety of translations and interpretations (for a list, see Mitton, pp. 207, 8). Some commentators, in spite of the apostle's application of Genesis 2:24 to Christ and the church, believe that it refers primarily to human marriage as the great "mystery." Others concede that though that may be true in itself, the phrase "but I say" (*egō de legō*) or, "it also applies," indicates that the marriage union serves as an illustration of something yet more meaningful. Beare paraphrases such thinking in the following way: "The mystery of the union of man and wife into one flesh is of far-reaching importance and clearly points itself toward some transcendental, eternal reality. I for my part take it to be a symbol of the union of Christ and the church" (Beare, p. 727).

5:33 / Lest the readers be too caught up in the mystical aspects of these thoughts, the author brings them back to reality: Nevertheless, or in spite of that application to Christ and the church in 5:32, **it also applies to you**. By doing this, he returns to the more practical and human considerations that initiated the discussion about husband and wife (5:22 ff.): **Every husband must love his wife as himself, and every wife must respect her husband**. Respect is a translation of the Greek *phobeō*, which, as in 5:21, also has the meaning of reverence. It is best understood as "awe," such as an individual would show before God (cf. Barth, *Eph. 4–6*, pp. 662–68 for a detailed explanation). Barth protests the equation of "fear" with awe, reverence, or respect, insisting that it be given an eschatological meaning as well, that is, "conduct that heeds the crisis of the present, the last judgment, and the ultimate triumph of Christ" (*Eph. 4–6*, p. 667).

This section of the household code ends in much the same way as it began—submission, reverence, and love. Throughout, the author has fluctuated between two analogies: At times the husband-wife relationship served an ecclesiological function by illustrating Christ's relationship to the church; at other times, the Christ-church analogy illustrated a domestic ideal. The end result is that one has a deeper appreciation and understanding of both relationships, even though the author's original intention was to enrich the understanding of marriage.

Additional Notes

In addition to the disc. and bibliography on the household codes in Chapters 18–21 on Colossians 3:18–4:1, see Frank Stagg, "The Domestic Code and Final Appeal: Ephesians 5:21–6:24," *RevExp* 75 (1979), pp. 541–52. On the use of traditional material in this section, P. Sampley, *And the Two Shall Become One Flesh: A Study of Traditions in Ephesians 5:21–33* (Cambridge: Cambridge University Press, 1971); Barth, *Eph. 4–6*, pp. 652–55; Mitton, pp. 208–10.

5:22 / For questions regarding the legitimacy of translating head (*kephalē*) as "authority," see the article by Berkeley and Alvira Mickelsen, "Does Male Dominance Tarnish Our Translations?" *Christianity Today*, October 5, 1979, pp. 23–29. The main point the Mickelsens make is that head "does *not* mean 'boss' or 'final authority' . . . but source or origin . . . or beginning."

5:26-27 / For arguments pro and con on the bridal bath, see R. Batey, "Jewish Gnosticism and the 'Hieros Gamos' of Eph. V. 21–33," *NTS* 10 (1963), pp. 121–27; C. Chavasse, *The Bride of Christ* (London: Faber & Faber, 1939); S. Hanson, *The Unity of the Church in the New Testament*. Barth argues against a baptismal interpretation of 5:26, 27, in his *Eph. 4–6*, pp. 687–700.

5:31 / On the use of Gen. 2:24 in Eph. 5:31, 32, see Lincoln, "The Use of the OT in Ephesians," esp. pp. 30–36. For additional thoughts on marriage, singleness, and individuality, Barth, *Eph. 4–6*, pp. 700–38; Stagg, "The Domestic Code and Final Appeal: Ephesians 5:21–6:24," pp. 547–48.

5:32 / Discussion on the concept of "sacred marriage" (*hieros gamos*) in Jewish and Hellenistic thought can be found in Barth, *Eph. 4–6*, pp. 738–44; Beare, pp. 726–28; and R. Batey, "Jewish Gnosticism and the 'Hieros Gamos' of Eph. v. 21–33."

23

Children and Parents

Children, it is your Christian[h] duty to obey your parents, for this is the right thing to do. [2]"Respect your father and mother" is the first commandment that has a promise added: [3]"so that all may go well with you, and you may live a long time in the land."

[4]Parents, do not treat your children in such a way as to make them angry. Instead, raise them with Christian discipline and instruction.

h. *Some manuscripts do not have* Christian.

I n 6:1–9 there is a continuation of these rules of conduct as they apply to children and parents (6:1–4) and slaves and masters (6:5–9). As in the section on the husband-wife relationship, there is the specific emphasis that the ethical life of the Christian is both grounded in and directed toward the Lord.

The superscription of submission out of "reverence for Christ" in 5:21 serves the entire code. Wives are to submit to their husbands as to the Lord (5:22); children are to obey their parents "in the Lord" ("it is your Christian duty," 6:1); fathers are to raise their children in the discipline and instruction "of the Lord" (6:4); slaves are to obey their earthly masters "as though they were serving Christ" (6:5) as his slaves (6:6). Masters, likewise, are to let Christ, the Master in heaven, govern their attitude and conduct toward their slaves (6:9).

It is possible that such rules of conduct were given as part of the catechetical instruction to newly baptized believers, but it is not necessary to conclude that the author is here addressing the congregation during a baptismal service. Nor does the inclusion of children in such instruction mean that infants were baptized. The primary concern is to demonstrate the kind of personal and domestic unity that should exist among Christians in the church.

6:1 / Although the author is following Colossians 3:20–21 rather closely, there are some significant differences in this epistle. Children are exhorted to **obey** their parents because **this is the right thing to do.** Obedience to parents is considered to be a self-evident and morally acceptable thing to do.

The phrase **it is your Christian duty to obey your parents** is somewhat redundant and changes the meaning slightly. Probably it comes from the Greek "in the Lord" that, although it is a disputed reading, is retained in such versions as the RSV and NIV. If retained, it makes obedience a Christian as well as a universal obligation. The statement does not clarify the Christian status of parents.

In Colossians, children are to obey "always," that is, in everything. Mitton suggests that the change in Ephesians would be appropriate "where the children addressed may have pagan parents," thus necessitating "an obedience which does not contravene a primary obedience 'to the Lord.' " (p. 210). Though obedience to parents is a universally acceptable principle, there are conflicts when Christian children are required to submit to parents who have no Christian commitment and whose moral standards run counter to Christ's.

6:2-3 / **"Respect your father and mother"**: Since this quotation from Exodus 20:12 (cf. Deut. 5:16) does not occur in the Colossians parallel, it is reasonable to assume that the author of Ephesians is either relying on a different tradition or making a point specifically appropriate to his audience. Obedience to this commandment carries the promise of prosperity and longevity. By **the first commandment that has a promise added** the author must mean first in importance with respect to children, because the second commandment, which prohibits idolatry, is followed by God's promise to show his steadfast love to those who love him and keep his commandments (Exod. 20:6).

Initially, Exodus 20:12 referred to the promised land that God was giving to the children of Israel. Also, it would have been older children who were called upon to honor their parents by obeying and exercising care and responsibility for them. Ephesians shortens the phrase "in the land that I am giving you" (Exod. 20:12) to "in the land." The promised land is replaced by a more general or universal conception. God rewards a society or a community in which obedience and respect are practiced.

It is difficult to demonstrate the fulfillment of this promise in a society where such a promise of reward does not always seem to hold true. Most commentators, therefore, interpret the author's intention in general rather than individual terms. "Then what is promised," claims J. Stott, "is not so much long life to each child who obeys his parents, as social stability to any community in which children honor their parents. Certainly a healthy society is inconceivable without a strong family life" (p. 241; cf. also Foulkes, p. 165; Mitton, p. 212, for similar applications).

6:4 / The change from **parents** (6:1) to "fathers" (in RSV and NIV, following the Greek text) may or may not be significant. Does the author mean that whereas obedience is required toward both parents, it is the father's responsibility to administer discipline and nurture the child in spiritual things? This could attest to the strong patriarchal orientation of the first century in both Jewish and pagan society. A Roman father, for example (*pater familias*), exercised a rigid and sovereign control over his household (Stott, p. 245; Barclay, p. 208). The GNB **parents** takes this to be a case in which the word "father" is used but both parents are meant.

Negatively, **parents** are exhorted to avoid making their children **angry** (from *parorgizō*, "provoke to anger"). Obedience can be expected, but it cannot be demanded by provoking, exasperating, or irritating children or causing them to be angry (Col. 3:21 adds "or they will become discouraged"). Positively, parents are urged to **raise them with Christian discipline and instruction**.

The verb for "raise" (*ektrephō*) has the meaning of nourish. Though it can be used for bodily nourishment and care (5:29), it applies also to the care given to the entire person. Such nurture is given through Christian discipline (*paideia*) and instruction (*nouthesia*). These exhortations for catechetical instruction may be related to the baptismal nature of the epistle. This may be one reason why this verse is omitted in Colossians; another could be that Ephesians was written considerably later than Colossians and thus reflects an increasingly parental and church concern for children.

Some commentators make a rather rigid distinction between the two categories of nurture that are employed, suggesting that *paideia* means training by disciplinary action and *nouthesia* refers to verbal instruction (Foulkes, p. 166; Stott, p. 248). Such distinctions, according to Mitton, are a little "strained," although "the words together suggest both the inculcation of patterns of behaviour worthy of a Christian and also verbal instruction about the contents of the faith" (p. 213).

24

Slaves and Masters

Slaves, obey your human masters with fear and trembling; and do it with a sincere heart, as though you were serving Christ. ⁶Do this not only when they are watching you, because you want to gain their approval; but with all your heart do what God wants, as slaves of Christ. ⁷Do your work as slaves cheerfully, as though you served the Lord, and not merely men. ⁸Remember that the Lord will reward everyone, whether slave or free, for the good work he does.

⁹Masters, behave in the same way toward your slaves and stop using threats. Remember that you and your slaves belong to the same Master in heaven, who judges everyone by the same standard.

Most of the things that were said about slavery in the exegesis of Colossians (Chap. 21) and Philemon applies to Ephesians as well. But though the Colossian code was directed specifically toward the need for order in the church, the code in Ephesians appears to be more general in nature and to conform to the writer's concern that there be unity and understanding within the Christian community as believers seek to serve Christ within the guidelines of the principle of submission (5:21).

6:5 / The slaves who are being addressed are Christians. This means that their life has a new center of reference and that their ultimate loyalty is directed toward the Lord, who puts new meaning into their earthly responsibilities. Consequently, they are to **obey** their **human masters** as though they were serving Christ (6:5); they are to consider themselves "as slaves of Christ" (6:6) and perform their duties as though they served "the Lord, and not merely men" (6:7).

Fear and trembling appears to be a common expression in connection with obedience (2 Cor. 7:15; Phil. 2:12). To some, this may connote cowardice or submission occasioned by severe oppression. But it is more likely that reverence and respect for those in authority is meant. Slaves, in spite of their newly found freedom in Christ, need to remember that they have not been freed socially from the institution of slavery. Disobedience to one's earthly masters could still result in severe punishment (cf. 6:9, "stop using threats"). Service to earthly masters is to be rendered with the same kind of sincerity (**a sincere heart**) that governs one's service to **Christ**.

6:6 / The previous idea is carried over into this verse, where sincerity is defined as enthusiastic behavior (**with all your heart**) without any attempt to attract human attention (**not only when they are watching you**) or any desire for human **approval**. This, states the author, is God's will for them: By serving in this way they do **what God wants**.

This, to be sure, is a revolutionary transformation of the work ethic and has many implications for labor relations today. For a Christian, there is no distinction between the secular and the sacred. "The Christian's ideal is for his daily work, seen or unseen by men, to be accepted as the *will of God*, rejoiced in and done not by constraint or carelessness but because it is his will" (Foulkes, p. 168).

6:7 / This verse essentially repeats—and thus re-emphasizes—the thought in the two preceding ones. Work that is done cheerfully (*eunoia* carries the idea of zeal and enthusiasm) has to come from the heart. That inner conviction that is brought about by a new relationship to Christ and new attitude toward work enables the slave to perform his or her responsibilities with enthusiasm.

6:8 / As in Colossians (3:24), the **reward** motif is introduced into the discussion as a reminder that there is more to life than poor working conditions or one's paycheck. In Colossians, there is a direct connection to the future inheritance that the faithful receive ("you will receive what he has kept for his people") because the problem of injustice seems to have been more pronounced (3:25). In Ephesians, the emphasis is upon the **good work** that is performed by **slave or free**: Both will be rewarded by the Lord.

6:9 / **Masters** are exhorted to **behave in the same way** toward their slaves. This means that the Lord expects sincerity, cheerfulness, and a detachment from earthly attention and approval from them as well; they are Christian masters and so their believing slaves share the same heavenly Lord (**remember that you and your slaves belong to the same Master in heaven**). "In civil law, the slave had no rights as against his master, but under Christianity the obligations are reciprocal" (Beare, p. 735). A higher social or economic status is of no advantage in the Christian community as far as one's relationship with the Lord is concerned. Christ **judges everyone by the same standard** (lit., "before him there is no partiality," *prosōpolēmpsia*).

Slave owners who became Christians had to make a radical change in their attitudes and behavior toward their slaves. One common way of controlling their labor force was by threats—threats of death, punishment, or sale. This practice, states the apostle, must be terminated (**stop using threats**). Service must be earned; it should not come through the fear of reprisal.

Although the author does not abolish the institution of slavery, this new relationship between slave and master ultimately led to its demise. In connection with this, J. Stott notes that the gospel, with its teaching of equality, justice, and brotherhood, "lit a fuse which at long last led to the explosion which destroyed it" (p. 257).

Additional Note

6:9 / In line with this, Frank Stagg makes a prophetic observation: "Slavery sooner or later had to come under the judgment of the Christian conscience. What about male domination or any other denial of the full personhood of any person?" ("The Domestic Code and Final Appeal: Ephesians 5:21–6:24," *RevExp* 75 (1979), p. 550).

25

The Christian's Armor

Finally, build up your strength in union with the Lord and by means of his mighty power. [11]Put on all the armor that God gives you, so that you will be able to stand up against the Devil's evil tricks. [12]For we are not fighting against human beings but against the wicked spiritual forces in the heavenly world, the rulers, authorities, and cosmic powers of this dark age. [13]So put on God's armor now! Then when the evil day comes, you will be able to resist the enemy's attacks; and after fighting to the end, you will still hold your ground.

[14]So stand ready, with truth as a belt tight around your waist, with righteousness as your breastplate, [15]and as your shoes the readiness to announce the Good News of peace.

[16]At all times carry faith as a shield; for with it you will be able to put out all the burning arrows shot by the Evil One. [17]And accept salvation as a helmet, and the word of God as the sword which the Spirit gives you. [18]Do all this in prayer, asking for God's help. Pray on every occasion as the Spirit leads. For this reason keep alert and never give up: pray always for all God's people. [19]And pray also for me, that God will give me a message when I am ready to speak, so that I may speak boldly and make known the gospel's secret. [20]For the sake of this gospel I am an ambassador, though now I am in prison. Pray that I may be bold in speaking about the gospel as I should.

Since the imagery of war and armor is quite prominent throughout the NT, this section in Ephesians does not specifically represent any new teaching. Paul, for example, speaks of his own Christian life as a spiritual fight (1 Cor. 9:24–27). The author of the Pastorals encourages Timothy to "run your best in the race of faith" (1 Tim. 6:12) and, in an age of apostasy, to let the apostle's words "serve as weapons in order to fight well" (1 Tim. 1:18, 19).

On several occasions Paul even identifies the weapons that the Christian is to use. Because the battle is a spiritual one, he says, "the weapons we use in our fight are not the world's weapons but God's powerful weapons, with which to destroy strongholds" (2 Cor. 10:4). He exhorts the Romans to "take up weapons for fighting in the light" (Rom. 13:12), whereas his admonition to the Thessalonians is to "wear faith and love as a breastplate, and our hope of salvation as a helmet (1 Thess. 5:8).

There are at least two possible sources for this kind of imagery. The original and most immediate source of inspiration may be the pieces of armor that the Roman armies used. Paul had sufficient opportunity to observe such armor on the soldiers who were guarding him in prison. But although the Roman military power is the nearest at hand, the author of Ephesians undoubtedly is working from concepts that had been fairly well established in the church.

The most obvious starting point for this biblical imagery lies in Isaiah 59:17, where God is pictured as the warrior who arms himself for battle: "He will wear justice like a coat of armor and victory like a helmet. He will clothe himself with the strong desire to set things right and to punish and avenge the wrongs that people suffer." In the prophecy of Isaiah 11:5, it is the Messiah who comes for war and judgment: "Righteousness shall be the girdle of his waist, and faithfulness the girdle of his loins" (RSV). This imagery is carried into the Apocryphal literature, where it states that the coming of the Lord and even all of creation will be armed for battle (Wisdom of Solomon 5:17–20). The idea of the heavenly armor originates in these OT sources and reaches its fully developed form in the NT picture of the Christian warrior.

Apart from the idea that the Christian life can be considered as a battle or a fight, it is likely that these exhortations were particularly useful when Christians were being persecuted. In 1 Peter 4:1, for example, the believers are exhorted to "arm themselves" (RSV) spiritually for the suffering that awaits them.

In Ephesians, the Christian warrior is exhorted to "put on all the armor that God gives" (6:11) for the battle against the forces of wickedness. Here there is no indication of persecution or suffering. The exhortation clearly is intended for the present life of the church, although mention of the coming evil day (6:13) brings in an element of the future as well. The author indicates that this is his final exhortation to the readers (6:10). Thus, they who are already in Christ by virtue of their baptism are to continue to find strength for their new life "in union with the Lord" (6:10).

The numerous references to "stand" (6:11, 13, 14) emphasize the theme of watchfulness and steadfastness that characterizes this early catechism (cf. 1 Cor. 16:13; Col. 4:12; James 4:7; 1 Pet. 5:8, 9). Although the NT often speaks about an "inner warfare" caused by the "passions of the flesh" (Rom. 7:23; Gal. 5:17; 1 Pet. 2:11; James 4:1), the enemies that the readers of Ephesians are to resist are spiritual in nature and include the Devil and "wicked spiritual forces in the heavenly world, the rulers, authorities, and cosmic powers of this dark age" (6:12).

There is very little evidence to indicate whether such an exhortation was connected specifically with baptism. Although baptism would be a suitable occasion to remind new Christians that they have spiritual armor to face the world, there is little to commend this connection in Ephesians. The most tangible evidence in this respect is found in Ignatius' letter to Polycarp: "Let your baptism be your arms; your faith, your helmet; your love, your spear; your endurance, your armor" (6.2).

The most that one can say about the author's final exhortation in the Epistle to the Ephesians is that it is built upon traditional imagery of the Christian warrior and early catechetical material on steadfastness and watchfulness in the Christian life. This section could, as Mitton suggests, pick up the warnings that the author developed in 5:3–20, or even in 4:25–31, where the readers are admonished not to give the Devil a chance (4:27). The exhortations in 6:10–22 provide specific ways in which evil can be thwarted (p. 219).

6:10 / **Finally**, that is, this is the last or concluding exhortation. The phrase **build up your strength in union with the Lord** is not a plea for self-effort. The verb *endynamoō* is a present passive that literally means "be made strong in the Lord continually." The next phrase indicates that this empowerment is possible because of the resources that the Lord supplies—**by means of his mighty power**.

Within this verse there are three Greek words for power—*dynamis, kratos,* and *ischus*. Distinctions between these words are not always possible or necessary; the message that comes through is that God's resources enable the believer to face evil. They are the same words that are used in 1:19 to describe the spiritual gifts of the believer (indicative); now believers are exhorted to experience the effect of that power in their daily life (imperative).

6:11 / **Put on** is a common expression in Ephesians and Colossians and is used, as has been seen, in the context of baptism (4:24; Col. 3:10,12). The aorist tense indicates that the author is thinking of a specific time or situation when this took place in the believer's life. "This would fit a baptismal occasion when the new Christian is ready to step out in his new venture of Christian discipleship" (Mitton, p. 220). **Stand**, as noted above, was a common theme in the catechetical instruction of the early church.

The reader's equipment is **all the armor that God gives,** literally, "the armor of God" (*tēn panoplian tou theou*). English translations usually add **all** (GNB), "whole" (RSV), or "full" (NIV). Such words, however, are redundant, because *panoplia* means "full armor," and give the phrase a wrong meaning. The author is not emphasizing the completeness of the armor, for to do so would have meant the addition of several other items; rather, he is drawing attention to the *quality* of the armor—its divineness (**armor of God**) or, as Barth proposes, the "splendid Armor" (*Eph. 4–6*, p. 793).

This spiritual armor is necessary so that believers can stand against **the Devil's evil tricks**. *Methodeia*, from which we derive the English words *methodical, planning, inquiry*, and so on, also means "cunning, subtlety, and scheming cleverness"—hence **evil tricks** or "wiles" of the Devil (RSV). The language is quite similar to another exhortation in Scripture: "Be alert, be on watch! Your enemy, the Devil, roams around like a roaring lion, looking for someone to devour" (1 Pet. 5:8).

6:12 / In addition to the Devil, believers face a host of wicked spiritual forces, described as **rulers** (*archōn*), **authorities** (*exousia*), **and cosmic powers** (*kosmokrator*) **of this dark age**. J. Stott gives a rather striking and complete picture of the evil forces that believers face: "The enemy," he states, is "powerful," "wicked," and "cunning," (pp. 263–67). No wonder, then, that believers are summoned to build up their strength and to "put on God's armor." "Only the power of God can defend and deliver us from the might, the evil and the craft of the devil" (Stott, p. 266).

By stating that the believer's warfare is not **against human beings** but **cosmic powers**, the author is utilizing the same cosmic mythology that he used earlier (1:21; 3:10) and that is found in other parts of the NT (Rom. 8:38; Gal. 4:3; Col. 1:16; 2:15, 20; 1 Pet. 3:22). Basically, these classes of evil spirits are a comprehensive designation for the enemy that Christians face. By belonging to the **heavenly** order they are nonmaterial or superterrestrial: "Though their present domain extends over the earth, their origin and base of operations lie beyond this world" (Mitton, p. 222). Only Ephesians uses the term *kosmokrator* (a compound noun made up of *kosmos*, "world," and *kratos*, "rule"). It is a title that was applied to a number of pagan gods (Beare, p. 738). Here, it is used to affirm that these evil powers exercise their authority in the world (*kosmos*) and thus over the believer.

The thoughts that this passage elicit take the reader back to Ephesians 1:21, which describes Christ's victory and exaltation over these evil forces. Believers who are "in Christ" through their faith and baptism share in that victory and exaltation (2:1–10). In Colossians, Christ's victory and authority over evil powers is stated even more emphatically (1:16; 2:15). The main point of the epistle is that, by virtue of Christ's work, these spirits no longer exercise any control over the believer—"You have died with Christ and are set free from the ruling spirits of the universe" (2:20). Nevertheless, believers are admonished continually to "become" what they "are" (the tension between the indicative and imperative).

In 6:12, the evil and cosmic powers are presented as still exercising power over the believer even though they have been defeated by Christ. They are still active; they continually attempt to regain their once-eminent position; they are a constant threat to the believer's spiritual welfare. This is why the readers are exhorted to utilize the armor that God has given to them.

6:13 / **So put on God's armor now**! The imagery of "putting on" the different pieces of armor may come from observing a soldier dressing himself or being dressed for battle. But given the nature of the Christians' armor and their having received that armor when they became believers, it is unlikely that one should think of the Christian soldier as gradually dressing him- or herself to face Satan. To "put on" (6:11, 13) is a call for believers to utilize what they already possess.

The coming **evil day** commonly is interpreted to mean some future eschatological conflict (Mark 13; 2 Thess. 2:8–10; 1 John 2:18; 4:17) or the final battle of Armageddon (Rev. 16:12–16; 20:7, 8). True, believers are warned in Scripture to prepare themselves for eschatological judgment, but this is not what appears to be in the apostle's mind; he sees the conflict as a current crisis and so admonishes them to be ready **now**. The coming **evil day** is a reminder of the ever-present reality of wickedness and temptation. Those equipped with God's armor **will be able to resist the enemy's attacks**.

When such assaults come, believers are assured that the Devil will not be able to move them—**and after fighting to the end, you will still hold your ground**. Though the context of the passage emphasizes "readiness" and "firmness," the use of *katergazomai* has the meaning of combat leading to victory (contra Barth, *Eph. 4–6*, pp. 765,766). The result of this combat, however, is not progress in conquest but the strengthening of one's position (**hold your ground**). Moule reminds readers that the picture of the battle in Ephesians is not a "march" but "the holding of the fortress of the soul" (p. 151). Here, "The scene is filled with the marshalled host of the Evil One, bent upon *dislodging* the soul, and the

Church, from the one possible vantage-ground of life and power—union and communion with their Lord" (p. 154).

6:14 / Having discussed the benefits and the need for preparedness, the apostle finally describes the individual pieces of God's armor that form the believer's equipment. Again, there is no attempt to be complete, since a number of items are omitted (cf. disc. on 6:11; also Beare, who quotes Polybius' account of the armor carried by the Roman spearman, p. 740). But this does not mean that the believer is inadequately equipped, since the author believes that the six items he lists are the essential ones: The **belt**, **breastplate**, shoes, shield, helmet, and sword are used to picture **truth**, **righteousness**, the Good News of peace, faith, salvation, and the word of God.

In interpreting these, it is wise to heed the advice of C. L. Mitton: "It is, however, a mistake to overelaborate the precise correspondence in each case. . . . The emphasis is rather on the total equipment. Just as the soldier in physical warfare needs all six items, if he is not to be needlessly vulnerable at some points, so the Christian needs each piece of spiritual equipment for his struggle" (p. 223). **So stand ready**!

First, stand ready **with truth as a belt tight around your waist**: In a culture where the people wore long loose-fitting robes, it would be necessary to bind such garments close to the body when quick action was required. Here, the believer is summoned to stand, therefore, literally, "having girded (*perizōnnumi*) your loins in truth" (cf. RSV; the meaning is the same as in 1 Pet. 1:13, where the phrase "loins of your mind" is used). "This means getting rid of anything which might be a hindrance in the struggle against evil, eliminating an easy-going casualness which might make him less than ready for the fray" (Mitton, p. 225).

Truth could carry two meanings: It may be a specific reference to the Good News that is the true messsage (Col 1:5), or to such equivalent concepts as genuineness, faithfulness, reliability, and integrity. If the gospel or correct doctrine was intended, one would expect to see the article ("the truth"). This verse could be an allusion to the previous emphasis on truthfulness and integrity within the body of Christ (4:25 ff.; 2 Cor. 6:7).

Second, stand **with righteousness for your breastplate**: Righteousness is one of the qualities of the divine warrior (Isa. 11:5; 59:17); in 1 Thessalonians, faith and love are the breastplate (5:8); as God's servants, writes Paul, "We have righteousness as our weapon, both to attack and to defend ourselves" (2 Cor. 6:7). In NT usage, righteousness (*dikaiosunē*) can mean the justification of the sinner as well as the moral quality of godliness (*dikaios*). Stott takes the expression to mean righteousness of character and conduct and quotes G. G. Findlay for support: " 'The completeness of pardon for past offence and integrity of character that belong to the justified life, are woven together into an impenetrable mail' " (p. 279). In either case, righteousness constitutes the breastplate that protects his heart.

6:15 / Third, there is **peace**, which is the **shoes** for your feet. The Greek uses an aorist participle (*hypodeō*), which conforms to the idea that this has already taken place—thus the RSV "having shod your feet with the equipment of the gospel of peace." This piece of armor testifies to the Christian warrior's **readiness to announce the Good News of peace**. The phrase is similar to the description of God's servant, the Messiah, in Isaiah 52:7: "How wonderful it is to see a messenger coming across the mountains, bringing good news, the news of peace" (also Rom. 10:15). Earlier in the epistle, the author stated that "Christ came and preached the Good News of peace to all" (2:17).

In the context of Ephesians, peace was proclaimed to the Gentiles (those "far off") and the Jews (those "near"), and it became a reality when they were reconciled to each other through Christ (2:15). In this verse, the emphasis seems to be on the immediacy of the spiritual battle that all believers face and their readiness to announce the Good News that Christ has defeated these evil forces of darkness. If *en hetoimasia* is understood as "steadfastness" rather than "readiness" (so Barth, *Eph. 4–6*, pp. 770–71), the shoes are more a defensive weapon enabling the believer to stand and resist the Devil. In either case, the establishment of peace in the world depends upon the defeat of all spiritual evil that destroys that peace.

6:16 / Fourth, **carry faith as a shield**: According to ancient historians, the large door-shaped protective shield was composed of two layers of wood covered with a flame-resistant hide. The **burning arrows** that the enemy shot would strike the shield and burn out without penetrating it. **Faith**, claims the author, acts like an impregnable shield and will extinguish all the **burning arrows shot by the Evil One**. Faith is complete confidence and reliance upon God to give his warrior the victory.

6:17 / Fifth, **accept salvation as a helmet** (cf. 1 Thess. 5:8): In the case of the divine warrior (Isa. 59:17), salvation is the helmet that God wears as he goes forth in battle against his enemies. In that context, the helmet symbolized God's "power and readiness to save others," not protection, as in Ephesians (Beare, p. 743; also Moule, p. 157). As protective headgear, the helmet guards "the centre of life. The sense of salvation puts life beyond all danger" (Wescott, p. 97).

The use of **accept** or "receive" (*dechomai*) is significant. Earlier, the writer used "put on" (*enduō*) (*analambanō*) for the other pieces of armor. So far, one could picture the soldier dressing himself and attaching each piece of armor carefully. Beare suggests that once a soldier was fully clad the helmet and sword would not be taken up from the ground by himself but would be handed to him by his attendant or armor bearer (Beare, p. 743). By analogy, **salvation** and **the word of God** are gifts that believers *receive*. Salvation is a gift of God, and "there is no doubt that God's saving power is our only defence against the enemy of our soul" (Stott, p. 282).

Sixth, and finally, **accept . . . the word of God as the sword which the Spirit gives you**. An issue related to this verse is how to interpret the phrase "the sword of the Spirit" (*tēn machairan tou pneumatos*). Is it "the sword which consists of the Spirit, or the sword which the Spirit provides?" (Mitton, p. 227). And how does this relate to the next phrase, literally, "which is the word of God"?

The best explanations take the sword as that which is given by the Spirit (GNB) but which is identified as the word of God—the sword (**which the Spirit gives**) is the word of God (for Biblical examples comparing speech to a sword, cf. Ps. 57:4; 64:3; Isa. 49:2; Heb. 4:12; Rev. 1:16; 2:16; 19:15). The **word of God** is not only the gospel (1 Pet. 1:25) but all of the words of God that come from his Spirit. "Salvation *is* the Christian's helmet, the indwelling Spirit *is* his sword. The Spirit gives him the word to speak" (cf. Mark 13:11, and Isa. 51:16; Houlden, p. 339; also Mitton, p. 227).

6:18 / Although the military imagery continues into this verse—**do all this**, that is, arm yourselves and **keep alert**—the prayer to which the readers are summoned should not be taken as a seventh piece of the Christian's armor. God has given his splendid armor to the believer, but the "putting on" and the utilization of that armor in battle calls for discipline in prayer and reliance upon **God's help**. According to Stott, "Equipping ourselves with God's armor is not a mechanical preparation; it is itself an expression of our dependence on God, in other words, of prayer" (p. 283).

The prayer that the believers are admonished to utter has some significant qualities about it. First, it is to be unceasing: **Do all this in prayer . . . pray on every occasion**. The idea is that the Christian warrior, although heavily armed, can only stand firm against his or her enemy through the agency of prayer. The praying that is done is **as the Spirit leads**, literally, "praying in the Spirit." To do so is not to be transposed into some ecstatic or euphoric condition beyond the senses but to live in the realization that the Spirit is the believer's helper (5:18) and intercessor (Rom. 8:15, 16, 26, 27). "It is an approach to God relying not on our own piety, but on the help which God in his Spirit offers to us" (Mitton, p. 228).

The Greek, and most English translations (RSV, NIV), employ the two expressions "prayer" (*proseuchē*) and "supplication" or "request" (*deēsis*). The feeling of most commentators is that "prayer" is always used for God, whereas "supplication" may be used to address either God or mankind. The GNB **asking for God's help** takes the Greek as a request to God and not as intercession on behalf of human beings.

Second, prayer is to be intense: **Keep alert and never give up**. In other words, maintain a spirit of watchfulness and perseverance. A Christian warrior must not be caught off guard. This exhortation toward constancy and watchfulness in prayer and the Christian life is common to the NT (Luke 18:1; Rom. 12:12; 1 Cor. 16:13; Phil. 4:6; Col. 4:2; 1 Thess. 5:17; 1 Pet. 5:8). But since this phrase falls between two other exhortations, it is not entirely clear where "perseverance" (**never give up**) belongs. Should it go with the idea of praying constantly with all alertness, or does it relate to the following phrase, in which believers are summoned to intercede for others? Beare suggests that alertness refers to the believer's spiritual conflict but that this, in turn, leads to "persevering intercession on behalf of all his comrades in the fight" (p. 746).

Third, prayer is unlimited: **Pray always for all God's people** (the saints). Since all believers are involved in a spiritual battle, prayer must transcend its narrow individualism and encompass the entire body of Christ. As a member of an army, believers must manifest a concern for all who are fighting along with them. Here the apostle's concerns are not unlike those in 1 Peter, where, in a similar context of warning his readers about the Devil, Peter writes: "Be firm in your faith and resist him because you know that your fellow believers in all the world are going through the same kind of suffering" (5:9).

6:19-20 / The thought of Christians praying for one another leads the apostle to think of himself and the personal needs that he has for prayer as well. (Cf. this pattern in Col. 4:3; 1 Thess. 5:25; 2 Thess. 3:1. This verse is almost identical in substance with Colossians 4:3.) Basically, the apostle has two requests: First, **pray . . . that God will give me a message when I am ready to speak**. Literally, the phrase reads, "Pray . . . so that a word (*logos*) may be given to me to open my mouth." According to Abbott, " 'Opening the mouth' is an expression used only when some grave utterance is in question" (p. 189). God is the giver of this special utterance, but the apostle knows that he is the bearer of it.

Second, he requests boldness to **make known the gospel's secret** (mystery). This concern is repeated in the next verse, thus indicating the burden that the apostle felt for a clear presentation of the gospel. The **secret** is used on other occasions in the epistle to mean the unity of Jews and Gentiles in the body of Christ (3:3–6, 9). Although he is an **ambassador** in chains (*hylasis*) because of the gospel, he envisions further opportunities to serve as the Lord's representative.

Additional Note

6:12 / In addition to disc. and bibliography on principalities, powers, etc., on 1:22; 3:10, and Col. 1:16; 2:15, 20, see D. E. H. Whiteley, "Ephesians vi. 12—Evil Powers," *ExpT* 68 (1956–57), pp. 100–103. Whiteley sums up the teaching of 6:12 this way: "Because Christ is One with God, and because we are members of Christ, the whole power of God is behind us in our struggle with the Evil Powers" (p. 103). Another helpful source dealing with the struggle of believers with evil powers that have already been defeated by Christ is O. Cullmann's *Christ and Time* (London: SCM, 1951 ed.); Cullmann's analogy of "D" and "V" Day has become famous.

Final Greetings

Tychicus, our dear brother and faithful servant in the Lord's work, will give you all the news about me, so that you may know how I am getting along. [22]That is why I am sending him to you—to tell you how all of us are getting along and to encourage you.

6:21–22 / Ephesians ends in a rather unexpected and uncharacteristic way: First, the personal references to Tychicus and some specific congregation(s) conflict with the impersonal and universal nature of the epistle. The most that one can say is that Tychicus, who is the bearer of Colossians and Philemon, may be taking Ephesians to the congregations in Asia Minor as well. Here Tychicus is considered a **dear brother and faithful servant** who will give news of the apostle's situation in prison.

Second, there is the problem of verbal correspondence with Colossians. Mitton has noted that "thirty-two consecutive words in Ephesians are identical with a similar number of words from Col. 4:7–8" (p. 230). Although there are many other similarities between these two epistles, there is little doubt that in this section the author is copying verbatim from Colossians.

Closing Benediction

May God the Father and the Lord Jesus Christ give to all Christian brothers peace and love with faith.	²⁴May God's grace be with all those who love our Lord Jesus Christ with undying love.

6:23-24 / These closing verses contain the familiar virtues of **peace**, **love**, **faith**, and **grace** that have occurred throughout the epistle. This benediction has a twofold application: First, peace, love, and faith are extended **to all Christian brothers**, that is, members of a local Christian community; second, the benediction of **grace** is much more general, being extended to **all those who love our Lord Jesus Christ**, that is, members of the universal church.

The benediction includes the unusual phrase **undying love**. *Aphtharsia*, which carries the meaning of immortal, incorruptible, or imperishable, may be just another way of saying forever. The GNB (as RSV, NIV) takes this word in connection with love, meaning that God's grace is for those who love the Lord forever. Some commentators, however, feel that this makes an unjustified distinction between two kinds of love—eternal versus transient—and connect it instead with God's grace. This has the effect of applying the word to God's unlimited grace rather than to man's love (so NEB: "God's grace be with all who love our Lord Jesus Christ, grace and immortality"). As such, the epistle ends with the same theme with which it began—God's grace (1:1, 2).

Abbreviations

ATR	*Anglican Theological Review*
BibSac	*Bibliotheca Sacra*
BibTod	*Bible Today*
BJRL	*Bulletin of John Rylands Library*
BZNW	*Beiheft zur Zeitschrift für die neutestamentliche Wissenschaft*
CBQ	*Catholic Biblical Quarterly*
CTJ	*Calvin Theological Journal*
cf.	compare
disc.	discussion
EQ	*Evangelical Quarterly*
ExpT	*Expository Times*
ff.	following pages or verses
HTR	*Harvard Theological Review*
IB	*Interpreter's Bible*
Interp	*Interpretation*
JBL	*Journal of Biblical Literature*
JETS	*Journal of the Evangelical Theological Society*
JSNT	*Journal for the Study of the New Testament*
JTS	*Journal of Theological Studies*
KJV	King James Version
n.	note
NASB	New American Standard Bible
NEB	New English Bible
NIV	New International Version
NovT	*Novum Testamentum*
NT	New Testament
NTS	*New Testament Studies*
OT	Old Testament
RB	*Revue Biblique*
RefThR	*Reformed Theological Review*
RevExp	*Review and Expositor*
RSV	Revised Standard Version
SBLDS	Society of Biblical Literature Dissertation Series
SBT	Studies in Biblical Theology
SJT	*Scottish Journal of Theology*
SNTSMS	Society for New Testament Monograph Series
ST	*Studia Theologica*
SWJTh	*Southwestern Journal of Theology*

TDNT	*Theological Dictionary of the New Testament*, edited by G. Kittel and G. Friedrich, and translated by G. W. Bromiley (1964–72)
TZ	*Theologische Zeitschrift*
v. (vv.)	verse(s)
ZNW	*Zeitschrift für die neutestamentliche Wissenschaft*

For Further Reading

Abbott, T. K. *Epistles to the Ephesians and to the Colossians.* Edinburgh: T. & T. Clark, 1924.

Allan, J. A. *The Epistle to the Ephesians.* London: SCM, 1959.

Barclay, W. *The Letters to the Galatians and Ephesians.* Edinburgh: Saint Andrew, 1959.

————. *The Letters to Philippians, Colossians, Thessalonians.* Edinburgh: Saint Andrew, 1959.

————. *The All-Sufficient Christ.* Philadelphia: Westminster, 1963.

Barth, M. *The Broken Wall.* Philadelphia: Judson, 1959.

————. *Ephesians 1–3.* Garden City, N. Y.: Doubleday, 1974.

————. *Ephesians 4–6.* Garden City, N. Y.: Doubleday, 1974.

Beare, F. W. "The Epistle to the Ephesians." In *The Interpreter's Bible Commentary*, vol. 10. Nashville: Abingdon, 1953.

————. "The Epistle to the Colossians." In *The Interpreter's Bible Commentary*, vol. 11. Nashville: Abingdon, 1953.

Bruce, F. F. "The Epistle to the Colossians." In *Commentary on the Epistles to the Ephesians and the Colossians.* London: Marshall, Morgan & Scott, 1957.

————. *The Epistle to the Ephesians.* London: Pickering & Inglis, 1961.

Caird, G. B. *Paul's Letters from Prison (Ephesians, Philippians, Colossians, Philemon).* The New Clarendon Bible. London: Oxford University Press, 1976.

Cannon, G. E. *The Use of Traditional Materials in Colossians.* Macon, Ga.: Mercer University Press, 1983.

Caragounis, C. C. *The Ephesian Mysterion.* Lund: CWK Gleerup, 1977.

Cross, F. L., ed. *Studies in Ephesians.* London: Mowbray, 1956.

Foulkes, F. *The Epistle of Paul to the Ephesians.* Grand Rapids: Eerdmans, 1963.

Francis, F. O., and Meeks, W., eds. *Conflict at Colossae.* Sources for Biblical Study 4. Missoula, Mont.: Scholars Press, 1975.

Hanson, S. *The Unity of the Church in the New Testament.* Lexington: American Library Association, 1963.

Houlden, J. L. *Paul's Letters from Prison: Philippians, Colossians, Philemon, and Ephesians.* Philadelphia: Westminster, 1977.

Kirby, J. *Ephesians: Baptism and Pentecost.* Montreal: McGill University Press, 1968.

Knox, J. *Philemon Among the Letters of Paul.* New York: Abingdon, 1959.

Leaney, A. R. C. *Timothy, Titus and Philemon*. Torch Bible Commentaries. London: SCM, 1960.

Lloyd-Jones, D. M. *God's Way of Reconciliation* (Ephesians 2). Grand Rapids: Baker, 1972.

_____. *Life in the Spirit* (Ephesians 5:18–6:9). Grand Rapids: Baker, 1973.

_____. *The Christian Warfare* (Ephesians 6:10–13). Grand Rapids: Baker, 1976.

_____. *The Christian Soldier* (Ephesians 6:10–20). Grand Rapids: Baker, 1977.

_____. *God's Ultimate Purpose* (Ephesians 1:1–23). Grand Rapids: Baker, 1978.

_____. *The Unsearchable Riches of Christ* (Ephesians 3:1–21). Grand Rapids: Baker, 1979.

_____. *Christian Unity* (Ephesians 4:1–16). Grand Rapids: Baker, 1980.

_____. *Darkness and Light* (Ephesians 4:17–5:17). Grand Rapids: Baker, 1982.

Lohse, E. *Colossians and Philemon*. Philadelphia: Fortress, 1971.

Mackay, J. *God's Order: The Ephesian Letter and This Present Time*. New York: Macmillan, 1953.

Martin, R. P. "Ephesians," *The Broadman Bible Commentary*, vol. 11. Nashville: Broadman, 1971.

_____. *Colossians and Philemon*. New Century Bible. Greenwood: Attic Press, 1974.

_____. *Reconciliation: A Study of Paul's Theology*. Atlanta: John Knox, 1981.

Mitton, C. L. *Ephesians*. New Century Bible. Greenwood: Attic Press, 1976.

Moody, D. *Christ and the Church*. Grand Rapids: Eerdmans, 1963.

Moule, C. F. D. *Ephesians*. Cambridge: Cambridge University Press, 1935.

_____. *The Epistles of Paul the Apostle to the Colossians and to Philemon*. Cambridge: Cambridge University Press, 1957.

O'Brien, P. T. *Colossians, Philemon*. Word Biblical Commentary vol. 44. Waco, Tex.: Word, 1982.

Robinson, J. A. *St. Paul's Epistle to the Ephesians*. 2d ed. London: Macmillan, 1909.

Schweizer, E. *The Letter to the Colossians*. Minneapolis: Augsburg, 1982.

Scott, E. F. *The Epistles of Paul to the Colossians, to Philemon, and the Ephesians*. London: Hodder & Stoughton, 1958.

Simpson, E. K. "The Epistle to the Ephesians," in *Commentary on the Epistles to the Ephesians and the Colossians*. London: Marshall, Morgan & Scott, 1957.

Stott, J. *God's New Society: The Message of Ephesians*. Downers Grove: Intervarsity, 1979.

Strauss, L. *Galatians and Ephesians*. New York: Loizeaux Brothers, 1957.

Summers, R. *Ephesians: Pattern for Christian Living*. Nashville: Broadman, 1960.

Thompson, G. H. P. *The Letters of Paul to the Ephesians, to the Colossians and to Philemon*. Cambridge: Cambridge University Press, 1967.

Vaughan, *Ephesians*. A Study Guide Commentary. Grand Rapids: Zondervan, 1977.

_____. "Colossians." In *The Expositor's Bible Commentary*, vol. 11. Grand Rapids: Zondervan, 1978.

_____. *Colossians and Philemon*. Bible Study Commentary. Grand Rapids: Zondervan, 1980.

Wescott, B. F. *Saint Paul's Epistle to the Ephesians*. London: Macmillan, 1906.

White, R. E. O. *In Him the Fulness*. Old Tappan, N. J.: Revell, 1973.

Wood, A. S. "Ephesians." In *The Expositor's Bible Commentary*, vol. 2. Grand Rapids: Zondervan, 1978.

Subject Index

Scripture Index

282

APOCRYPHA

EARLY CHRISTIAN LITERATURE

OTHER WORKS